The Comprehensive Guide To
Jig & Live Bait
Fishing
Secrets

The Comprehensive Guide To
Jig & Live Bait
Fishing
Secrets
by Babe Winkelman

Published by
Babe Winkelman Productions, Inc.
Brainerd, Minnesota

Book Design	Babe Winkelman
Cover Design	Duane Ryks
Photography	Charles Dunemann/Mark Strand
Artwork	Duane Ryks/John Norlin/Charles Dunemann
Writing	Babe Winkelman/Steve Grooms/Mark Strand
Editing	Steve Grooms/Mark Strand/Duane Ryks
Typesetting	Sentinel Printing
Layout	Duane Ryks
Keyline	Sandra Ryks
Printing	Sentinel Printing

Published by Babe Winkelman Productions
P.O. Box 407, 213 N.W. 4th St., Brainerd, MN 56401

Printed in the United States of America

First edition, 1986
Library of Congress Catalog
Card Number 86-051141

ISBN 0-915405-05-9

Library of Congress Cataloguing in
Publication Date

Winkelman, Babe
The Comprehensive Guide to Jig and Live Bait Fishing Secrets

Brainerd, Minnesota: Babe Winkelman Productions
ISBN 0-915405-05-9

It is with love, respect and admiration that I dedicate this book:

to Bill Binkelman, a wise and wonderful fisherman who has done so much to *create* the modern tackle and methods for jig and live bait fishing, that many of us now take for granted;

to my dad, who started all of this by taking me to the store to buy jigs, and then out on the water to learn to use them;

to my wife Charlie, a loving and caring partner in everything I do, from the house to the office to the fishing book;

to my daughters, Tanya, Jennifer, Jasmine and Donielle, who continue to provide the love and understanding that brings our family together;

to the staff of our growing company, whose loyalty and pursuit of quality helps me continue to believe in our dreams;

but mostly to my Creator, for giving me the chance to go fishing.

ACKNOWLEDGEMENTS

This book is, really, one of the first products to come from a growing company called Babe Winkelman Productions as much as from a man named Babe Winkelman. It represents the realization of a dream for me, of putting together a Research Team comprising the best angling minds in North America, for the purpose of teaching others how to catch fish.

Much of the information in this book is mine, of course, but there are also major contributions from an international legion of today's finest fisherman. It represents the beginning of the future direction of our company.

Bill Binkelman, for one, spent a good deal of time with us, discussing his ideas on fishing in general and jig fishing in particular. From the time he taught us all about fluorescent colors and how they catch fish, he has been sharing his knowledge. We all owe a big debt of gratitude to Bill.

There are others, many others, all over. Superb fishermen/teachers such as Spence Petros, Gary Roach, Randy Amenrud, Mike McClelland, Bob Probst, John Christianson, Duane Ryks, Wayne Ekelund, Dan Nelson, Hart Chesick, Elden Bailey, Jim Fofrich, and Jim Hayes. And there are numerous others. These people are all of the same type. They are sincerely interested in helping you catch more fish.

Nobody fishes alone, and nobody produces a fishing book alone. Under our roof, we have a team of fishing people who are also skilled at what they "really" do for a living. Duane Ryks heads the department that does all the illustrations and production. He is a proven pro who has done a wonderful job again. John Norlin has improved his skills as a fisherman and illustrator since he joined us, and his pictures will help you "see" the ideas we talk about in the text.

Mark Strand is a creative writer and photographer who has done much to see this book from the germ of an idea to completion. Steve Grooms, a writer who needs no introduction to fishing folks, also wrote a large part of the manuscript. Charles Dunemann, a talented illustrator, graphic artist and photographer, lent his hand to many areas as the book took shape.

Ray Eng, a resourceful and energetic researcher and photo assistant, was a steady hand from the beginning of the book's concept to the day it was done. And, as always, Sandy Ryks took everything these guys gave her and put her keylining touch to it, giving the book the "look" it carries with pride.

In addition to our immediate staff, there are numerous individuals and organizations that contributed greatly. Through their generosity, Gordy Vados, Vados Live Bait, Spring Lake Park, MN; Duane Shodeen, Minnesota Department of Natural Resources; Lester Cleveland, Dave Anderson, Fish Lake Live Bait, Harris, MN; Marv Koep, Nisswa Bait and Tackle, Brainerd, MN; Robinson's Wholesale Bait, Ronnie Anderson, Anderson Minnow Farms; and Audrey Halverson made the book more complete.

TABLE OF CONTENTS

FOREWORD

We all know how tough it can be to get the location of a secret spot from another fisherman. You stand a better chance of running into Santa Claus in July.

But more and more, fellow fishermen are becoming willing to share information on *how* to fish, and that's the important part anyway. You can always find your own spots.

In the 1960s and 70s, fishing techniques underwent a revolution. Equipment was refined and knowledge of fish behavior entered a new dimension. But the things that were learned weren't completely understood by more than a small percentage of fishermen.

The 1980s will surely come to be known as the period when fishing *education* catches up with the earlier explosion in knowledge. The same pioneers who spent years developing systems for catching fish will master the art of telling others what they know.

There is nothing that Babe Winkelman Productions wants to be known for more than leading this fishing education crusade. Gathering together the best, most accurate information on how to catch fish and giving it to you, free of half-truths and baloney, is our mission.

You can look forward, in the coming months and years, to being taught how to fish by the best of the best. The wheels I put in motion years ago have come to full speed, and the Babe Winkelman Research Team is now staffed with the finest all-around fishermen I could find. Their names are in the acknowledgements of this book.

Ultimately, the ones who will benefit most are you, the fishermen who don't get the chance to spend the time on the water necessary to become the angler that is locked inside. So take this research, this system, take everything these people have to offer, and adapt it to your personal fishing style. Let it draw out the master angler potential in you.

Back to the topic at hand. There is an old saying that a fisherman is a jerk on one end, waiting for a jerk on the other. Well, the truth is, if we all waited around until we felt a solid jerk on the other end, we wouldn't catch very many fish.

Most fish tell us in very subtle ways that they have taken our bait, and only through intense concentration and a lot of practice can we get good at knowing when.

Getting good, getting *very* good, at knowing when is part of what this book is about. In every volume of the *Comprehensive Guide* series, we strive to give you pieces of the system we have developed for catching fish under any conditions, in any type of water. This book is a critical piece of that system.

For, besides information on learning to detect subtle bites from fish, it gives you what you need to know to fish well with the two most effective tools ever devised for catching most species of fish: the jig and the live bait rig.

As I said, the goal of our company, and our burgeoning Research Team, is to teach you how to fish. That will take time, and a team effort between us and you. When you get there, please remember that it also takes time to grow a fish, and give serious thought to releasing some of them, unharmed and waiting for the fisherman who will come along behind you.

— Babe Winkelman

Chapter 1
A New Fishing System

On a hot weekend in 1963, Milwaukee angler Bill Binkelman decided to conduct an experiment.

It would change the nature of fishing forever. It certainly changed *my* fishing!

Bill was fishing Lake Okauchee, a lake near Milwaukee that was widely considered "fished out." Once in a while a walleye was caught from the shallows of Okauchee in the spring, yet most fishermen thought the lake had no walleyes.

Bill disagreed. Once he had caught a walleye in deep water when wind had blown his boat off the shallow bass structure he was working. Binkelman figured Okauchee just might have walleyes that never saw a hook because they lived in deeper water than anyone had fished. Remember, in 1963 almost nobody fished deeper than 15 feet.

Bill also had a new idea about how deep water walleyes might be caught. His rig included 4-pound line and a thin-wired, long-shanked #8 hook. The line was threaded through an egg sinker, with a split shot pinched on to make it a *slip-sinker rig*.

There was also something unusual about his bait. He was using a fat nightcrawler hooked lightly once in the nose. In those days, the only way crawlers were fished was by running a huge hook through them over and over, creating a gob that really turned on the bullheads. In 1963, the gear Bill used would have been considered too tiny and light for anything but sunfish.

Late in the afternoon, with his boat in 35 feet of water, Bill felt a bite. He set the hook against a solid weight that proved to be a 6 pound, 6 ounce walleye. Aha! There were walleyes here, and they could be caught in deep water. And a naturally-presented crawler on a slip sinker rig was the way to get them.

That fish was no fluke. Bill and some friends went on to catch 15 similar fish that famous afternoon. A new fishing technique had been born.

Shortly after that momentous fishing trip, Bill printed a fascinating little book called *Nightcrawler Secrets*.

Bill Binkelman beams over a massive stringer of walleyes. This catch, the first ever made with Bill's revolutionary live bait methods, changed the course of angling history. Photo courtesy of Bill Binkelman.

The Bill Binkelman Legacy

I'm proud to claim Bill Binkelman as a close friend. A true gentleman, he has been a major innovator and fishing educator. Bill was once described in a magazine article as "The Man Who Taught You How To Fish." And that's very close to the truth. You may not have heard his name before, but he is a major figure in the fishing revolution that made it possible for us to enjoy far better fishing than once was possible.

Bill is probably the main inventor of modern refined live bait fishing for fish on deeper structure. Several years of independent thinking and experimenting finally came together on that day on Okauchee. Bill went on to publicize his findings through books, especially *Nightcrawler Secrets*, and the magazine he founded, *Fishing Facts*.

It all came about in an interesting way. Bill Binkelman has long been an ardent fisherman. He went through a long period of frustration-...that period that so many anglers never leave. But by the early 1960s, by specializing on a few bodies of water, Bill turned things around. He began to taste success when he began to learn those little areas where fish could be found.

More and more, Bill came to realize the "expert" advice he read in outdoor magazines did not agree with the lessons of his personal experience.

In particular, Bill had learned that fish related to certain significant features on the lake bottom. Often those key spots lay in water that was fairly deep.

But no authorities were saying that...except a maverick named Buck Perry, who was promoting a lure called the Spoonplug. Perry had a number of radical ideas, including these:

- *Big fish like deep water most of the time;*
- *Fish are usually found in schools;*
- *Fish relate to bottom features, which Perry called "structure;"*
- *While fishermen complain of "bad weather" a lot, the real weather villain is the cold front; and*
- *By fishing with Spoonplugs at high speeds, it is possible to trigger reflexive strikes from fish.*

Bill's experience convinced him that Perry was right and the other authorities were wrong about how to catch fish. But there was one problem. After trolling Spoonplugs for two years, Bill gave them up in disgust. He said, "Some people like apples and some people like strawberries; I just *don't* like motor trolling."

What Bill preferred was fishing carefully with live bait. He pioneered live bait rigs. He did a great deal of the innovating with jig fishing, studying different head styles and patterns.

Through his patient work, Bill Binkelman pioneered many of the jigging and rigging techniques and concepts that will be presented in this book.

He did it by accepting Perry's structure fishing theories, but throwing out the Spoonplugs. Bill drew on his trout fishing fishing background to come up with natural, clean, light rigs for fishing live bait in a lifelike manner. He fished structure, but he did it as if he were fishing for trout.

Bill Binkelman and I have shared a fishing boat on several occasions. He is the consummate fishing educator, and it is a joy to spend time with him.

It was a simple idea, but like a lot of simple ideas it changed the fishing world.

One of the most important ideas Bill has passed on to modern fishermen is the need to pay attention to fine details of presentation. Today's emphasis on small hooks, light lines and presenting bait in a natural manner all come directly from Bill. He has been a fanatic about the quality of the live bait itself, inventing the techniques for "conditioning" crawlers.

People used to fish for bass and walleyes as if they were dumb, crude creatures. The attitude was: why worry about the size of your leader, when you were "just after walleyes" anyway? Bill noted, "If bass and walleyes are so dumb, how come almost nobody can catch them?" He approached these gamefish as if they had much of the wariness of trout. The results speak for themselves!

None of that would have mattered if Binkelman hadn't shared his ideas. But, as I said, he founded *Fishing Facts* magazine, and it grew to be a magazine with immense impact.

The Lindy Rig

Bill Binkelman has always been the kind of man who enjoyed working closely with friends, sharing information and theories. Among his early fishing friends were Ron and Al Lindner, fishing brothers originally from Chicago.

After the Lindners moved to Brainerd, Minnesota, to begin guiding, Ron invented the Lindy Rig. That was in 1967. The Lindy Rig was a variation on the rig Bill used on Okauchee, but it used a special "walking" slip sinker instead of Bill's bullet sinker and the Lindy Rig had a swivel clip instead of Bill's split shot stopper.

Of course, there is very little that is brand new in the world of fishing. The basic idea of a one-way sliding sinker had been around a long time. Bill Binkelman had introduced the notion of fishing for walleyes with a sliding sinker rig in "Nightcrawler Secrets," and he then called it "an old carp fishing trick." In a way, what was mostly new was the application of a slip sinker rig to deeper water walleyes and other lake gamefish. Nobody before had believed walleyes and bass and other lake fish were "smart" enough to mind a fixed sinker.

The Lindy Rig was basically an updated version of Binkelman's "Nightcrawler Secrets" rig. At the same time, it employed little hooks and light leader material so that the whole presentation was clean and natural. Never before had such a simple and effective live bait rig been sold, all pre- tied, in attractive packaging that explained how to catch fish with it.

Almost immediately, the Lindy Rig became famous. The Lindy Rig became popular at the same time people were discovering that "fished-out" lakes had tremendous fish in them. You just had to have the right tackle and know where to look.

The Lindy Rig was promoted with the promise that you'd catch more and bigger fish if you used it. And guess what, for once that promise was true.

By this time, the better anglers and guides had just gotten into using fishing sonar. Fishing sonar made it possible for them to work deeper structure with precision. They made some phenomenal catches of fish. The Lindy Rig wouldn't have caught on like it did if it hadn't been for the popularity of the early Lowrance "Fish Lo-K-tors."

Together, the sonar and the Lindy Rig formed the key ingredients of an incredibly effective *fishing system*.

The Lindy Rig owed some of its early success to a bunch of sharp guides who banded together to form the Nisswa Guide's League. Tips were shared back and forth. Someone discovered that boats would go slower and with more control if they were run backward, and soon *backtrolling* became part of the new live bait fishing technique.

Everything was coming together at one place and time: the right equipment, ideas and people. Suddenly people were catching stringers of good- sized fish of all species. And they didn't have to go to Canada to do it.

The Lindy Rig has a rich chapter to add to the annals of angling history.
Vintage photos courtesy of the In-Fisherman.

Then, drawing on his assortment of live bait rigs and jigs, he can fish in the most efficient way at all times.

Again, he rejects limits. If the fish are deep, he can fish deep. If they want a fast presentation, he can give it to them...with a variety of possible baits, with a variety of attractors in various colors. If they want a slow presentation, that is easy—perhaps a Lindy Rig, or a slowly-trolled jig, or perhaps a jig hopped vertically over and over.

Or maybe the fish are suspended. He can get at them. Even better, he can get at them with a variety of techniques. He might fish down to them with a weight-forward spinner or a slip-bobber rig. Or a jig, possibly with a spinner attached, tipped with several possible baits. Or he might fish up to them from the bottom with a Lindy Rig and any of several floats.

The whole technique is a system. Like other systems, this fishing approach has many components that fit together to cover all possible fishing challenges. Negative fish, fish in weeds, scattered fish, rough weather, tough lakes—all these are not obstacles but challenges which the total system can take care of.

In this book, I'll give you the guidance that will combine with your own experience to produce the kind of comprehensive fishing ability I'm talking about. It's the most valuable thing I can give you.

You'll know when you "have arrived." You'll be facing some difficult fishing problem, and you'll think, "I know how to beat this. In fact, I know *a bunch* of good ways of catching these fish!"

When you're not only that good, but good enough to choose the very best of your fish- catching options, you will be a master of the live bait rigging and jigging fishing system.

By then, you'll be writing books of your own!

This is the cabin in northern Minnesota where I learned to catch walleyes. Inside, I studied every piece of fishing information I could find. On the lake, I learned to use early depth finders to "hunt" for fish, and understand their world.

And that's just what I found in Bill Binkelman's book, *Nightcrawler Secrets*, which I bought in about 1965. Here was somebody willing to *share* secrets!

Unlike other authorities, Binkelman emphasized the importance of *locating* special places that would hold fish. That made sense to me, as I already suspected that finding fish was harder than catching them. Bill even seemed to know what sorts of places would hold fish. He wrote about the importance of the shape of the bottom of the lake, telling his readers what sorts of places fish hung out in. I loved this man many years before I actually got to meet him.

I became a ravenous reader of fishing literature, especially the articles in *Fishing News* (which became *Fishing Facts*). I read and re-read those articles as closely as a medical student poring over an anatomy text. I still have those dog-eared old magazines.

The big turning point in my fishing came when I combined the "Nightcrawler Secrets" techniques with my first sonar depth finder. Many readers of this book began fishing with the famous Lowrance "Green Box." Few of you probably know that it was preceeded by a "Red Box." Well, I had one of those.

I was so fascinated by what it told me that for a year I hardly fished...I just motored around watching the face of my sonar as it revealed the mysteries of the fishes' world. It blew my mind.

On Hay Lake, where we had our cabin, areas I assumed were terribly deep because they were in the center of the lake, turned out to be relatively shallow mud flats. Or I'd go to areas where I knew there was a rock bottom, and I'd get this big, bright signal back. I'd fix that picture in my mind. I'd remember what the sonar looked like as the

16

boat moved from the mud up over a rock pile. Then I'd go look at weeds with the sonar.

Those were exciting days! I lived to fish. I couldn't find enough time to study my depth finder. When I wasn't fishing I was reading about fishing. Pretty soon, I could catch more fish in our lake than anybody around. I still remember the day I caught my first limit of six walleyes. One of those fish went 8 pounds, and I can see that fish as clearly today as though it were in front of me.

The combination of my first sonar and the Nightcrawler Secrets style of fishing was deadly. When the Lindy Rig appeared, I dropped the Binkelman rig in favor of the convenience of the new rig.

The original Lowrance Green Box (left) was actually preceeded by a Red Box (right). I had one of the first Red Boxes, and it opened up a whole new exciting era of fishing for me.

Then I got into guiding, although there weren't many opportunities for that where I grew up. I had a little 12-foot car-top aluminum boat rig that I bought, used, for $100. Heck, I'd have fished with anybody who would share the cost of gas. It seemed too good to be true that someone would actually *pay me* to go fishing with them.

Soon I began making trips to Brainerd, where I talked fishing with the Lindners, Gary Roach and other good fishermen in the Nisswa Guides League.

Bit by bit, the pieces began to fit together. Every now and then I'd meet someone who was willing to share some more secrets. A friend of my father's, Orland Juelleum, knew how to catch walleyes by casting a jig (we always drifted with them). I can remember a string of walleyes he took that averaged seven pounds, doing that. He taught me a lot about jigging, back in 1963.

It was Orland, in fact, who started me thinking about how important color can be. He was catching way more walleyes than we were, but I knew he used the same bait. Then, one day, he told me his jig was the "Bumblebee" pattern, a yellow and black jig, not the blue and white "Bluetail Fly" I used. And he was right. When I began to fish the yellow and black jig in our lake, I began to catch more fish.

In a way, none of this learning was easy. There was a lot of bad information floating around in those days, "facts" that just weren't true. So for every four or five secrets of fishing I learned, I later had to un-learn two or three. More and more, I learned to be suspicious about anything I hadn't learned for myself.

But it doesn't seem right to talk about this being "hard" learning. It was fishing, and fishing is *fun*.

The Fishing Team

The sensational success of the Lindy Rig in the mid-70s caused the Lindners to start a tackle company. They joined with a businessman named Nick Adams to form the Lindy Tackle Company.

Eventually, Lindy was merged with a respected old tackle company, Little Joe, becoming Lindy-Little Joe. The Lindners left to start up a magazine.

Sales of Lindy Rigs in the early days were brisk, but there was a problem: there was a huge gap in knowledge between the fishing knowledge of a few "insiders" and the average angler. The big East Coast outdoor magazines ignored the structure fishing revolution. To tell the truth, *even today* I don't think they understand what has happened! To spread the word about the new fishing tactics and gear, Lindy created its famous Fishing Team.

The team had three purposes. One was educational. The average angler was hungry for knowledge about the new fishing techniques, so Team members wrote articles, fished with media people and gave seminars all around the country. Another purpose was to promote Lindy tackle. The third purpose was to test the company's products. A lot of companies claim to have field *testers*, but this one really did. When some piece of tackle didn't work right, the team told the factory about it in pretty blunt terms.

The team has been a Who's Who of angling. Team members, right from the first, were real fishermen, not figureheads. Some of my best friends have been on Lindy's team over the years, including such guys as Big John Christianson, Gary Roach, Wayne Ekelund, Randy Amenrud, Rod Romine, Dan Nelson and many others.

And the team is where I entered the story again. I'd gone from guiding to tournament fishing in the early 1970s, writing a few articles along the way. In 1972, I became a member of the Lindy-Little Joe Fishing Team. From that point on, fishing education has been the center of my work, just as fishing has been the center of my personal life.

Learn how to catch more & bigger fish!

Babe Winkelman

This is your chance to ask questions and get tips from a professional fisherman of the Lindy-Little Joe Fishing Team.

WED., JUNE 28
7:30 p.m.
at the
FALLS HOLIDAY INN
No admission charge!
Bring your friends!

FREE PRIZES FOR EVERYONE!
Register for these door prizes
- **Fly-in Fishing Trip**   • **4-$25 Savings Bonds**
- **Flight Bags**   • **Lots of Fishing Tackle**

Lindy®-LITTLE JOE®
FISHING TEAM
Member

Babe Winkelman

Spends 1000's of hours fishing every year. He has the answers. Learn how to read a lake, what tackle and bait to use, how to beat the odds. It's an actual fishing school.

Then..
Thurs., June 29
from
10 a.m.-4 p.m.
at
GATEWAY TRADING POST
You can talk to Babe about more fishing questions.

I am still proud of my early association with the Lindy-Little Joe Fishing Team. We had the same mission then as I do now: to help others catch fish!

You've probably seen the television commercial where the guy says, "I liked this shaver so well I bought the company!" Well, that's pretty much what happened to me, for in 1986 I acquired a major share of stock in my favorite tackle company, Lindy-Little Joe.

That's one of the reasons I'm writing this book, a book that might be even closer to my heart than the others I have written. I owe a *lot* to the tackle I'll be talking about here, mainly jigs and live bait rigs. Most of the fish and the fun in my fishing today comes from this tackle.

Before buying into Lindy-Little Joe, I had already begun assembling a Research Team of outstanding fishermen to work with me at Babe Winkelman Productions. These guys not only catch fish, but they're always asking questions and looking for new ways of doing things. This staff includes several guys who have tested their skills in the rugged world of tournament fishing. Some of them have been prominent in the recent history of angling, and they'll all take a part in changes to come.

I'm now in a position to combine the strength of the Lindy-Little Joe Fishing Team with innovative input from my own Research Team. It's an exciting time for me, my company and for the fishing public.

Lindy-Little Joe has been changing, too. The basic Lindy Rig has been modified in a bunch of ways that make it work well under many different circumstances. I'm especially excited about the latest developments in floating live bait rigs. Fluorescent colors have been added to various products, plus some other hot color ideas I'll get into later. Over time, the company has learned more and more about which hooks, leader materials, etc. work best. The result is a better product. The company's line of jigs has gotten stronger and stronger every year.

And much bigger things are to come! I'm currently working on the Lindy Rig Plus, a refinement on the original concept which has already been proving itself in our field research.

Hooks, lead and bait: the essential, common ingredients of the jigging and live bait rigging system.

Jigs and Live Bait Rigs

Notice something about live bait rigs and jigs, the subject matter of this book. They all have three things in common: a hook, some lead and some type of bait. Hooks, lead and bait. Oh, sometimes other elements are added, like bobbers or spinners or jig bodies, but the essentials are hooks, lead and bait.

What is so special about that?

Just this—most fish spend most of their time near the bottom. They might only be in four feet of water, but they'll be near bottom. Day in, day out, fish are more catchable on live bait than on artificials. So what is the most basic, reliable technique for catching fish of all species under all circumstances? *Put live bait on a hook and attach some lead to it so you will be fishing near bottom!* Boy, you can't get more basic than that!

We can add one more factor, the element of speed. A major limitation of many artificials is that they have to be fished at a certain speed. Often enough, that speed is faster than is right for the mood of the fish.

All of which is another reason jigs and live bait rigs work so well. With them, you can move live bait along the bottom in an attractive manner at very slow speeds.

No wonder jigs and live bait rigs catch fish.

Why Live Bait?

Why fish live bait when artificials are so good?

Well, let's take a look at the attractions of artificials. They've got a lot going for them.

Soft plastic baits like curly-tail grubs have excellent *action*. Some minnow-imitating soft plastic lures wiggle better in the water than most minnows. The same is true for some pork baits— they have fantastic action. Artificials like buzzbaits have deadly actions no natural bait can duplicate.

Every lure has a certain *vibration* pattern, and many are obviously attractive to fish. Presumably, some of the vibration patterns must be unique and hard for a natural bait to produce.

With all the commercial *scents* available to fishermen, it's easy to add a little flavor to any lure. I've got to think that artificials doped up with scent put out more scent in the water than many live baits.

With modern techniques, which apply finishes to lures with photographic processes, it is possible to make a crankbait with an extremely *lifelike appearance*. I've seen real perch that didn't look as realistic as some of the perch finish plugs.

Various spoons and spinners have terrific *flash*, just like many silver-sided minnows and other forage fish.

Some artificials—like soft plastics—even *feel* good in a fish's mouth.

So, again, why bother with live bait?

You might have noticed in the discussion above that I kept saying "some" artificials have this and "some" artificials have that quality.

Live bait has it all.

With live bait, you have total realism. Everything is right— appearance, size, color, action, vibration pattern, flash—it's all perfectly natural and attractive.

With live bait, you automatically have a bait that smells, feels and tastes right...better than any artificial.

With live bait, you automatically have attractive action. Often the action of live bait cannot be duplicated by artificials. A leech wriggling beneath a bobber is doing something no piece of plastic or pork could do when fished under a bobber. Live bait will often panic at the sight of a predator moving in. Man, that's an attractive action you can't get from any artificial!

I once fished some lakes on the Disney World property in central Florida, fishing big shiner minnows. We did a lot of moving around at first, looking for fish. By watching closely, I could tell where the big bass were by the way my shiner acted. Those shiners were talking to me. They talked to the bass, too, acting distressed and easy to catch. Some things you just can't do with artificial baits.

It seems logical to me that live bait puts out vibrations in the water that can not be duplicated by any artificial. Predator fish, using lateral line sensitivity, pick up those vibrations. Live bait can vary its vibration patterns in response to danger. When a big fish comes in range, the minnow starts to move in a panicky way. Hey, that's a response you can't get from an artificial.

Artificial baits in many cases look *as good as the real thing, and they do catch fish. But live bait has it* all: *appearance, size, color, action, feel, smell and taste.*

And let me say again, live bait has *everything* going in its favor. You get the perfect appearance, texture, smell, taste, vibration and action in the same bait.

Let's look at it in a different way.

Artificials really catch fish when they are aggressive.

I've had walleyes just about knock the rod out of my hands when retrieving a spinnerbait for bass. I've had bass snatch crankbaits out of the air. On the Great Lakes, I've seen trout and salmon so aggressive that it wasn't possible to get more than one line in the water because, as soon as a lure was down, the fish were trying to kill it.

Those times are fun. When you find fish in a chasing, aggressive mood, artificials are fast and fun to use.

But as readers of this book already know, there are *other* times, times when the fish are just so-so about feeding. Somehow it always seems "you shoulda been here yesterday."

Well, that would be nice, but today is today. For whatever reason, the fish are a little tough today, but today is the day you have for fishing. You might as well get on with it and make the best day of this you possibly can. And your best bet will often be live bait. It works on tough days.

I've got hundreds of examples, thousands of examples.

I remember one bass tournament I did badly in. In practice, I'd found a bunch of nice fish on a big flat. Wouldn't you know, just before the tournament a cold front swept in and fishing became just terrible. I stayed on my spot and died on my spot. Think I caught two little fish. After the tournament I was both mad and curious about what the bass had done, so I fished my same spot...only I fished a little deeper with a Lindy Rig and some salamanders. In a short time that evening, I caught and released two limits of big bass—fish that would have won the tournament, easily. They hadn't gone anywhere. They had just gone off artificials.

Live bait will usually outproduce artificials when fish aren't feeding aggressively. And that's a *lot* of the time!

Or put it this way: when the fish are really snapping, you don't have a problem. You can catch them, with live bait or artificials. When the going gets tough, though, the good angler gets going...and he will often do it with live bait.

Fishing well is a matter of beating difficult days, of solving problems. And live bait is probably the best single problem solver you'll find. Nothing takes the place of knowledge or skill. But if you combine knowledge, skill and decent equipment with the modern live bait tactics, you're set to battle the worst conditions.

Another example comes to mind. Quite a few years back, I'd been fishing a bay that I knew was just stuffed with bass, but on this one particular day I couldn't get anything to pop for me. Fishing was so slow, I went swimming for fun. I was using a snorkel and mask, paddling around over this weed flat I'd been fishing, when I began seeing lots of bass in the tops of the weeds.

Heck, the bass were still there. They were just negative.

I rigged up a fat crawler on a small Lindy Rig hook and fished it with no weight...just let the worm flutter and free-fall to the tops of the weeds. I caught about a dozen nice bass. More important, I learned a lesson. When things get tough, I fish harder and smarter, usually with live bait.

There are more reasons to use live bait. It's one I don't see people paying enough attention to. Live bait will help you catch *bigger fish*. I think everybody would rather catch big fish.

Understand, hardly a week goes by in the fishing season when I don't fish artificials. I have spent a lifetime mastering all types of fishing techniques, and don't mind saying I'm proud of my ability to handle artificals. I'm a versatile fisherman, and you should be too.

But an awful lot of my bigger fish have come on live bait, especially the bigger fish I've taken in water that has seen a lot of fishing pressure.

Big fish don't get big by making stupid mistakes. They are naturally more cautious than smaller fish. The aggressive feeders are the first to land on a stringer, while their careful sisters and brothers keep living and growing.

Live bait will take cautious, big fish. Live bait isn't *something like* what they feed upon, it *is* what they feed on.

With many species, big fish feed differently than when they were small. As young fish, they could afford to chase food, even when some chases didn't pay off.

A bigger fish has to play a different game. A big muskie or smallmouth literally can't afford to run around wasting energy as it

When fishing gets tough, nothing turns the trick as consistently as live bait.

feeds. It takes more energy to move a big body. There better be a payoff, much of the time, or the fish is losing ground in the game of survival.

Big fish do have some advantages. They get to occupy the very choicest habitat, the spots where they can feed with efficiency and safety. So with many species, the larger fish lie in ambush in the most ideal spots, making short attacks on big, vulnerable prey.

Live bait, especially *big* live bait, is ideal for catching cautious, "lazy" lunkers. Because you can fish live bait in one spot, and still have good action on your bait, you can take those fish that would just sit there all day watching artificals moving past.

I'll give you a good example. Northern pike make more of a distinct shift in feeding styles as they grow up than just about any fish. As we all know, small northerns are so catchable that they plague us when we're looking for other fish. Not big northerns, though. No way! Pike from about 16 pounds on up are very hard to catch (except on some Canadian wilderness waters) if you don't use live bait. Big pike feed less often and much more efficiently than little pike, and they are not nearly as vulnerable to artificials. But you *can* get them with big minnows fished carefully.

In the early 1970s I was trolling a Lindy Rig along a steep break when I felt a fish pecking on my bait, a big sucker minnow. I set the hook and quickly reeled in this small northern. He didn't even have the hook—he was too small—but was hanging on. I was laughing at that when this spooky shadow came sliding under the boat and swallowed my minnow *and* the little northern! I was one nervous guy, waiting to set that hook! I landed that fish, my first really big northern, and I learned another lesson. That big fish had been ignoring my sucker minnow for an hour because it wasn't big enough to be interesting.

A Few Words About Prejudice

I wish I didn't have to include this section.

For whatever reasons, there are a lot of anglers who seem to enjoy sneering at live bait anglers. In a word, that's their problem...not yours or mine.

Angling snobs say things like, "Using live bait is for fish hogs." Or, "Anybody can catch fish on live bait, but it takes skill to catch them on artificials." Or, "Sure, you might catch fish on live bait, but you haven't proven anything that way."

Hey, who's trying to *prove* anything? I go fishing to enjoy myself, not to prove something. And I don't mind admitting it is more fun catching a mess of crappies on a jig and minnow than catching nothing on a bare jig. Who is writing the rules of sportsmanship, anyway? If you hate fishing with live bait, I'm not going to call you names. Just do me the courtesy of not calling me names if I enjoy fishing with the full range of techniques, live bait included.

It is simply wrong and ignorant to claim that fishing with live bait doesn't require skill. Whenever anyone says that, I'm tempted to hand them my rod and live bait and say, "If catching fish with live bait is so easy, let's see *you* prove it!"

Fishing skill is something you develop from study, thought, hard work and experience. It has nothing to do with your choice of technique. There are skillful artificial anglers *and* artificial anglers who can't catch diddly-squat. There are klutzy live bait anglers *and* live bait anglers whose competence is awesome. Izaak Walton (who was a skilled live bait angler) understood all that 300 years ago, but today some people have strange ideas.

Nor is it true that live bait anglers are fish hogs who kill too many fish. I've known thousands of fish hogs who wouldn't touch live bait, plus countless live bait anglers who are great conservationists. If you fish live bait carefully, you can almost always return fish in good condition. Don't confuse ethics with technique.

Isn't it perfectly obvious? A good angler might be the master of live bait *or* artificials. But a great angler is master of both...and sharp enough to know when to use which technique.

A good angler is a good angler and a snob is a snob. There's no need to worry about what other people think.

My fishing buddy, Spence Petros, recently told me a story that relates to this. I've had the same experience, time and again, and have written about at least one occasion in *Bass Patterns*. I knew how Spence's story was going to turn out before he got halfway there.

Spence was fishing a private lake in central Florida with a friend and a local angler, who was the host for this expedition. They hoped to catch some of the big bass that lake was known for. At the host's request, the three fishermen threw plastic worms up on a weedy flat for hours and hours, but caught nothing.

Spence began to talk about getting some live bait, but the host refused to even listen to such talk. There'd be no live bait used in *his* boat! On and on they fished, getting zipped, until Spence insisted on going to town for bait. He came back with two dozen golden shiners.

With Spence running the electric trolling motor, they put out Lindy Rigs with light sinkers, just enough weight to get the shiners down without inhibiting their action.

All this time, the host sat in the boat without speaking to Spence and his buddy. He was totally grossed out by the thought of live bait fishing. He had his arms crossed on his body, and he sat there scowling at the center of the lake. Not talking.

The first pass along the edge of a deep channel in the flat produced nothing, though at one point Spence's shiner began to jump around a lot.

Spence knew what that meant, so he went back. The first bass went 5 pounds. They came back again, and that time took a 7 pound, 6 ounce bass. On their next pass, Spence and his buddy had a double-header.

Finally the host spoke, "Give me one of those damned Yankee rigs!"

A huge Florida bass Spence Petros caught using live shiners, fishing over the same water that produced nothing with artificials!

27

The System

It is critical that you understand the way live bait rigs and jigs fit together with several other critical elements to form a *complete fishing system*. These are the two deadliest ways of solving fish-catching problems, especially when put together in an overall system.

Another key element is the right kind of boat. By that, I don't mean a Ranger boat, though that is as right as you can get, but a boat that has the right characteristics and which has been properly rigged.

As I'll be emphasizing a little later, "right rigging" mainly means that the boat has the kind of sonar that tells the complete story of what's happening in the underwater world. That, plus the boat must be set up so it can move with precision, forward or backward, at a full range of speeds.

And there is no more key element than the knowledge of how to use this equipment, which is the point of this book. Your head is still the most important fishing aid you have.

A skilled angler, armed with the full array of jigs and live bait rigs, has at his command a versatile collection of effective presentations. If he's got a good boat and the skills needed to run it, he can *do anything he needs to do* to catch fish. He knows no limits.

That means he can put that boat where it has to be, exactly, under all kinds of circumstances.

The skilled angler has the right equipment and the knowledge to use it properly.

A Passion For Fishing

At about the same time as Bill Binkelman was making his break-through catch on Okauchee, a teen-aged kid was desperately trying to learn how to catch walleyes on the little Minnesota lake where his dad was building a cabin. I remember that struggle well, for I was that kid.

I'd been taught that the best way to get walleyes was with a Little Joe Bluetail Canadian Fly (a jig) with a sucker minnow on it. My dad and I used to drift across the center of the lake, dangling those jigs below us.

To call our boat control "primitive" would be to praise it. We had no maps to show us the shape of the lake, so we assumed it was deepest in those spots farthest from shore. We went where the wind sent us, though we learned in time that certain spots produced more fish. We didn't know why. That didn't matter much, for unless the wind was from the right direction we couldn't fish certain spots anyway.

Man, did we work hard to catch fish! Somehow we'd caught on to the importance of depth. Since we didn't have a fishing sonar, we took depth soundings by hand. By tying weighted lines to bleach bottles and setting them afloat, we could find the dropoffs. We were doing things the hard way, but at least we were asking the right sorts of questions. Even then, I had the idea that locating fish was the biggest challenge, and I knew depth had a lot to do with where fish held.

It seemed to me then that there must be some *secrets* that would unlock the puzzles of fishing and let me catch fish regularly.

Chapter 2
Understanding and Finding Fish

Let's establish some important points.

Most fishermen pay too much attention to *presentation*—their lures and retrieves—and far too little attention to the problems of *location*.

That is pretty understandable, but it's a classic case of putting the cart before the horse. *You can't catch 'em until you find 'em!* If you are sitting right over some fish, you might catch some with a screwball choice of lure or bait. Heck, I see that happen all the time. But if your boat is nowhere near a fish, which is the case with so many fishermen, you won't get any even if you "fish" with blasting caps.

I guess many people find the location part of the problem dull. They'd rather read about magic lures.

Well, I'm not going to put my name on a book that avoids talking about what I know is most important. After all, almost all of this book will be devoted to presentation of live bait. We simply have to talk a little about the part of the game that most people handle badly.

There are many, many different ways of catching fish, but they all start with *finding fish*. To do that, you need to know some things about how fish operate in their watery world.

If you really know all this stuff, you can skip this chapter. But I'm warning you, if I see you on the water, I'll give you a pop quiz on this stuff!

For a more complete treatment of these concepts, you should see my books *Bass Patterns* and *Walleye Patterns*.

It doesn't matter how well you present your bait, if you don't put it down in front of the fish.

Understanding Fish

Fish are cold-blooded creatures with small brains. Don't ever think in terms of "outsmarting" a fish. Even if your IQ is somewhere in the single figures, you are smarter than fish. Instead of brains, fish have instincts and keenly tuned senses. They have evolved over the centuries until they are extremely well adapted to their watery environment. Brains would just get in the way if they had them.

The real contest, then, is between your brains and the fishes' senses, wariness and instincts for survival. Not the fishes' brains. But don't take too much comfort from that. Any adult gamefish has already beaten long odds in the game of survival. It is a wary animal living in total harmony with its environment.

An adult largemouth bass, for example, knows how to use the cover in its lake or reservoir to feed with maximum efficiency. Quite a few bass spend much of their time in places where you couldn't place a bait unless you went down in a scuba outfit and shoved it in there by hand. Many of these fish are highly aware of boats and even understand that boats are a threat to them.

You need to understand the basic nature of fish, particularly the species you're fishing for. You have to understand its basic habitat needs and the kinds of food it depends upon. Fish have a sort of annual calendar, a cycle of activity and priorities that governs their activity. Then you have to consider the particular lake (or reservoir or river) you are fishing. What does it have to offer the fish you seek?

Knowing what the fish need and what the lake offers, you have a strong starting point for beginning the search for those fish. Then its a matter of carefully sorting out the possibilities.

The Senses of Fish

Fish have all the senses we humans have, plus an extra one. Fishermen screw up when we try to understand fish because we just can't get it through our heads that the basic senses of fish are *different* from ours!

Mostly they are different because water isn't air. Water does not carry light as well as air and is normally full of suspended particles that really cut down on light penetration. Air doesn't carry scent or transmit sound waves nearly as well as water. And objects move through water far more easily than in water.

Two senses, *touch* and *taste*, are relatively unimportant to fish.

There are exceptions. Catfish and bullheads, for example, depend on the sense of feel to help them move in lightless, muddy water. Their barbels are a special feeler device.

Catfish and bullheads also use their sense of taste to determine what is food and what is not. But most fish don't depend much on their sense of taste. Scientists tell us most fish species have few sensory receptors in the mouth area, so they receive little information that way. That fits with the observations of fishermen.

The sense of *hearing* in fish is important in a limited way. Fish have ears in their heads that pick up certain high frequency sounds. Clicks and scrapes are the sort of harsh, high frequency noise fish pick up with ears. High frequency sounds, like the noise of a trolling motor being slammed into its bracket, are danger signals to fish.

The sense of hearing, in other words, allows a fish to pick up on possible trouble. It is not a primary way of locating prey. That's one reason I've never been a big fan of crankbaits with loud rattles, for those high pitched sounds are what fish associate with threats, not a meal. Frogs and minnows don't rattle.

Fish are highly aware of what's going on in their world. They take any potential threat very seriously. A great many anglers I take out in my boat don't seem to realize how touchy fish are about unnatural noises.

The *lateral line perception*, on the other hand, is quite important for allowing gamefish to sense the presence of food. This is the ability of a fish to perceive low frequency pressure waves. Lateral line perception is something in between feeling and hearing. If you close your eyes and wave your hand near your face, the wind you feel is like the sound waves a fish senses with its lateral line.

With some species, such as largemouth bass, northern pike or walleyes, lateral line sensitivity is highly developed. Blindfolded largemouth bass have caught minnows in aquarium studies, snatching them as deftly as if they had perfect vision. Fish can "hear" a plastic worm wiggling in the water with this unique sense.

Fish species are quite variable in the acuteness of lateral line sensitivity. Even within a species, individual fish vary according to how well they can use lateral line sensitivity. Largemouth bass in clear water rely on their eyes to feed, so lateral line sensitivity in them is undeveloped. Bass feeding in dirty water, on the other hand, have acute lateral line sensitivity, as that is critical for their survival. A bass taken from clear water and blindfolded has difficulty locating minnows in an aquarium. Eventually they will learn to use lateral line sensitivity to feed.

In a school of minnows, perch or other small baitfish, there will often be a sick, weak or injured individual. When a predator comes into view, that unfit fish is apt to panic and send out erratic sound pulses that call attention to itself almost as if it were advertising. That's all part of Nature's plan.

Lateral line sensitivity not only supplements vision, but directs feeding within a school. In general, lateral line perception is much more important than humans generally recognize.

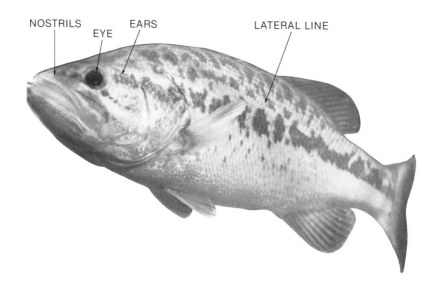

NOSTRILS   EYE   EARS   LATERAL LINE

The senses of a fish.

The sense of *sight* is extremely important to most fish.

Each species has slightly different eyes. Walleyes and saugers have eyes especially adapted for dim light vision. Their eyes sort of bounce the light around to get maximum information from it. Northern pike lack that special dim light perception ability, so they rarely feed except when the sun is up. Stream trout have eyes like microscopes, because feeding in current forces them to make thousands of quick decisions about what is food and what is not.

All fish tend to be nearsighted, for fish are intensely concerned about close objects and not concerned with objects that are farther away. Water is dense. Moving quickly in it requires great expenditures of energy. Neither food nor predators at a distance are much of a factor for fish.

For you or me, a semi truck coming at us in our lane of the highway is something we care about, even when it is 100 yards away. It's different for fish. A watery predator doesn't launch an attack from 30 yards away; 30 inches is more like it.

And fish simply can't see far in water anyway, for much water carries so many suspended particles that close range vision is the only important vision. Until you have done some diving, as our Babe Winkelman Research Team has, you might find this hard to appreciate. In some lakes, you can't see your hand if you extend your arm...and that's without considering timber, weeds or brush.

One big lesson in all this is that anglers rarely understand how close they have to get their lures to fish. Unless fish are in an aggressive mood, lures or baits more than a few inches away might just as well be on the other side of the lake.

Most gamefish are predators that have a blend of two- and three-dimensional vision. But, by far, the greatest percentage of their sight is two- dimensional, with the three-dimensional vision limited to a small area directly in front of them, where they feed.

Fish of forage species have eyes set well to the sides of their heads, the better to see predators coming. Predator fish have eyes set forward, the better to capture their prey with three-dimensional vision. Compare the location of eyes on the heads of northern pike and bluegills.

Too much used to be written about fish not having eyelids, a theory that seemed to explain why many predator fish lurk in shade. Actually, fish like bass and muskies have several ways of accomodating high light levels. Many predator fish use shade to hide in until their prey comes close. They only act as if they can't tolerate sunlight.

Fish can see colors—it's been proven time and again. Not all fish see colors the same way. Walleye eyes are primarily sensitive to greens and oranges. Bass eyes are most sensitive to reds and yellows.

You'll find controversy about the importance of the sense of *scent*.

Many fish, such as salmon, use the sense of scent to help them migrate across the ocean and return to their natal streams. Research has even shown that such lake gamefish as largemouth bass can return to the same site where they spawned before, probably through he use of scent.

Chemicals emitted by fish are important for controlling their social relations with fish of their species. Scientists and anglers alike know that scents can be "turn-off" or "turn-on" factors. Fish can communicate fear to each other. Some spawning behavior is regulated by scents.

One of the best examples of a negative scent is the scent put out by northern pike and muskies. It puts off such fish as bass. If you are trying to catch walleyes or bass and you get a pike or a musky, it will pay to put on a new lure or carefully wash and mask the scent on your lure.

Fish also use scent to locate prey. Trout, salmon and catfish are outstanding examples of species that sometimes depend heavily on the sense of smell when feeding.

Experienced anglers argue about whether it is more important to cover up bad odors or put out attractive ones. I believe both factors are important at times. Don't expect commercial scent products to make you a good angler, but they are one more tool to use in tough circumstances. I've seen commercial scents attract fish to a lure, many times. Often, though, it might be just as important to use a good soap, such as Lindy's No-Scent Soap, to avoid putting negative scents on your offering.

The Annual Cycle

If you understand the *annual cycle*, you'll know the priorities concerning fish at a given time of year. That's critical to finding them. Different species have slightly different annual calendars, but the basics hold true for all fish.

Winter is a time of inactivity for most species. In the icy water, a fish's metabolism slows down so much that it doesn't need much food. A small meal takes days and days to digest. That's good, because cold fish are not capable of running down much food.

That's good for another reason, too, for a lake's supply of food will be lower in winter than at any other time. Insect activity is minimal. Minnow schools have been depleted by summer and fall predation. Frogs and crayfish are hibernating.

Not all fish respond to winter's cool water the same way. Northern pike like it cold, so they go on feeding when other species are sluggish. Lake trout and eelpout are such cold-loving fish that they are more active under the ice than the rest of the year.

Spring is a crazy, fast-changing time. As the water warms up in the shallows, many fish change location drastically. Meanwhile, the spawn (in spring for most fish) has a powerful influence on fish behavior.

Some fish (like northern pike) spawn just before or after ice-out. Others (primarily walleyes) do so very soon afterward. But many species (bass, crappies, bluegills) hit the shallows for a pre-spawn feeding binge as soon as those areas become warm.

Understanding the fish's annual cycle is critical. Knowing the changes in location and behavior of the species you're after helps you stay on the fish as the seasons change.

Early in the spring, the weather switchable and fish might be forced to move a lot. They might be in the shallows, only to be driven out to the nearest dropoff by a cold front. Eventually things stabilize and the process of warming goes more steadily. In lakes or reservoirs, the process is much the same. The shoreline shallows in back bays, marshes, coves, boat canals and similar areas are the first to warm and first to attract fish.

As I said, fish come in to feed, though this early pre-spawn movement is often labeled a "spawning" movement by anglers. In the warming water, insects start moving. Minnow schools work on the insects. Frogs and crayfish crawl out of the ooze. Life resumes.

Fish of many species are highly catchable before the spawn because they are feeding aggressively and there is little food available to them. Water temperatures in spring are colder than fish prefer at other times of year, so you can often find fishing action by finding the warmest water around. For example, a cove that is three degrees warmer than another might have much faster bass or panfish fishing. Similarly, spring trolling for salmon can depend on finding water two or three degrees warmer than the surrounding water.

Spawning fish have a single-minded focus on the business at hand. They can rarely be caught, which is probably the way it ought to be.

The spawn of most fish is triggered by water temperature, but other factors are important. Usually it takes a certain water temperature in conjunction with day length and even moon phase to make the spawn take off.

The main thing to understand is that spawning does not all happen at once for fish of a given species. The spawn will go in fits and starts before and after the main bulk of fish (of a species) spawn. Fish like crappies might spread out their spawning in one lake over a period of six weeks.

That is a protective mechanism. If every smallmouth bass in a lake, for example, spawned at exactly the same moment in a given lake, that whole year's nesting effort could be wiped out by a single storm or cold snap.

The spawn is very difficult on fish, especially the females. With walleyes, males and females need time to recover after spawning; with bass, the females drop into deeper water while the males guard the nests. Fishing seasons are often set to open at the time most fish have just recovered and are ready to be active again.

Great fishing often occurs when the fish have all recovered from spawning. The food supplies in most lakes are low, yet the fish are super hungry. As the water warms, they need more and more food. And at the same time, most predator fish start using deeper water. Deeper water will become attractive to predators as deeper weeds begin to form.

Fish at this time are *feeding to grow*. That is, they are feeding in the most efficient way possible. Some species (smallmouth) stay at home, working the best feeding situations in a narrow area. Others (northerns, largemouth bass) might move around from spot to spot, taking advantage of the best feeding situations available.

And here are some examples. Some crappies are spawning in a marshy bay; several muskies hang right behind them in deeper water, swinging through from time to time to grab an easy meal. A rock pile has more crayfish in it than good hiding places; the local smallmouth are there to bring things back in balance. Mayflies begin hatching, popping out of the silt to float helplessly to the surface; a school of walleyes chops at them as they hatch and even when the mayflies are struggling in the surface film. Smelt come downriver after spawning in a Great Lakes stream; lake trout are waiting for them at the river-mouth.

As spring fades into summer, the water continues to warm and vegetation reaches its full development. Fish move to their summertime habitat. Lakes that will "thermocline"—divide into a three-layered thermal structure—will have done so. Everything stabilizes.

Just where the summertime habitat will be is not easy to say. Walleyes start off the year using shoreline areas and points, later moving to mid-lake structure...*if* there is any. Many lakes lack mid-lake structure. Largemouth bass make similar moves in many lakes, staying in or near heavy weeds much of the time, but in many lakes bass are obliged to take the most protective cover not being used by big northerns or walleyes.

In other words, where the fish go depends on the basic nature of the fish, the habitat in the lake, the nature of the lake's forage and the amount of competition exerted by other predator fish.

Summer is a time of relative stability. For several weeks, fish movements are regular and not hard to predict. Many fish move, but their movements are not as radical or hard to predict as they can be at other times of year. In particular, summer fish don't do a great deal of vertical moving (changing depths radically). Weather changes cause constant fluctuations in their mood, but enormous changes in location are not common.

In most lakes, fishing for bass, walleyes and northerns becomes more difficult in the middle of summer because so many young minnows and other little fish have grown to the size where they make a good meal. In lakes around my Brainerd home, this change often comes in the second week of July or so.

Fish continue to feed to grow throughout the summer. As the nights turn chilly, summer's great abundance of food fades. Natural mortality and persistent predation have beaten down the supply of small fish. There are still bonanza feeding situations, as when the frogs run into marshy bays to hibernate for the winter. The fish adapt to the new conditions, making the most of what their environment offers.

Fall sees many other changes. Dying weeds make some key feeding areas inhospitable, driving such fish as panfish and largemouth bass into deeper water. Many lakes in fall lose the three- layered thermal structure they had much of the year. Fish are more free to move shallow and deep, and they do move a lot in their quest for food. Fall fish often hold along steeply sloping structure, partly because they often make major vertical movements in fall.

In rivers and flowages, cold weather brings other changes. Walleyes begin to migrate toward the headwaters in what seems to be an early anticipation of the spawn. In reservoirs, both largemouth bass and shad concentrate in deeper holes, usually in the main lake area, where they will spend the winter.

In fall, fish switch feeding modes into what I call *feeding to fatten*. Fish are still looking for special feeding situations, but now they definitely prefer *larger* meals. I don't suppose they know winter is coming, but they feed as if they were pigging out in anticipation of the long cold winter. This is the time for anglers to use huge baits and hunt for a trophy. As in spring, fishing is better on warmer days.

And then winter...and the return of quiet times.

Activity Moods

Fish have moods. They can be aggressive, shy or anywhere in between.

We should distinguish between mood and behavior that is caused by population dynamics. In some little lakes, northern pike populations often get out of control. The fish won't be big, but they are plentiful and they will be amazingly aggressive. In such a lake, you can have northerns go sailing through the air to grab your lure as you pull it out of the water.

Similarly, in Canadian waters it isn't rare to see fish actually fighting to get to your lure. As a hooked fish runs around under your boat, other fish will try to steal the lure from its mouth.

Situations like those certainly represent aggressive fish, but their aggression is not the result of mood. Those fish have been thrust into a super-competitive situation where they can't afford to exercise the normal degree of caution on feeding.

Mood is something else. Mood is a predisposition to attack a lure, and it varies in most gamefish populations. A fish in an aggressive mood is primarily concerned about attacking food. A fish in a negative mood is primarily concerned about something else *getting him*.

When fish are aggressive (which isn't a large share of the time), they might chase down your lure even if you cast some distance away from them. When a lure hits somewhere near them, aggressive fish will wheel to face it and you'll often see wakes homing in on your spinnerbait or jig as you retrieve it.

Aggressive fish often honk down your whole bait in one decisive gulp. They can hit so hard you might have the rod knocked out of your hand. A northern pike might bash your spoon four times on the same retrieve, then finally nail it and get hooked. A bass or walleye will grab your jig-and- minnow and run quickly with it to get away from other fish in the school.

These are fairly rare but memorable moments. When fish are aggressive, you can (and *should*) use fast, noisy baits—something like a buzzbait, for example. You want to appeal to their aggressive side and you want to cover water quickly.

Fish exhibit different feeding "moods" at different times. Most of the time, they aren't very aggressive, and will scrutinize your bait closely before deciding to ignore or bite it.

Let's go to the opposite extreme.

When fish are negative, they hardly move at all to take a bait. Sometimes, in fact, they are bugged by the presence of your bait and will move off. I've banged my Lindy Rig sinker on the backs of walleyes that weren't in the mood to take. If you cast over shy fish, they might be spooked into running to deeper water by the sight of your lure in the air.

Negative fish are much better caught on live bait than artificials. Even then, you'll need to use smaller live baits, presenting them slowly and very close to the cover or structure where the fish are holding. Live bait anglers have to let negative fish play with the bait for a long time before setting the hook.

While aggressive fish often can be taken on a wide range of presentations, negative fish typically have a very specific notion of what they'll pop for. It's easy to get the wrong idea. You try and try to get some fish to move, but they just sit there, blips on your sonar. Then you change the type of minnow you're using, or you go to a slightly lighter jig, or you put a new color of spinner on your rig...and *bang, bang, bang!* That was it!

Fish are rarely super shy or super aggressive; usually they're somewhere in the middle. They are fairly catchable, but not pushovers.

Every day you go fishing, you need to determine the mood of the fish. If they are aggressive, you can fish fast and cover a lot of water. If they are off their feed, you'll need to be extra cautious, slow and methodical.

Mood Influences

Why do fish change moods? Sometimes we can seem to tell, and sometimes only the fish seem to know why they have changed aggression levels.

Most fish seem to respond to several influences that we can trace. The big mood influences are *hunger, weather, water temperature* and *the spawn.*

We already know that spawning fish have their minds on something other than eating. And fish right after the spawn are trying to recover from the grueling exerience (spawning is so rough on some fish that they die afterwards).

Weather is the main influence on mood throughout the summer (and, actually, at other times of year). Weather is a weird variable. I don't completely understand it, and I won't trust anybody who says he does! East winds are bad for fishing. I don't know why. They just are.

The most common weather influence on mood is the *cold front.* You know—a storm system moves through, then the next day the sky is deep blue, the clouds are miles high, the weather is delightfully cool…and the easy fishing you were enjoying a day or two ago is gone.

Cold fronts are likely to move fish mood in a negative direction. Some fronts are harsher than others. Worst of all is a succession of frequent fronts, so that just when the fish are coming out of the postfrontal slows, another front hits. The longer it has been since a front last came through, the better the fishing.

Let me make two quick points on cold fronts. Not all fish are equally affected by them. Largemouth bass and walleyes are much more sensitive to fronts than northern pike, for example, and Great Lakes salmon and trout may not be affected at all.

Second, even after a bad front, fishing is not impossible. You fish more carefully, you change tactics, you do what you have to do…but you can catch fish. I've taken some beautiful fish in the middle of postfrontal conditions.

Storms are another weather phenomenon which influence mood. Again, I don't completely understand this, but the earliest stages of a rainstorm are often fantastic for fishing. Fish will be as positive as they can get.

A severe thunderstorm approaching on the Red River in Manitoba. Weather has a tremendous affect on fish location and feeding moods.

Water temperature also affects fish mood. Maybe it would be more accurate to say extra cold or warm temperatures reduce fish activity. It is possible (particularly in southern states) for water temperatures to go so high that fish are reluctant to move, except maybe at night. But usually a fish can move deeper to avoid hot water temperatures.

More often—every winter, spring and fall— the water is at the cold end of what fish can tolerate. In general, fish in too-cold water feed lightly. A spell of warm weather or some special source of hot water (like a warm stream entering a lake) can produce dynamite fishing.

Finally, hunger obviously relates to fish aggression levels. A hungry fish is more apt to chase your lure than a full fish. Fish can be hungry when food supplies are low...or when competition for food is severe.

Fish don't chase food on a continual basis but seem to feed in intense periods, then go dormant for a period of time. For reasons I can't explain, fish don't make these transitions from inactivity to activity on an individual basis but as groups. A whole school of fish will turn on at once, perhaps coming in out of deep water where they were susupended to suddenly rip up the baitfish along a reef. And when the fish of one species turn on in one end of the lake, it's often true that the fish of that species at the other end are also going. We don't know why.

The World of the Fish

Lake and River Classifications

Every lake is to some extent unique, but there are very important ways in which lakes are the same. The most basic division of all lakes is based on how fertile they are. Any lake can be ranked on a scale from: *oligotrophic* (the least fertile), *eutrophic* (most fertile) or *mesotrophic* (somewhere in between).

No need to get nervous about those strange scientific names. Most fishermen already understand these three types of lakes.

Oligotrophic lakes are clear, rock-bound, sterile waters like many Canadian lakes. They seem to be an angler's heaven until a few float planes have landed, and suddenly they might be fished out. These lakes are very limited in terms of the fish life they can sustain. They are a good example of a "fragile" natural resource. They typically have lake trout, northerns and walleyes in them. Any lake with lake trout, in fact, is basically an oligotrophic lake.

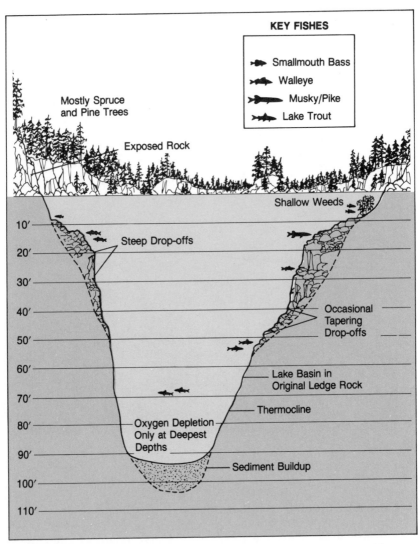

Oligitrophic lakes are characterized by deep basins and infertile water. They are, by nature, best suited for fish like lake trout but can also support small populations of walleyes, smallmouth bass and northern pike.

Eutrophic lakes are soupy, shallow, warm lakes that often carry big algae blooms most of the summer. They are loaded with food, but they often support undesirable fish like bullheads, carp and tremendous populations of stunted panfish. Some, however, are also great large-mouth lakes. You don't expect very much *structure* on eutrophic lakes, as they tend to be bowl-shaped lakes with silty bottoms (I'll define structure in a moment).

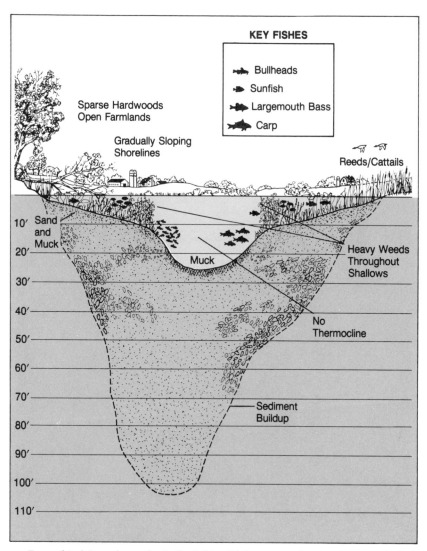

KEY FISHES

- Bullheads
- Sunfish
- Largemouth Bass
- Carp

Sparse Hardwoods
Open Farmlands

Gradually Sloping
Shorelines

Reeds/Cattails

10' Sand
and
Muck

20'

Muck

Heavy Weeds
Throughout
Shallows

30'

40'

No
Thermocline

50'

60'

70'

Sediment
Buildup

80'

90'

100'

110'

Eutrophic lakes, the geologically "oldest" lakes, are rich in nutrients and often low in oxygen, especially in the latter stages of the eutrophication process. The water is off-colored and by summer becomes thick with algae, which limit oxygen levels. These lakes are often referred to as "bass and panfish lakes" because, of the desireable species, they support best.

A great many fishing lakes fall in the middle, mesotrophic category. They are reasonably clear but have good weed growth. They hold walleyes, northerns, sunfish, perch, crappies and bass— either smallmouth or largemouth or even both. Many mesotrophic lakes have fairly firm bottoms with a decent amount of structure. I'm fortunate enough to live right among some of the nation's best mesotrophic lakes, but they are found across the continent.

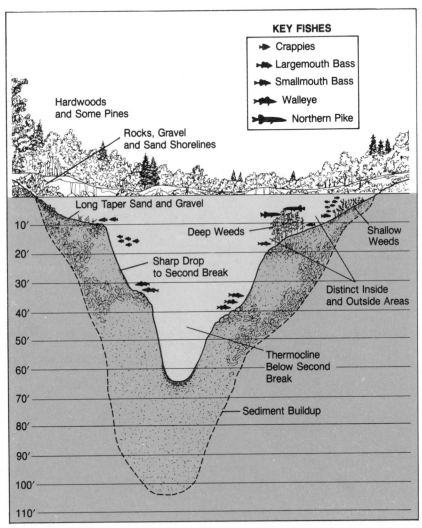

KEY FISHES

- Crappies
- Largemouth Bass
- Smallmouth Bass
- Walleye
- Northern Pike

Hardwoods
and Some Pines

Rocks, Gravel
and Sand Shorelines

Long Taper Sand and Gravel

Deep Weeds

Shallow
Weeds

Sharp Drop
to Second Break

Distinct Inside
and Outside Areas

Thermocline
Below Second
Break

Sediment Buildup

Mesotrophic *bodies of water have medium fertility and can support a wide range of fish species. They are the ideal environment for naturally-reproducing walleye populations. They can also hold good numbers of smallmouths, largemouths, muskies, northerns, crappies and sunfish. As a rule, mesotrophic lakes have ample and varied weed growth, and can have large basins of shallow, medium-depth and deep water.*

We have to be careful about generalizations here. Some lakes fit in two categories. A popular lake near Minneapolis, Minnetonka, is actually a series of bays; at its upstream end, Minnetonka is a series of eutrophic bays, but it concludes downstream in a series of bays that are mesotrophic. Oligotrophic wilderness lakes commonly have some mesotrophic bays, or a mesotrophic lake might have eutrophic sections.

Rivers don't fit the same kind of categorization, though some people have tried to do it. Rivers take their character in a variety of ways: the volume of water they carry, the speed of the current, the amount of structure they hold, the fertility of the soil they drain, the basic temperature of the water, etc. I've never seen a classification system on rivers that seemed to work.

Fish in rivers relate to structure just as fish in lakes do, but they also are powerfully influenced by *current*. The impact of current on all sorts of structure or obstacles produces lots of little edges, where slow and fast water come together, and those are the key spots for finding river fish. You get nowhere fishing rivers until you come to terms with current.

Flowages and reservoirs have some of the characteristics of rivers and some of lakes. The main consideration is how much current effect there is in a given area. If there is much current, fish will behave like river fish; if the current is negligible, fish act just as they do in a lake.

Thermal Layering

In late spring or summer, many lakes settle out into three layers. The warmest upper layer, the *epilimnion*, has plenty of oxygen, but might be too warm for such fish as walleyes. The lowest layer, the *hypolimnion*, is very cold. As time goes on, the hypolimnion gradually loses its oxygen. In between those two layers is a thin *thermocline* in which the water temperature drops suddenly.

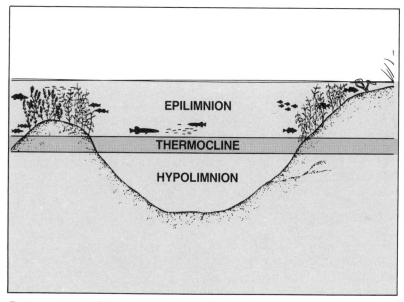

During summer, lakes sometimes stratify *into layers of water density and temperature. The middle layer, or* thermocline, *is a thin band separating the warmer epilimnion from the colder hypolimnion. A thermocline may set up and break up several times during the season. In many lakes, the hypolimnion is devoid of oxygen, so fish are in or above the thermocline.*

47

In lakes that develop thermoclines, much good summer fishing takes place in or just above the thermocline. Fish *can* survive in the hypolimnion, but few gamefish go there. For one thing, to move quickly from the warmer water above into the icy hypolimnion can cause potentially fatal thermal shock.

Fish do pass through the thermocline; I see them do it on my graph from time to time. But many fish hold in or just above the thermocline. At first, the cold water below the thermocline has plenty of oxygen. In time, as plants and algae die and decompose in the depths, they use up the oxygen and there is no way it can be replenished.

That means that many fish (walleyes, bass and panfish) behave as if the summer thermocline is the lower limit of the lake. They just don't go lower than that as a routine practice. When fish are down in the cold water below the thermocline, they are certainly not very catchable...I've found that out, often enough. The one exception to that rule is the lake trout, a fish that loves icy water.

In fall, when the layered structure breaks down, a lake is temporarily homogenous, both in oxygen content and temperature. Fish are free to move anywhere they please, and they do move.

Remember, not all lakes thermocline, and not all gamefish are found above the hypolimnion. In oligotrophic lakes (which, remember, have few nutrients), the oxygen does not get consumed in the cold hypolimnion. Fish can live there, and that in fact is where lake trout stay when the surface water is warm. There is also evidence that large northern pike live below the thermocline in the hot months.

Water Clarity

Water clarity has an impact on fish and fishing.

Most water has some amount of suspended matter in it. Light transmission is reduced by those particles, making the underwater world darker. But there are big differences in lakes on this point.

In the crystal clear waters of some Canadian lakes or Lake Superior, fish see well but know they can be seen. In such water, fish are usually wary and hard to approach, often sticking tightly to cover or deep water.

When feeding, fish in clear lakes rely on their eyes more than other senses. Since the light penetrates deeper, weeds grow at greater depths. While you might rarely fish deeper than 12 feet in a lake with dark water, in a very clear lake it wouldn't be strange to fish 30 feet down or more for smallmouth bass or walleyes. In my experience, fish in clear lakes tend to feed deliberately. Walleyes in very clear water often revert to night feeding.

You have to be more careful about approaching fish in clear water. If you are Lindy Rigging for walleyes, you might need to have a lot of line out behind the boat, and even then you'd want to use an electric trolling motor. If you're pitching jigs for smallmouth bass in clear water, your

Fish that live in very clear (left) and murky (right) waters are faced with differing environments. They adapt to life in very different environments.

casts might need to be longer and your line lighter. In clear water you pay attention to the presence of shadows, and you make a special effort to fish tight to cover. I could tell you about times when I could tell I was spooking fish in 30 feet of water, and I was using my trolling motor!

Fish in turbid, dark water are a different story. They'll roam around in the security of the dark water, paying less attention to the need to get under logs or deep in the weeds. You can put a boat right on top of them without spooking them. They may, however, have difficulty locating prey or your lure, and they'll make more use of other senses, especially their lateral line perception.

You can catch these fish with very short casts, but you might need to use noisy lures or lures that are fluorescent or even phosphorescent. For example, a classic technique for catching largemouth bass in turbid water is to cast noisy crankbaits so they riccochet off timber and draw strikes from fish that "hear" them with lateral line sensitivity. I've done well on walleyes and other fish with Lazer Tail jigs, soft plastic jigs with phosphorescent tails.

Water clarity is not the only factor that causes the underwater world to be bright. Because of the position of the sun, more light comes into the water in summer than in spring or fall. Since light levels are less harsh at dawn and dusk, many predator fish are far more active then. Sky cover obviously affects how much light hits the water. And a ruffled, choppy lake surface admits far less light than a glass-smooth surface.

All these factors have to be put together and balanced out. The clearer a lake is, and the brighter the conditions are, the deeper fish will tend to hold.

That doesn't mean high winds and dark skies automatically mean fish will be shallow and active. In a lake with murky water, high winds can be bad because the reduced light levels can make it difficult for even walleyes to feed. Yet on a lake across the road with very clear water, a "walleye chop" on the water might mean lower light levels and a welcome pick-up in fishing action from walleyes.

Predator/Prey Relations

The predator-prey relationship is no joke to the fish. They are locked in a constant struggle for survival, during which they may be eaten by a bigger fish at any moment. As a fisherman, you must learn to appeal to their instinct to prey on other things, while at the same time avoid spooking them.

Fish don't live alone in water. To understand how fish operate and where they'll be, you have to consider the mix of species persent.

It helps to know what predators are in the lake. If you're looking for largemouth bass in some lakes I know, it is important to realize that there are lots of big northerns in those lakes. Because of the northerns, the bass are forced to live in shallow water—sunfish water—in order to keep from becoming a meal.

Knowing the main food species also helps. If you are fishing Lake Erie where walleyes feed heavily on suspended schools of smelt, you'll be fishing mid-depth water; walleyes in a lake with a perch forage base will primarily feed near the bottom.

For example, I just fished two nearby Ontario lakes for big northerns. One lake had a forage base of whitefish. The whitefish were feeding in shallow, sandy-bottomed bays with timber, working on the insects there. Since the whitefish were up in the shallow timber bays, that's where the northerns were. The other lake was food-poor, so northerns were forced to eat each other or the walleyes in that lake. There we caught northerns fishing rocky reefs where walleyes might be found, though some northerns were in grassy bays feeding on smaller pike.

Predator-prey relationships will change with the season, even week-by-week. When the frogs start running into the shallow bays in fall, bass and even walleyes will act like there is no other food and no other place for them to be. They take advantage of that feeding situation as long as it is prime, then move on. The best feeding opportunities are always changing. The fish are always on top of them.

Structure and Cover

Structure and cover are two elements of the underwater world that make certain areas much more attractive to fish than others.

Structure refers to significant features or changes in the bottom. A reef is structure, as is an island or a point. Others include humps, saddles, holes, dropoffs and flats. A change in bottom composition—like from silt to gravel—can be considered structure; it is a significant change that attracts fish.

Fish are attracted to structure for two or three big reasons. First, most structure offers some handy options on depth. A hump, for example, allows a walleye or northern to feed in food-rich shallows...and yet they can always slip off into the security of deep water without travelling far.

Structure also makes for *edge effects*, and all animals are attracted to edges. Hunters know the importance of edges for concentrating grouse or almost any game, and it is no different with fish. An edge represents the coming together of two types of habitat. It is a meeting point, an area where fish naturally congregate.

Finally, it's clear that most fish like to "relate to something" rather than occupying a space in empty water. A point or a reef is something like a home base or a center of activity for fish.

Cover satisfies different needs. Cover is usually some sort of vegetation—trees, brush or weeds—in the water. But some rocks can be cover, or manmade objects such as riprap, docks and old auto bodies.

Cover offers predators both security and a place to launch an ambush. A pile of sunken brush in front of a dock in a reservoir offers crappies security, plus the branches concentrate food for the fish. From a good bunch of weeds or some timber, a predator fish can feed efficiently. He can eat without being eaten.

Let's sharpen up our notion of cover. A bunch of weeds is cover. A stand of timber is cover. But fish will see cover with more precise eyes. They are extremely aware of little places where weeds or timber might be especially thick and protective. If you lived in a weedbed for even a week, you'd have that same kind of awareness. Since you don't, you have to use your imagination a little.

Fish are highly aware of two common features of cover that all good anglers also recognize. Whether you are talking about timber, weeds, brush or some other kind of cover, a universal feature would be a *point* or projection extending off that cover. Fish naturally concentrate on or in points of cover.

An *inside turn* is a small opening along the edge of cover. It is the opposite of a point in shape, but identical in its ability to concentrate fish.

Both points and inside turns feature the edge effect I talked about earlier. Two habitats are meeting. Points and inside turns made excellent ambush spots.

Fish often concentrate in points or inside turns. As a rule, on a given day fish of a given species will be either on the points or inside turns of cover...not both. So largemouth bass will be on the points or tucked up in the inside turns, not in both places at once. But if bass are in the inside turns, northern pike might be on the points.

Some fish species, of course, don't rely on cover. Walleyes don't normally use weeds very much. But when walleyes are stocked in weedy bass lakes which lack traditional walleye structure, they will take up residence in the weeds, for that's where the food is. Salmon are typical of fish that simply chase down their food rather than ambushing it from cover (which is one reason they have the muscles to fight so well).

For many fish, the single most important key to finding them is locating those *structure-cover combinations* that offer them everything they want. In most lakes, there are a whole *lot* of places a fish can be. To find them, you have to find the combination of cover and structure that offers the most optimum circumstances for fish. It isn't enough to know bass are in "weeds" on "points." In a lake with a decent amount of structure and weed growth, the bass are probably concentrated in certain kinds of points at a particular depth in a particular type of weed. As an angler, you need to expand your awareness of the ways these various factors combine.

You usually can't find fish by simply finding some gross object in the water—a reef, or a big weedbed, for example. You then have to find the small places on that larger object that concentrate fish. On the reef there might be a little finger of rubble projecting into deeper water. In the weedbed there might be some extra heavy clumps of weeds. Find something like that, and you are looking in the right sort of place.

Cover and structure can exist in greater or lesser quantities. Some lakes have a bewildering variety of structure, while others are featureless saucers. Some lakes have tremendous amounts of cover, while others are cover-poor.

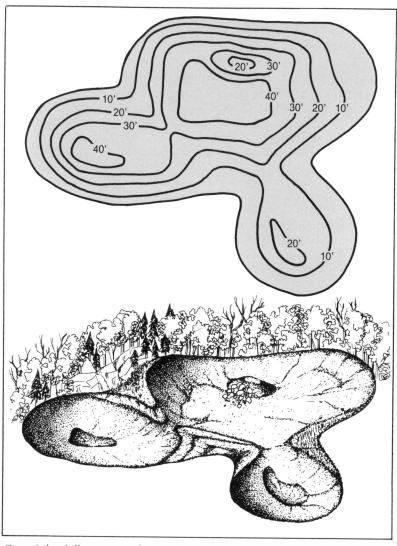

One of the skills you must hone to become a successful fisherman is the ability to read a topographic map of a lake and picture the major structural elements it shows. Examine this two-part illustration closely. It shows you the actual lake bottom (below) that the map represents. Teach yourself what all the lines on the map mean, and then practice finding major structures on an actual lake with your sonar.

Here's a good general rule: the less cover or structure a lake has, the more important the little bits of them become. If a small lake has one little reef, you'll sure want to work that reef carefully. On the other hand, when structure and cover are abundant, fish get to choose which of all the great-looking structure they'll use. Then, to find them, you have to find exactly the *ideal* combination of structure, cover and water depth.

The Importance of Depth

Almost always, the first critical step in finding fish is to learn *how deep they are.*

Deep water represents security to fish, and that is terribly important to them. They have many escape options in deep water, plus they don't have to worry about attacks from the air. Much of the time, deep water is more comfortable for them because light levels are not harsh and the temperature will usually be right.

But if a fish goes too deep, it might run out of oxygen or cover. Weeds can only grow so deep in a lake, then they stop. In many lakes, the shallows are the big food-producing areas, so big fish lying in deep water would be a long way from their "kitchen" areas.

So every fish in every body of water has to choose its depth carefully. They'll be responding to a whole lot of factors at once: water temperature, weed growth, light penetration, escape options and the presence of food. At times fish of a species will stack up a certain depth with eery consistency. Other times the factors that would concentrate them are not working together, and you'll find some fish shallow and some deep.

My point is simply this: the search for fish has to deal with the all-important issue of depth. If you ask me where I just caught a 6-pound largemouth, I would start the description by saying, "In 19 feet of water, right by...." If you're telling me about the 9-pound walleye you just caught, don't tell me it came from in front of the cabin where the mean dog lives; tell me how deep that walleye was. That's not the only thing I want to know, but it's the first thing!

Getting the depth right is the most important single step in finding fish. That is why the invention of a fishing sonar was absolutely necessary before modern fishing techniques could be developed.

Pattern Fishing

Some people get frustrated with careful, qualified statements with a lot of "some fish" and "might be" or "at times" statements. Okay, here comes a big, fat, unqualified statement. *There's only one smart way to fish, the way all good anglers fish.* It's called *pattern fishing.* Amazingly enough, pattern fishing works when you're trolling blue water for tuna or casting tiny dry flies for brown trout in streams.

It all boils down to three basic ideas:

- *At a given time, most fish of a species will be found in a certain kinds of places.*
- *At a given time, most fish of a species will be vulnerable to certain kinds of presentations.*
- *Every day, the challenge to every angler is to work out two patterns, the locational pattern and the presentational pattern.*

Let's take those ideas in order.

Fish are in certain types of places, not scattered randomly all over the lake. When you go fishing, you've got to find the kinds of places will be that day—what depth, what kind of structure, what kind of cover.

And there will be a pattern to their location. Not every fish will be in identical cover, etc., but usually there will be one or two or three definite types of spot where the fish will be concentrated.

This is true no matter what kind of fish you are dealing with. There will be a regularity, a pattern, to the places you find fish.

You always start off with guesses about where the fish are, then you refine those guesses by systematically checking out the possibilities. You know what season it is and therefore what the fish will have as their priorities. You know how warm the lake is, how dark the water is and what kinds of structure and cover options the lake offers the fish. You know whether recent weather has been favorable or unfavorable. You can tell whether the light levels are so bright as to push the fish deep.

So you go fishing, not to catch a fish so much as to *find a fish*. If you pay attention and fish systematically, you will get a fish or at least a strike. The process of homing on the location is now well along!

You also need to identify the best presentation. That is, you need to identify the best lure or bait to use, as well as how fast to move it and with what kind of action. Every time you catch a fish or even just get a light pickup, you are gathering information that points toward the best presentation.

The important thing is to *move* until you contact active fish and to *move systematically* from one type of spot to another. And when you get any indication you have found fish you can often switch emphasis to your presentation.

While you are moving to nail down location, you also should be working systematically to learn the presentation that best suits the fish. It helps to have different fishermen in the boat working with different baits until you're sure enough of the right presentation that everyone can swing over to it.

There can be several locational patterns for the same species of fish, and any number of effective ways of catching them. But if you work systematically, you will find the most productive pattern for both location and presentation. Keep alert, for patterns change. You might have to start fishing a little deeper or maybe switch colors, etc.

Pattern fishing doesn't remove all complexity from fishing. It just forces you to look at all the little factors that are so important, trying hard to identify exactly where the fish are concentrated and exactly what they seem to want.

Pattern fishing isn't just a way of fishing. It is *the* way to fish.

Attitude

There are many differences between a great angler and a guy who occasionally has a good day. One has better equipment and more refined skills. He can get on fish a lot faster than most anglers. He fishes more often and has a better feel for what's happening to his live bait rig. He hears more of what his jig is telling him. And so forth.

But one big difference is *attitude*.

If you don't insist on good fishing, you aren't likely to get it.

That's the trouble with so many fishermen— they don't expect to do well, so when they don't do well it is hardly a surprise. *They settle for bad fishing.*

Oh, if they happen to stumble into a hot situation, they'll happily catch fish and feel like heroes for a few days. But they don't hit the water with the attitude that they expect—even demand—the very best fishing possible that day. And if they don't insist on the best action possible, they won't get it.

Let's say a pair of fishermen find a shoreline point where a Lindy Rig baited with minnows produces two small walleyes one morning, in three hours of fishing. If they're like many guys, they'll probably spend the rest of the morning working that spot, over and over. After all they caught fish there and they didn't catch anything anywhere else.

If they're like many anglers, in fact, they'll be back the next day and the next. Each guy is taking a walleye or two a day.

They have *settled for* bad fishing.

That's not for me. I get enough slow fishing without settling for it, because some days I just can't hit it big no matter how hard I try. But my point is this: at least I'm going to ask for the very best fishing possible each day, not settling for the stuff that comes easy.

If I pick up a couple of small fish in an area, I might be encouraged to switch presentations to see if something better is there to be caught. Or I might zip across the lake to an entirely different sort of spot and check it out. Or I might run my boat up on the trailer and fire on over to another lake rather than dying on a lake that isn't doing anything.

I am *not* going to be happy to flog unpromising water for hours and hours.

I don't want two little fish, I want six big ones. If I don't get them in spite of my best efforts, fine. I'll be thankful for another wonderful day on the water. But I basically expect a lot from the water and from myself. If I settled for bad fishing, I'd be cheating myself and all the work I've put into developing myself as an angler.

Expect good fishing every time you go fishing. Raise your sights a little. Be grateful for every fish that comes your way, but try always to make better fishing happen. Don't settle for mediocrity in your fishing, for that's a way of accepting mediocrity in yourself.

Ask and ye shall receive. If you don't settle for bad fishing, you will have more good days.

Chapter 3

Live Bait: Let's Get it Straight

Lowering a bait into the water is the moment of truth in fishing. All of your planning is over: you've picked the water you're going to fish, you've decided somehow that it's worth your time to fish at the spot you are now over, and you are all rigged up.

Are you forgetting anything?

Does the live bait you are sending down there to represent you look like the man of the hour? Does your minnow look lively? Did your leech wiggle so hard you could barely get it on the hook? Does your nightcrawler look like a weightlifter, all pumped up and ready for action?

If your live bait looks like it just went 10 rounds with the champ, you are kidding yourself if you think it's going to catch a lot of fish. If the fish are really on, ready to bite anything that isn't attached to the lake bottom, you might get a few bites on a nightcrawler that couldn't crawl across the bottom of the boat. But if they aren't, if the fish are in the mood they usually are in, you might as well be home watching television.

It's important to always keep a fresh, spunky offering in front of the fish. One of the things that separates great fishermen from others is the *amount* and *variety* of live baits they bring with them, even for a day's outing. They change leeches frequently on their live bait rigs, not just after one has become chewed until it looks like a piece of beef jerky. And if leeches don't do the trick, they have some minnows waiting in a nearby bucket.

When they go out early in the season, they don't just take one type of minnows. They might have fatheads, redtail chubs, and some shiners along, or some similar assortment. And, even though minnows are usually the best choice in early season, there is usually a container of nightcrawlers somewhere in the boat, if you look close enough.

You get the idea. This is just one more of those *little* things I talk about so often. You have to buy live bait according to what you can afford, of course, but if you can keep a good quantity and variety on hand and experiment as you fish, you will automatically have an advantage over fishermen who don't.

There's more to picking out, catching, and caring for live bait than most people realize. You shouldn't just walk into a bait shop and buy the first box of nightcrawlers you grab, and you shouldn't have the bait salesman fill your bucket with minnows until you've had a look at what kind of condition they're in.

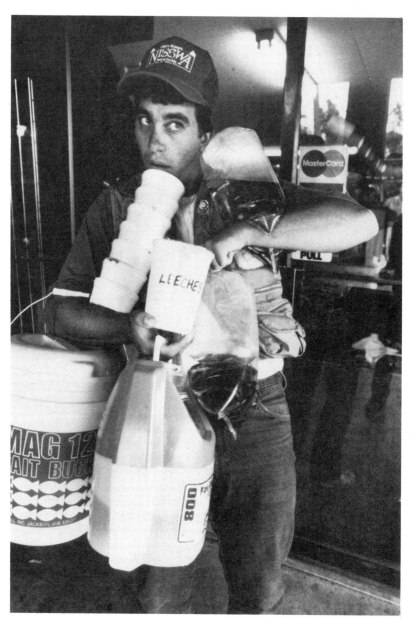

Once you buy bait, it doesn't just take care of itself, either. Believe me, the crew and I have learned some valuable lessons these past years, as we travel the country filming the *Good Fishing* television series. We usually try to bring our own supply of live bait, and we now have our own special aerated coolers that are constantly iced down and checked as we go from stop to stop. The water is changed only when we can be sure the new water won't kill the bait, which means doing it at a lakeshore or good bait shop.

Most bait is fragile and needs to be kept in certain ways to stay alive and healthy. Learning about live baits is a very important step to becoming a better fisherman.

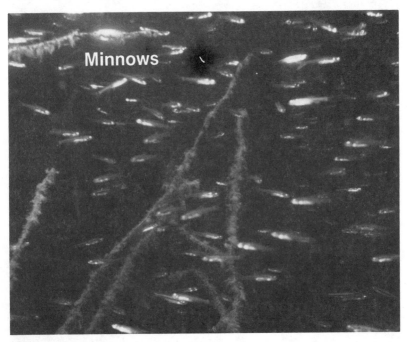

Keeping Minnows Alive

Bait dealers are good at keeping minnows alive. They have to be; their livelihood depends on it. If they can't keep minnows for a fairly long time, in healthy condition, they won't have anything to sell their customers, and they won't be eating very well.

But as soon as you buy some minnows from a bait dealer, the minnows become your problem. *You* must now care for them, or they will die or just sit there when you want them to wiggle and struggle on your hook.

There are some common things that kill minnows, or at least make them "wimpy" baits, that you can learn to avoid and watch for. With careful attention to common sense care, you can keep minnows alive and jumping while you're out fishing, and can even keep them until you go out fishing again.

Probably the most important thing to consider when trying to keep minnows—and all live bait for that matter—alive and healthy is the *oxygen* factor.

It *almost* goes without saying, but minnows need oxygen to live. Water temperature has a lot to do with the oxygen content, because cold water can hold much more oxygen than warm water. At 90 degrees F., for example, water holds 7.3 parts per million (PPM) oxygen, compared to 13 PPM at 40 degrees F.

If you crowd too many minnows into one little bait bucket, they will soon exhaust the supply of oxygen and die. It's a good idea to only keep a few dozen of most minnows in a bucket.

If the water gets too warm, it won't hold as much oxygen. Warmer water also raises the metabolic rate of the minnows, forcing them to take in more oxygen. In this kind of environment, minnows will die off very quickly. Simply keep the water cool and the battle is almost over, as long as the minnows aren't overcrowded.

During the spring, fall and winter, low oxygen levels are not normally a problem. About the only thing to worry about at those times of year is overcrowding. To avoid this, don't buy any more minnows than you need at any one time.

Learn to keep an eye on the oxygen situation in your minnow buckets. Remember, healthy minnows swim to the bottom of the bucket. If your minnows are at the top, sucking for air, that should be a big clue that it's time to get them some!

Tips on Caring for Your Minnows' Oxygen Needs

• If you are going to be driving for more than an hour or so to get to the lake, especially in hot weather, have the bait shop pack your minnows in an oxygen bag. Better bait shops will offer this service. The salesman will put the minnows in a small amount of water in the bottom of a large plastic bag, then fill the bag with oxygen, closing it with a sealing ring. As long as this bag is kept out of the sun and heat (the plastic bag magnifies the effects of sun), minnows can be kept alive for days until you are ready to fish.

• Use an aerator or pump-aerator combination to keep fresh, oxygen-rich water in your bucket. Simple aerators keep the existing water mixing with the surrounding air, which increases the amount of dissolved oxygen.

There are a few cautions about using an aerator. Number one, don't use one that is too big and powerful for the amount of water you are aerating. If the motor churns up the water too much, it can actually cause it to become supersaturated with nitrogen, killing the minnows. Use common sense in evaluating this. You should see a steady bubbling, not a heavy churning that creates a foaming of the water that you can't see through.

Number two, remember that aerators cause a current flow in the water, which the minnows have to swim against. If you subject minnows to too strong a current for much time, they can get physically worn out and perform poorly as bait.

Aerator-pump combinations not only circulate the existing water in your minnow bucket, but also are capable of pumping fresh water in to replace the old. This is the sort of system found in a boat livewell, and there are several available on the market. The best line of aerators I've ever found, from simple ones to more elaborate pumps, are made by Marine Metal Products Co., Inc., 1222 Range Rd., Clearwater, FL 33575-5074.

Aerated buckets and oxygen bags are essential for keeping minnows healthy during transport and fishing.

• Built-in baitwells right in the boat are the handiest, surest way to keep bait alive and in good condition. My new Ranger Fisherman has one built in near the rear driver's seat, and it is one of the nicest features of a super boat. It has an aerator-pump system built in, along with a drain plug. It never tips over and spills, and you can choose to pump fresh water continuously or occasionally over your bait, or in hot weather seal it off and control the temperature of the water with ice cubes.

• O-tabs are little tablets that fizzle like Alka Seltzer, setting up a cascade of bubbles which raise oxygen levels.

They have been around for a long time. They were invented in 1939 by a chemist named Carl Pemble. What they are is a combination of chemicals that react with water to release (not produce) oxygen from the chemicals. The reaction gives off a small percentage of carbon dioxide, but this has never caused a problem with minnows.

O-tabs are most useful in warm weather, when oxygen levels in minnow buckets can be very low. They last for up to 36 hours, but are most effective for the first three or four hours. To use them, remove the lid on the small can and place the rest of the can into the bait container, open side up. It will start bubbling.

• Do whatever you can to keep the water cool and out of direct sunlight. Keep the lid on your minnow bucket or keep it in the shade if you are fishing from shore. Add ice cubes slowly if the water gets too warm.

Water Purity

Chlorine may be a wonderful and necessary purifier of our drinking water, but chlorinated water kills minnows and other live baits, such as leeches. Never put your minnows in ordinary tap water that contains chlorine; use lake or well water, if available.

If you must use tap water, dechlorinate it by letting it stand overnight (the chlorine will evaporate from the water), or by using the drops or tablets aquarium owners use for the same purpose.

Another thing that affects water purity is the amount of time your minnows have been in the bucket, and how warm the water is. When left in the same water too long, oxygen isn't the only problem facing your minnows. Warm water, which speeds up the metabolism of the minnows, also presents a purity problem. In warmer water, the minnows' own waste products can contaminate the water. Change it or cool it down before it gets to that point.

Water Temperature

In general, the preferred water temperature for most minnows is 50-60 degrees F. It is important to realize, though, that a drastic *change* in water temperature can spell doom for your minnows as surely as the water being too warm or too cold can. A quick change in water temperature, anything over about 10 degrees, might not kill the minnows immediately, but it surely will within a day or so.

Water temperature problems are almost nonexistent during the colder months in spring, fall and winter, but are ever-present and can cause serious problems during the hot summer months.

To prevent problems with water temperature, *temper* the water your minnows are in. If you are going to put minnows into water that is more than 10 degrees different than what they are in, gradually raise or lower the temperature the minnows are in by adding small amounts of ice or adding warm (not hot) water while mixing constantly. Try to get the water to within 5 degrees of the water in the other container if possible. To help you do this, keep an inexpensive thermometer in your tackle box at all times.

This is another area where common sense can avoid big headaches. During the hot summer months when surface temperatures in lakes have risen dramatically, avoid placing floating minnow buckets directly in the lake. The difference in the temperature of the lake compared to that the minnows came in can be as high as 30-40 degrees. When you bring minnows from a bait shop out onto the lake, let the warm air temperature gradually temper the water in the floating minnow bucket. Again, check the water temperature in both the bucket and the lake with a thermometer.

Dark metal and plastic minnow buckets absorb heat. If you take a dark bucket that has been sitting in the sun or the trunk of your car into a bait shop and the bait salesman immediately puts water and minnows into your bucket, it won't be long before the water has heated up enough to kill the minnows.

If you use one of these types of buckets, make sure the bait salesman rinses the bucket in cold water. It's best, in fact, to leave cold water sitting in the bucket for a few minutes, to cool it down. Then, dump out the water and replace it with new, cold water before putting minnows in the bucket.

By far the best minnow bucket is the old standby champion, the white styrofoam. A white insulated bucket that holds a lot of water and has a secure lid can keep water and minnows cool for a long time, even in direct sun. With just small amounts of ice added through the day, the minnows will stay ready to go for extended periods.

Regardless of the type of bucket you use, keep the lid on and the bucket shaded from direct sun as much as possible.

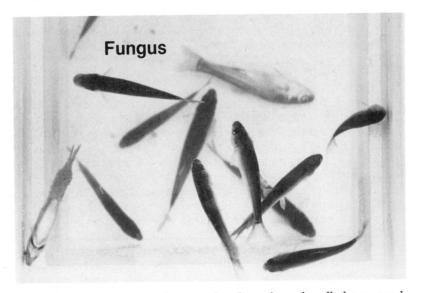

Fungus

Fungus can grow on minnows that have been handled too much when being captured, placed in poor water conditions, or in any way stressed. Excessive or rough handling removes slime from minnows, making them vulnerable to fungus growth.

If you leave minnows in your bucket until they die and get that "fuzzy" growth all over them, or even if your last batch of minnows had the slightest fungus problem, wash and rinse your bucket thoroughly before putting new minnows in it. Use baking soda to disinfect and clean the inside of the bucket if possible. This prevents fungus and disease from contaminating the new minnows.

If the minnows will be used that day, a small amount of fungus is not a big problem, unless it detracts visually from the natural appearance of the minnow.

The real answer to preventing fungus is proper handling and storage of minnows, by *both* the dealer and the fisherman. If a certain dealer in your area consistently has fungused minnows, buy them somewhere else.

Bait dealers often add softner or canning salt to minnow tanks to prevent or eliminate fungus growth. Salt stimulates the production of slime on the minnows, which fights fungus and other diseases.

If you are trying to store minnows for a long time, or have some with a fungus growth on them, you may want to experiment with giving them a "salt bath." One recommended ratio is one tablespoon of salt for every five gallons of water. The salt will not kill the minnows, and exposing them to it once should help the situation.

Other additives that help keep your minnows healthy are available at most bait shops. Bait Saver and similar products contain salt and other ingredients that minimize fungus and other problems.

Catching Your Own Minnows

At any time, catching your own is economical. Minnows, especially some types, can be expensive.

But, before you start plucking minnows from public waters, you must understand your state's laws regarding catching and transporting live baits. There are many restrictions, and yes, bait dealers have to get permits from the state and must follow the rules, also.

There is something really satisfying about catching fish on minnows that you also caught yourself. Most of the time, I buy my minnows from local bait dealers, but sometimes catching your own minnows is either a good option or the only one available.

In some cases, fishermen don't even have access to a bait shop.

In some cases, the minnows naturally occuring in a given lake are different than those available at local bait shops. If you want to match the natural forage, you have no choice but to catch your own.

In some cases, minnows are so easily caught or trapped, in such good numbers, that it's foolish not to.

Trapping Minnows

There are available, at most bait stores, scaled-down versions of the round trap used by bait dealers to catch minnows. Dealers will usually be glad to show you a thing or two about how to use it, and give you some tips on where to set it, etc.

First, bait the trap with bread crumbs, crackers, or oatmeal. Then, find some minnows. Sounds tough, you say? Think back to some of your local fishing excursions. Where have you seen big groups of minnows in shallow water? Would it be likely they'd be there now? If you really are starting from scratch in your search, try placing the baited trap on the edge of weedlines, against banks of rivers, or along shorelines.

Mark the location of your trap by attaching a rope with a float of some kind to the trap. Check your trap every day and immediately remove any minnows, or they will just die a needless death in the trap.

Here are two versions of the round trap for catching minnows. On the left is the scaled-down version normally used by fishermen to catch a small supply. On the right is a full-sized round trap used by bait dealers.

Seining Minnows

Most bait stores also sell seines. They are available in many dimensions, but again, you've got to check local laws regarding the use of seines, as there tend to be restrictions on how big a seine you can use, and in many cases seines are illegal.

Many minnows can be caught quickly and in good numbers using seines. In fact, a few hours of seining with a friend can be an exciting outing. As you come to the end of each pass, it's like raising up a sealed box from the bottom of the ocean. There might be a treasure in there, or it might be a bust!

Minnow seines come in various sizes. But they are all made of a fine-mesh netting, usually 1/4-inch cotton or nylon. They have floats running the entire length of the top of the seine, and lead weights strung along the bottom to keep the net down.

On each end is a pole which one of the seiners holds on to and pushes downward on, to keep the net flush to the bottom of the lake or river. If you don't keep the net tight to the bottom, minnows will swim underneath the seine.

Take your seine and your partner to shallow areas of lakes, backwaters or eddies in rivers, and small ponds where you suspect there might be minnows, and start working.

Before you do anything, make sure you have enough buckets to hold as many minnows as you need, without overcrowding. Take the temperature of the water in the lake, pond or river, then fill your minnow buckets with that same water. Don't leave them in the sun, though, or they will quickly get too warm! You should have a cooler with some ice in it if it's a hot day, so you can keep the minnows you catch in a comfortable condition.   Plan each pass of the seine before making it, and try to have the ending point at a gradual bank or shoreline, to make it easier to sort and load your catch.

Don't make long runs. As a minnow is captured, it is tumbled over and over, as if it's in a washing machine. It fights the seine, and each time it rubs against the net, slime comes off. That could contribute to the fungus problem I talked about earlier.

Work quickly to the end point of the pass, and then lift both ends of the seine in unison, but *don't* lift the seine out of the water. Sort the minnows while they are still in the water, but safely in the seine. If you are having trouble grabbing the minnow buckets, holding the seine up tight and then sorting the minnows, try putting one end of the seine up on the bank and weighing it down with a few rocks. Then, one person holds the other end of the seine so it is tight but the minnows are still in the water, while the partner sorts the minnows and puts the ones you want in buckets.

A last, but very important point: as you remove the minnows from the seine and put them in buckets, handle them as little as possible, using only a soft net to dip them with.

Umbrella Nets

Umbrella nets can be very effective for catching minnows off docks and larger piers. They are made from nylon netting, and are usually four feet square. A metal frame keeps the net open.

After being baited with crackers, bread, or oatmeal, they are simply lowered into the water in places where there are schools of minnows. When minnows are directly over the net, just raise it back up as fast as you can, before the minnows escape.

Types of Minnows

How many types of minnows are there? Lots. How many are worth talking about as fishing baits? How much time do you have?

I am going to go over just the more commonly-used and sold minnows. There are others, I know that, but I want you to finish reading this and get out on the water before your children have children who have children who are college age!

Fathead Minnows

Fatheads are probably the most commonly used minnow for fishing, partly because they are so easily and widely available. They spawn in shallow water up to eight times per summer, making them one of the most prolific fishes. They are available to bait dealers—and fishermen—in large quantities year-round.

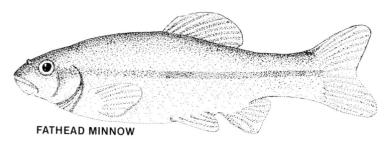

FATHEAD MINNOW

Fatheads are effective on many species of fish, and are available in a wide range of sizes, up to 3 1/2 inches long. The smaller ones, from 1/2 inch long to slightly larger, are often referred to as "crappie minnows."

In the South, fatheads are called "tuffy" minnows by many people.

They are popular also because they are durable, able to tolerate lower oxygen levels than many other varieties of minnows. Because they are so oxygen-tolerant, fatheads are easily transported by dealers and fishermen, and more fatheads can be safely kept in a bucket than other minnows that need more "living space."

Almost all bait shops have a good supply of fatheads for sale, regardless of season. Fatheads are normally separated into small (crappie minnows), medium and large sizes, so just pick the right size for the fish you are after.

As with all minnows, take a look at them before buying. If most of them are at the bottom of the tank, that's a good sign they are healthy. Minnows that are up at the top of the tank, sucking for air, probably need oxygen or are sick.

Shiners

Just the name evokes images of something that would catch fish! Shiners shine and dart and wiggle when they're at their best, and fish find them hard to resist.

There are many types of shiners found in the United States, all of which are in the genus *Notropis*. That's why you'll sometimes hear shiners referred to as "Notropis minnows."

Shiners have a reputation, and in many cases well-deserved, of being fragile. Many varieties are hard to keep alive even under ideal conditions, and when summer comes and the lakes and rivers warm up, it can be easier to revive a mosquito that you smashed against your arm than it is to keep a shiner alive very long after you hook it and send it down!

Shiners also require more care in storage than other minnows. In fact, they are treated with kid gloves from the moment your bait dealer even decides he's going after them.

The availability of shiners at the bait shop depends much on whether your dealer is able to get out and capitalize on the shiner spawning run.

Usually, minnows reside in deep water of lakes and rivers, but when they get ready to spawn, they come into the shallow warm water of shorelines and swim or "run" parallel to the shore, looking for a place to spawn. At these times, they are easily captured. Seining works well at these times, but it does put more stress on shiners than trapping.

Common shiners, as their name suggests, are very abundant, probably the most commonly sold and used shiner as fishing bait. They are a fragile minnow that won't live long once hooked, and need to be cared for carefully in the bucket.

Common shiners are usually 3 to 5 inches long, very silvery in color (they are often called "silver" shiners), with a broad body. Some people, in fact, actually fish for common shiners!

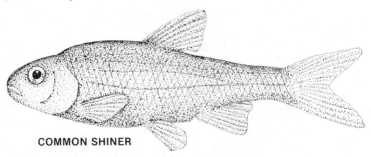

COMMON SHINER

The name game doesn't stop with those two, in fact. Many people also call these minnows "river shiners." By any of the three names, it can be a good bait.

Golden shiners are probably the hardiest of the shiners. As their name suggests, they have a golden-colored body. They are also deeper bodied than many types of shiners.

In bait shops, golden shiners are usually available, graded, from about 2 to 4 or 5 inches long.

Because they are so common in so many fishing lakes, golden shiners are something fish are used to seeing—and eating. They are often a good choice for fishermen trying to match the natural food a lake contains. And, obviously, because they are easier to keep alive than other shiners, they are a good choice in the warmer months.

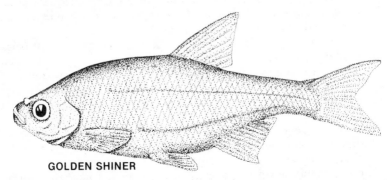

GOLDEN SHINER

In the Southern United States, golden shiners are by far the most widely used minnow by fishermen. Dealers spend more time breeding and raising them than any other bait. Anderson's Minnow Farms in Arkansas, as an example, sold over a million pounds in one year.

This is another minnow that people sometimes fish for, using small hooks and live bait.

Emerald shiners are found in both lakes and rivers, and get their name from their translucent coloring (green on top, silver on the bottom). Big schools of these minnows will roll on the surface, and their appearance will suggest a big bunch of emeralds.

They come 2 to 4 inches long, and are sometimes sold as fathead minnows. If you get some in your fatheads, don't sweat it. Emeralds are good bait!

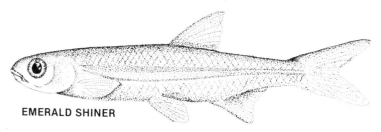

EMERALD SHINER

Spottail shiners can be excellent bait, when you can get them. They are one of the least durable of the shiners. They don't live well in polluted waters, but good numbers can be found in clean lakes and rivers.

The name, as you might guess, comes from the black spot at the base of their tail.

Suckers

White sucker minnows make excellent bait for a variety of fish. Bigger suckers are deadly for fish like northern pike and muskies, and the smaller minnows are excellent bass baits. They will catch other fish, of course, but these are the species they "specialize" in taking.

Suckers are one of the most durable minnows available to fishermen. In the wild, they use their thick and fleshy lips to forage on the bottom of lakes, rivers and streams. They actually perform an ecological service, cleaning up rough vegetables and waste products.

Before and after spawning, suckers are a greyish-white color along the sides, with a darker back. During actual spawning time, they change to a greyish brown color with black bands along the body.

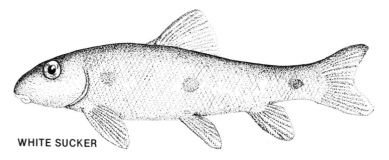

WHITE SUCKER

Because they are so easily raised commercially (dealers can get as high as a 94 percent hatch rate), suckers are normally available at most bait shops.

That doesn't mean they are inexpensive! Sucker minnows can be among the most expensive items in the minnow tanks, especially if nearby commercial hatchery operations have had a recent disaster.

Sucker fry are produced by hatchery experts, in the same way gamefish fry are. Fry are stocked in rearing ponds, which allow them a chance to grow without much threat of predation. From spring until ice forms on the pond, the fry will grow to an average of 4 inches long. They must then survive the winter before being trapped or seined and offered for sale at bait dealers.

A big threat to these stock ponds is a winter kill. The ponds are very vulnerable to freeze-out, because they are not extremely large or deep. Often, whole crops of suckers are killed off during a bad winter.

This is the reason that, at times, suckers are hard to come by and bait shops may not have any. In the long run, the cost of commercially raising suckers and the cost of occasional die-offs account for the fact that suckers can be expensive bait.

Chubs

Scientists know the *redtail chub* by the name hornyhead chub. They are found primarily in rivers of the Midwest. Dealers seine them in the rapids of smaller rivers after chumming for them with clams.

They are a dark minnow, like a fathead, but have reddish fins and tails. They range in size from 3 to 6 inches in bait shops. They are very effective bait for many species of fish, and are a favorite of many jig fishermen because of their tough skull that helps them stay on the hook long after other minnows have been knocked off.

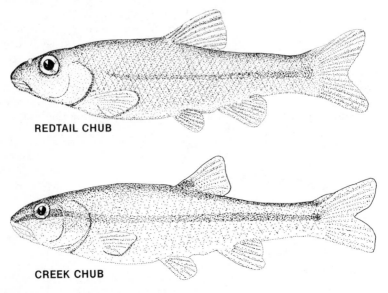

REDTAIL CHUB

CREEK CHUB

Creek chubs, or "silversides" as they are sometimes called, are a close relative of the redtail, and are often sold interchangeably with them. A creek chub has lighter, more silvery sides than a redtail, and a dark spot at the front base of the dorsal fin.

Dace

Southern redbelly dace are known to many fishermen as "rainbow chubs." They are usually trapped by dealers in fall or winter.

One of the most colorful of all minnows, the males have a beautiful red belly, and two dark bands on each side. Females have a yellowish belly. Although smallish (they don't get much larger than 3 inches), they are a popular and effective bait, partly because they can tolerate a broader band of water temperatures than most minnows, from 34-90 degrees F.

The *northern redbelly dace* is a very close relative, with a slightly different mouth and head shape. Both are good baits.

There are other types of dace used as bait, such as the *finescale dace*, especially in parts of Canada.

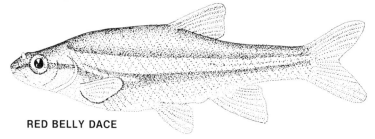

RED BELLY DACE

Goldfish are popular baits for Southern and Eastern fishermen. Any kid knows what they look like, but for you adults, they look like a carp, except they range in color from bright orange to olive.

Traditionally, goldfish were used primarily as catfish and black bass bait, but have recently been used quite a bit for striped bass.

They are easy to raise artificially, taking only three or four months to go from newly-hatched fry to 4- to 6-inch minnow ready for sale. Goldfish are a very durable bait, and live a long time after being hooked.

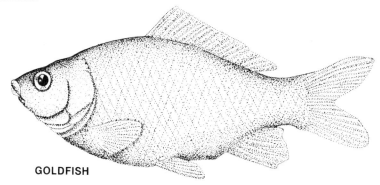

GOLDFISH

Nightcrawlers

Nightcrawlers are one of the most commonly used live baits by fishermen throughout the United States and Canada. They have many uses besides live bait. Commercially, they are used as a high-protein food source. Educationally, they are used as many science students' first introduction to the wonders of dissection.

Their biggest role, however, is as a benefit to plant life and the general health of the earth they live in. They condition the soil as they burrow through it, leaving behind rich nutrients from their excretions and opening the earth to needed oxygen.

It takes a while to grow a big, fat nightcrawler. They grow about one inch per year. Many of the biggest 'crawlers used as live bait are imported from Canada.

There is hardly a bait that is easier to buy and keep in large quantities, and you can do more for *after* you buy it, than nightcrawlers. Their ability to catch fish is unquestioned, but there is a lot you can do to ensure that all of that ability is present in your nightcrawlers.

Bedding: Home of the Nightcrawler

The first thing you can do to ensure fat, healthy 'crawlers is give them a decent place to live. Bedding, the name given to the various compounds used to store nightcrawlers, can be either a hospitable home where the critters can grow and flourish, or a death trap. Much has to do with the type and size of container the bedding is placed in, and much also with the makeup of the bedding itself.

A good bedding supplies a proper amount of moisture, food, and an adequate oxygen supply. Any bedding material, in order to supply a *proper* amount of moisture, should be moist, not wet. Some containers, such as the small, individual dozen packages used in bait shops, are for very short-term storage, for example. That sort of environment is not suitable, nor intended, for long-term storage and health of the nightcrawlers.

Bedding made from ground-up newspaper is good for short-term storage. It should be moistened with water, with the excess being drained off before the nightcrawlers are placed on it. This type of bedding provides moisture to keep 'crawlers plump, and has plenty of air space for oxygen.

There are several brands of commercial bedding available, and that is probably the best way to go. When mixed with water and squeezed to remove excess moisture, then placed in an insulated storage container, bedding provides a wonderful environment for the 'crawlers.

Some commmercial beddings have food added to them. With others, you have to buy the food separately. I have been impressed with a new bedding, called Worm Paradise. It is distributed by H.T. Enterprises, Rt. 1, Box 94A, Eden WI 53019. You add water to make a damp mixture, as you do with any commercial bedding. The food is in the bedding. You never have to add anything; there is ground newspaper, natural foods, everything in the package as it comes. The food supply lasts an entire summer.

You can simply add ground, moistened newspaper and a mixture of rich organic material to a commercial bedding. That works well for short- and long-term storage, because it provides all the essentials, moisture, oxygen and a natural food supply in the organic material.

Bedding can be a home or a death trap for nightcrawlers. Keep it moist, but not wet, and provide the 'crawlers with food if you are storing them long-term.

Most dealers, in fact, transport nightcrawlers in nutrient-rich dirt or moss that is wrapped in damp newspaper. The newspaper keeps light out and provides moisture, and the dirt provides a natural food source.

Keeping Nightcrawlers

Nightcrawlers are one of the easiest baits to keep in large quantities, but there are basic things to know about their proper storage and conditioning. One of the most important is temperature. Proper storage temperature is between 40 and 60 degrees F., with about 50 degrees being optimum.

The container you keep your 'crawlers in doesn't have to be deep, but it should be insulated, and large enough to handle the number of nightcrawlers you want to keep. A good rule of thumb is that the container should hold one pound of bedding for every 100 nightcrawlers. It should also have air vents to allow oxygen to get in even when it's covered. A lid is important, especially if it is dark where you keep the nightcrawlers. When it is dark, they will sometimes try to crawl out of the container.

Don't forget: the bedding should be moist, not wet.

When you place nightcrawlers into a storage container, do it in the light, and put them on top of the bedding. Don't mix them down into the bedding. Let them crawl down in there by themselves. Healthy nightcrawlers will want to avoid the light, and will soon crawl down. Any that stay on top, unless they are obviously healthy, are probably sick. Throw any sick ones away. Dead nightcrawlers create heat and a gas that soon spreads throughout the whole bunch, and you've got a container full of dead and stinking nightcrawlers.

Nightcrawlers are far healthier if they are fed, but they can only ingest very tiny objects. The way they normally feed is to burrow through dirt, breaking it down as they go, eating natural foods along the way. Ground-up corn works well as a food, but it has to be ground extremely fine, into a powdery dust.

In a quality bedding, kept moist and fortified with food, nightcrawlers can be kept for a year or more. They will simply get bigger and more "wiggly" the longer they are cared for properly, and even runty 'crawlers can be made into champions. If you are going to try to keep large numbers for a long time, you might want to get an old refrigerator, and equip it with a thermometer. Keep the temperature as close to 50 degrees F. as you can, and you won't be disappointed the night before the big trip.   Just remember that if you keep your 'crawlers in the dark, you need to keep a lid on them, or they will remind you how they got their name.

Conditioning Nightcrawlers

If you are going to fish with a batch of nightcrawlers right away, there's not a whole lot you can do to improve their condition, but if you are waiting at least until the following day and maybe longer, you can look at the 'crawlers you have as "raw recruits" you are about to whip into shape.

Strictly speaking, a nightcrawler that has been cared for in the way we just described in "keeping nightcrawlers" *is* a conditioned 'crawler. Often, people discuss this topic separately from storage; they talk about it as a magical process they do after they are done storing nightcrawlers and just before they fish with them.

But, if we can agree that a conditioned nightcrawler is one that is big, fat, juicy and full of wiggle and squirm, we can also agree that proper storage will, by itself, condition nightcrawlers.

It takes a while, though, for this natural conditioning process to take place. What if you are faced with a bucket full of wimp 'crawlers that you want to use as bait the next day? Or, even worse, in a couple hours?

There is a quick-conditioning method that works wonders.

Try leaving small, scraggly-looking 'crawlers in a cooler with water and ice cubes in it, covered with newspaper, overnight. You will be absolutely amazed at what they look like in the morning.

The caution I leave you with here might be obvious by now: putting nightcrawlers from a warm environment directly into a near-freezing one won't probably condition them. It will probably kill them. Put them first in a bucket of cool water, then cold water, and then into the ice bath. And if you put them in ice water, make sure you keep the water cold all day.

I've already said that it's a good idea to take a close look at nightcrawlers in a bait shop before buying any. Open the containers and uncover the 'crawlers. They should be plump and wiggly; when you lightly pinch them, they should squirm and move. If not, you may have sickly nightcrawlers on your hands, and you shouldn't buy them.

Before buying nightcrawlers, open the containers and look at them. Pinch a few; they should be lively.

No matter how many you buy, have at the ready a container with cool, moist bedding. Transfer the nightcrawlers immediately out of the container they come in, into the bedding. Those small containers are a quick ticket to dead 'crawlers when they go outside into the heat.

If you fish with nightcrawlers a lot, you might want to consider buying them in quantity. As I've said, they are easy to care for, as long as you follow the basic rules.

In bulk, nightcrawlers are sold by the *flat*. Each flat should contain 500 'crawlers. Before purchasing a flat, ask to see four or five of them. Some flats have bigger, livelier nightcrawlers in them than others.

There is no reason not to buy nightcrawlers in bulk. If you properly store them, you can have a good supply of giant fish-catchers, all waiting to be taken to the lake.

One final tip: set up a small cooler, that you can add a small amount of your bedding to, to take a few dozen nightcrawlers at a time out fishing. If it's going to be a hot day, a few ice cubes in a plastic bag can be put in the bedding to keep it cool.

Catching Your Own Nightcrawlers

If you have some extra time on your hands at night, especially after a rain or right after you water the lawn, you can have a productive hour or so picking your own nightcrawlers.

Nightcrawlers, as their name gives away, come out of their underground living quarters at night, to breed and migrate. They typically come up when the earth's surface is wet. Wet soil must make it easier for them to move about, or make them feel more comfortable.

There is really only one period of the year when you don't want to pick 'crawlers for long-term storage. In the early spring, for about six weeks after the ground has thawed enough for nightcrawler activity to pick up, you will find them and can pick them for immediate use. But after their winter hibernation, they are weak and need a period of activity before adapting to the change in season and once again becoming firm, lively and strong.

And now...tips for your next nightcrawler hunt. You want to look for them at night, with the aid of a flashlight. But not just any flashlight. White light will spook 'crawlers, and they will get back down their hole before you see them.

Cover the lens of a flashlight with a red cloth or cellophane filter. A flashlight attached to your forehead is best, because it leaves both hands free, one to hold the container and one to pick up nightcrawlers. Use a container with moist, cool bedding in it, and holes to let oxygen in.

Nightcrawlers are surprisingly fast and evasive. Sound spooks them as well as white light, so wear tennis shoes or something equally soft, and be quiet as you move about looking. In a split second, they can be back down their hole. They often sit on top of the earth with their tails still in the hole.

When you spot a 'crawler, quietly move close to it and grab it below the collar (actually, grab it as close to where the 'crawler meets the ground as possible), so if you grab it too hard you won't injure vital parts. Grab the nightcrawler quickly and firmly, but not too hard. If it is partially buried in the ground, don't jerk it up, because you will break it in half every time. Nightcrawlers have very strong muscles and resist you until the bitter end. Simply maintain your firm hold on the nightcrawler until you feel it relax, and then it will easily slide up out of the hole.

If you do break one off trying to pull it up, throw it away. It will soon die, causing other live nightcrawlers in your container to die also.

In general, older, more established lawns hold more nightcrawlers than newer ones do. Golf courses and baseball fields are also excellent places to spend a few nights looking for this ready source of free live bait.

Leeches

Leeches are loved by those fishermen who understand what they are and what they stand for, and how deadly they are. It hasn't been that many years since the leech became a popular bait, so it is understandable that many people are still afraid of them, refuse to handle them without asbestos gloves on, or won't even get in the same boat with a dozen leeches.

Ribbon leeches, the ones you want to use as bait, are *not* bloodsuckers. They are not even the same animal. Sure, they have *suckers* which they use to attach themselves to things, but they don't suck the blood from living creatures. They will not put on a death lock and cause you to pass out from loss of blood if they try to attach to you as you hook them on. They have a rather weak grip, and just fall off most of the time after a few seconds.

After you get used to handling leeches, in fact, you will find yourself reaching into the bucket and grabbing a handful, and then picking out the one you want. They are actually easier to handle than many other live baits.

Leeches feed at night, on decaying plant life, dead fish and other decaying organisms. Many people still believe they are a predator to fish, but this is simply not true.

Once you get used to handling leeches, it is simple to grab a handful and pick out the one you want to fish with.

So how can you tell the difference between a leech and a bloodsucker?

Ribbon leeches are firm to the touch, versus bloodsuckers, which are mushy and soft. Ribbon leeches have visible edges on each side when they roll up into a ball, versus bloodsuckers which roll up into a perfect ball with no edges. Simply poke the outsides of the two critters, and you will feel an obvious difference, without having to get near the suckers, which are located at each end on the inside.

Medicine leeches and horse leeches are two varieties of bloodsuckers. Medicine leeches are easy to identify and avoid: they have a black back and orangish belly, with rows of red dots down their backs. If you pick them up, they are very mushy compared to ribbon leeches.

Ribbon leeches, unless water conditions become poor, will contentedly stay in a container of water. Horse and medicine leeches, which have a stronger sucker than ribbon leeches, will often crawl out of even the tallest bucket. By leaving the top off your bucket, or just watching which ones try to scale the sides, you can figure out which are the bloodsuckers and toss them away.

Believe me, there is a huge difference in which ones the fish will bite! Here at Babe Winkelman Productions, we have large tanks in our office that we use to observe fish. As an experiment, we will go back to the tanks on lunch hour and toss out a half dozen ribbon leeches. *Bam,*

bam, smack! they are gone in about two seconds. Everything, from sunfish to crappies to walleyes to northern pike, attack them first and ask questions later.

But, even if you have the fish built up to a frenzy, you can toss in a bloodsucker among a bunch of leeches and the fish will avoid it! They will occasionally put their mouth up to it, but they will not take it in. Fish simply *will not* eat bloodsuckers.

Leeches, on the other hand, don't live for more than a minute in any water where fish swim.

MEDICINE LEECH (BLOODSUCKER)

RIBBON LEECH

Caring for Leeches

Because leeches are most available, and most used, during the late spring through hot summer months, it is imperative that you know how to take care of them—and that you do.

Keep leeches in a container with water. The water must be free of chlorine, which kills leeches. Either use lake or well water, or dechlorinate your water as described in the section on caring for minnows.

A general rule is that every half-pound of leeches needs at least a quart of water. I normally give them a little more than that, just to be sure.

Keep the water cool. If you can, just leave the leeches, covered, in your refrigerator. This lowers their metabolism, so they are less active and excrete fewer waste products into the water. Leeches also require less oxygen and won't need to feed if kept cool.

Change the water frequently, say every two to four days. If you are out in the boat and the leeches' water gets warm, you may have to change it several times during the day. Whenever the water gets a milky color, it needs to be changed.

Always wash your hands before handling the leeches. It's a good policy to keep contaminants away from them. It may take you a while to get used to doing this, but occasionally you should clean the leeches by rinsing them under cold water (free from chlorine, of course), gently rolling them in your hand to take off excess slime.

As soon as you buy leeches, and while storing them, check for dead or near-dead ones. Continually discard them; death is catchy with leeches, as it is with nightcrawlers.

Above all, pay attention to how your leeches are acting. If they seem alive and are staying at the bottom of the container, everything is probably fine. But if they are constantly trying to crawl out of the water and onto the sides of the container, that means they are hurting! It could be from low oxygen levels, uncomfortable water temperature, or impure water. Changing the water, and keeping it cool, will solve most problems.

Transporting Leeches

Keeping leeches comfortable and healthy while transporting them long distances is fairly simple. Many of the requirements, in terms of water temperature and oxygen, are the same as for minnows. Read that section if you haven't already.

If you will be driving for a day, let's say, have the leeches packed in an oxygen bag, as described in the minnow section. During the hot months, put the bag in a cooler with ice, and close the lid. During the spring and fall, a cooler is not necessary (although leeches are not always available in the fall).

When you have the leeches in the boat, or while fishing from shore, keep them in an insulated (styrofoam is best) bucket with a good lid on it. When it's hot out, add ice to the water to keep it cool, but make sure the ice was made with water containing no chlorine.

Buying Leeches

As I recommended for the other live baits, take a good look at the leeches in the dealer's tank before buying them. Are they lively and swimming around? When you swish the water, do they swim or do they wash about the tank like dead leeches?

Touch a leech or two. They should be firm.

If you are just going out fishing for the afternoon or something, simply buy a couple dozen or so leeches and use them up. But because leeches, like nightcrawlers, are fairly easy to care for, there's no reason not to buy them in larger quantities.

You will often see signs advertising leeches for sale by the pound or half-pound. How do you know whether you are getting a good deal?

How many dozen leeches are there in a pound? It varies, depending on the size. The following figures are not absolutes, but they give you a pretty good estimate:

How many leeches to the pound?

Size	Approximate number
Jumbo	7-9 dozen
Large	10-12 dozen
Medium	13-20 dozen
Small	20 dozen & up

You have the right to see the leeches weighed when buying by the pound. Many dealers weigh leeches in advance of busy times, in order to save time for the customers. Most dealers are honest, but when it comes right down to it, you might look at a container and not miss as much as a quarter-pound, which is a lot of leeches. Don't make it a habit to go in and demand to have the leeches re-weighed in front of the whole county, but if you suspect a pound might be "light" don't be afraid to ask to have it weighed.

When you watch leeches being weighed, make sure all water is drained out of the serving net before the leeches are put on the scale. Water is heavy, and it won't catch fish.

How Leeches are Trapped

The ribbon leech lives in ponds, lakes and rivers, but it is trapped only in waters that contain no gamefish and have lots of decaying vegetation and good algae growth.

In spring, when the water temperatures in their northern pond homes get up to about 50 degrees F., dealers set traps for them. Leeches are impossible to find and trap in fall and winter. In fact, adult leeches die in late summer or fall, explaining why it is hard to buy good, lively leeches then.

Leeches are night feeders, so the traps are set in the daytime and checked before it gets too light in the morning. Dealers normally use cut-up dead fish they catch in their minnow traps, such as suckers, carp, or bullheads. This is where fishermen who try to catch their own leeches often make a big mistake: they try to catch them using live minnows as bait. Leeches, as I've said, won't feed on anything living.

Leech traps are made from coffee cans that have the plastic lid on one end, and a fine-mesh wire funnel on the other; dark-colored garbage bags; and gunny sacks. Leech trappers simply tie a rope or string to the trap, leading to a visible float on the surface. That way, they can easily find all their traps in the early morning light.

Bait is placed in the traps, and at night, when leeches feed, they find their way into the can or bag and attach themselves to the bait.

If you want to try trapping your own leeches, probably the easiest way is to tie a rope to a gunny sack, put some dead fish or liver in it, toss a few rocks in to weigh it down, and dump it into a likely spot. Go ahead and tie the top of the bag shut; leeches will have no problem working their way through the fiber of the gunny sack to get to the bait.

The best time to trap leeches is in early spring, after pond temperatures get up to 50 degrees F. Leeches will "run" through early summer.

Check your trap before the light gets too bright in the morning, and your first supply of "homemade" leeches, in all sizes and colors, might be waiting to be taken home.

Chapter 4
A Controllable Boat

Boat control is terrifically important in jigging and live bait rigging.

Some fishermen are happy if they can get the boat where it ought to be much of the time. They've got it backwards. To fish efficiently, you want total control of your boat, so it is where it should be and moving the way you want it to move...*all the time*.

The first time you come through an area—like a stretch of shoreline—is the most important. You want to work each bit of cover right, *the first time*, when it is most important.

You can't get that kind of total control with any single boat control method. Backtrolling is a great way to run a boat, but it's just one of many ways. You want to master a whole set of techniques. Then, on the water, you should be able to switch from one to another instantly.

That's why I want to talk in terms of a total boat control system. You want perfect control all the time.

Wherever you want to put your boat, you should have the equipment and technique to put it exactly there, with a variety of methods, not just one. Then you choose the best method to suit the circumstances.

Some people find this boring, I guess, but I don't. There's a certain sense of satisfaction in running a boat under control, with precision. If you don't get a real kick out of making a perfect run along a tricky bit of deep structure, so that the boat is never out of position...well, you're wired different from me.

Boat control is fun. And boat control is critical to catching fish, which is the point of the whole thing.

You achieve good boat control in four ways:

- you need to choose a suitable hull;
- you have to match that hull with the right outboard;
- then you need to rig up the boat so it can be controlled; and
- finally, you need to develop technique.

Hulls For A Controllable Boat

A good boat for the total angler has to be capable of moving forward *and* backward, slowly *and* under control. And, of course, it has to be safe. It should be comfortable to fish from and should let you operate efficiently.

Having said only that much, we've already eliminated about 90 percent of the boats on the market as unsuitable.

You need to choose a boat with size that's appropriate for the water you fish, keeping in mind how much of a load you'll carry. The fellow who fishes sheltered 200-acre lakes in northern Wisconsin won't need as much boat as the guy who fishes some huge windswept reservoir with two partners, a full livewell and a lot of electronic gear.

People usually discuss boat size in terms of length. We talk about "16-foot boats" as if that specified how big the boat is. It doesn't. Some narrow and low-sided 16-footers don't belong on anything but protected waters. Other 16-footers are so seaworthy they are perfectly safe to fish the waters of the Missouri River or the Great Lakes...if used sensibly.

There are a lot of boats to choose from, but few of them are capable of doing all the things necessary to make them efficient fishing rigs.

Fishermen should pay more attention to width. Staying with the example of 16-foot boats, I can name some that are 66" wide as well as some that are 84" wide. Do those extra 18 inches make much of a difference? You better believe it! Remember, each extra inch of width should multiplied by 192 (the number of inches of length in a 16-footer). Those extra inches add up and give you buoyancy and storage space. Don't forget that width is as much a measure of boat size as length.

There's a problem with some wide boats. Some have seats placed where a live bait angler can hardly fish from them. The sides of the boat are too far away from the seat to reach with a rod tip. This is worse if the sides are also high.

Before you buy any boat, *fish* in it. Or at least insist on sitting in the boat in the dealer's showroom. Think carefully about how well the seats and other parts are laid out for fishing. Where would the tackle boxes go? The batteries? Gas cans? Take the time to see how well the boat will accept the kind of gear you carry.

It's hard to give guidelines for the *depth* (or height—they're the same) of a good boat. I really can't see that this dimension of a boat can be reduced to a number. Hull shape has to figure in here, so it all gets complicated. You face a dilemma: you want a dry boat with high enough sides to keep out waves when you fish, yet you don't want any more "sail area" than absolutely necessary. The sail area is the profile your boat presents to the wind when you are fishing. A bass boat has very little sail area, while a high-sided 18-foot aluminum boat represents the other extreme.

Too much sail area makes it impossible to backtroll with precision. If the wind is forever knocking the front of your boat to one side or the other, you can't hold a good course no matter how carefully you steer from the back. Certain boats, mostly glass boats, are favored by serious live bait fishermen because they "track true" (which just means they have little sail area).

Fiberglass boats have an advantage over metal boats because they have complex hull shapes that offer both a dry ride and low sail area. When you look at an aluminum boat in the water, it looks pretty much the same at rest or on plane. Glass boats are different. A good fiberglass boat with a modified V hull will sit low in the water during fishing, presenting little sail area, then rise up out of the water when planing to give you a safe, dry ride.

There's another difference that relates to complex hull design. Metal boats try to keep you dry by putting a high metal wall between passengers and water; the best fiberglass boats do it by directing splash and spray away from the boat. Ask any of the guys who have owned both types of boats. The better fiberglass boats are much drier than the best of the aluminum boats.

Ask them also about the fishing positions of different boats. Some boats force you to hold your rod tip up high, a long way off water. That's *not good*! You want to run live bait rigs with your tip almost in the water, minimizing the amount of slack line that the wind can get at.

The biggest boats give up something in maneuverability. The heavier your boat is, the more sluggish it will be on turns. And when backtrolling with big outboard motors, you'll find the motor won't turn sharply enough to let you follow a tricky, curving contour line. For safety reasons, bigger tiller outboards have limitations on the arc they can turn; in other words, you can run around in a much tighter circle with a 20-horse than with a 55-horse because the bigger motor has been limited by the factory to give it less steering arc.

Boat size is a frustrating issue. We *all* want a big boat so we can have storage room and safety. But bigness carries a price. When you move into a bigger boat you have to get a bigger motor, bigger trolling motors, more gas storage room and more batteries. Next thing you know, you seem to be back pretty close to where you started with storage room, but with a very heavy boat.

To my mind, the best boats for fishing all techniques, live baits and artificials, *start* with the very biggest 14-footers. On smaller waters, a big 14-footer with a full 20-inch transom and a 15- horse will be extremely responsive and fishable if you don't carry too many people or too much gear.

Most of the good fishing boats come in at around 16 or 17 feet, and it's no coincidence. That's a very good compromise. A well-proportioned boat of that length gives you safety, storage room and fishing performance that are hard to beat.

Some 18-footers work well enough for live bait fishing, but at this size you begin to get into problems. There aren't many tiller motors that will handle these big boats. If you're trying to push 18 feet of boat loaded with gear with a 45- or 50-horse outboard, your boat's going to feel "piggy" and underpowered. Boats that big are also not as precise when backtrolling complicated structure. They have a lot of sail area, plus they are too heavy to respond quickly to new steering inputs.

But let's be realistic. If you fish big waters and don't do a lot of precise backtrolling, an 18-footer will let you go out with two buddies and fish in safety. On really big lakes and reservoirs, where long runs and high waves are normal, you simply have to work with big boats.

And never forget, safety is the first consideration. There's no such thing as an unsafe but good fishing boat. If a boat isn't truly safe, it isn't worth buying...it isn't even worth accepting as a gift.

Tiller Versus Console Steering

Console steering boats have several obvious advantages over tiller controls. They are:
- Since your weight is forward in a console boat, your boat will be rated for a bigger motor, which gives you more speed;
- The forward steering position is safer at high speeds than the tiller seating position because you see forward better;
- If your boat splashes a lot, the console position will keep you drier, too; and
- It's nice to have the console to carry gauges and fishing aids (like gas gauges and sonar, etc.).

But console boats have some serious disadvantages, especially for the live bait angler. Some of them are:

- Because of the "slop" in the throttle and steering, you simply cannot backtroll precisely through a console;
- Consoles tie up a lot of precious boat space and deny you access to the storage that would otherwise be available on the right side of your boat;
- The big outboards on large console boats might not troll down well, forcing you to use a second motor for fishing.
- Your fishing position is much more natural and comfortable with a tiller than with a console.

Controlling a Console Boat

In spite of the problems, many people feel they need the size and speed of a bigger console boat. They've worked out a number of answers to the problems of boat control.

For example, on the Missouri River, where running distances can be long and the waves are usually brutal, big boats with consoles are the standard. Guys out there usually control their boats from the bow with big troll motors, trolling forward. That requires a tremendous amount of battery power, but if you get the biggest deep cycle batteries and maintain them carefully, you can fish all day between charges with this kind of equipment.

The speed of a console boat is an asset when fishing big water. Here, I am running across a Canadian lake fishing walleye spots that are well-spaced.

As we'll see, this boat control system can run into trouble in high waves. It works, but is less than ideal. Yet if I had to fish big reservoirs where 20-mile runs to the fishing grounds in 25 mph winds are common, this would be an attractive setup to me. In fact, I own a Ranger 372-V which I use when I'm working big lakes where I know I'll be making long runs.

Some guys like to use a big motor to run to a fishing spot, then switch to a smaller outboard for trolling. These small tiller-controlled outboards sit off to one side or the other of the big motor. Often, your seating position for running the little motor is less than ideal, but the system works. It isn't easy to get a splash guard that will work well around two outboards, but it can be done.

Do-It-All Boats

Let's sum up what we've discussed so far. The ideal live bait boat for most anglers is one that can be run with a tiller outboard of 60 horses or less. These boats backtroll with precision and they're sure my favorites.

Remember though, ideally we are looking for a boat that will go forward and backward, slowly and with control. The best boats for going backward are tiller-operated boats of moderate size.

Let's quickly discuss the advantages of the *backtrolling* boat control system. Remember, it's always easy to get a boat to move fast, but getting a boat to move slowly enough is often hard. That's where backtrolling shines, because:

- the transom slows down the boat;
- motors are geared to run more slowly in reverse than in forward;
- your steering is far more precise when going backward because the turning is being done by the leading end of the boat; and
- when backtrolling, the boat operator has control—*instant* control—of speed and direction in one hand, leaving one hand free to fish.

So a good boat for rigging and jigging should be a backtrolling boat. No other control system offers the same degree of complete, precise control.

Okay, what kind of boat is suitable for backtrolling? To perform well at backtrolling, a boat should have tiller operation and a 20″ transom. It should be seaworthy without too much sail area. That's the basics.

For comfort and fishing efficiency, it should have a flat and open floor, a carpet and good swivel seats. A good livewell. Decent storage areas for gear, plus sensible places to put batteries and gas.

But I want *more* from my boat. I want to be able to fish forward, too. I love to jig, and much of my jigging is done while moving forward slowly with the trolling motor. For that, I want a raised front deck with a clean floor. I want a good mounting area for the trolling motor, plus a spot for a bow sonar unit.

When fishing on more confirmed waters, it's hard to beat the versatility of a tiller-controlled boat with electric motors front and back.

We're talking about a backtrolling boat that also carries a bass-style front deck. There's no generic name for these boats, but they're the type of boat I do most of my fishing in.

The key thing is the way this kind of boat lets me choose from the whole range of boat control techniques. I can troll forward or backward from the stern. I can sneak around silently without using my hands by using the bow trolling motor. It's all there. I'm in control.

Put it all together, and you have a great boat for all forms of live bait fishing...and most any other sort of fishing, as well. Such a boat exists. There are several pretty good ones, in fact, but I have a clear favorite. Pardon my pride, but I helped design the new Ranger Fisherman.

The Ranger Fisherman

A number of years ago, I worked with Forrest Wood and his talented crew at Ranger Boats to bring about a new boat. In fact, the Ranger 1600 was a new *type* of boat, the first boat ever designed specifically to be fished forward and backward.

As you might know from watching my television shows, I fish from the Ranger 1600 *a lot*. It is a great little boat which has helped me catch fish of all species all over the country and several Canadian provinces. When I go to work, the 1600 has been my "office" for the last several years!

The interior of the Ranger Fisherman is roomy, comfortable, functional, safe, and chock full of "fishing" touches that it make it the serious fisherman's dream boat.

But over the years I've sometimes wished my 1600 was a little bigger and better able to turn away high waves. While it never let me down in bad weather, I wanted a bigger margin of safety in heavy seas. I wanted a somewhat larger boat. And I had some new ideas I wanted to see put into effect.

So, starting several years ago, I began working with Ranger to design a boat that would represent everything a lifetime of fishing had taught me would be desirable. We met time after time to debate specifications and performance requirements. For a long time there was serious doubt the boat would be built because Ranger wasn't sure they could produce a hull that performed the way we wanted it to *and* have the extra flotation qualities needed to make it as safe as other Rangers.

I'm happy to report, the boat was built. It is called the Ranger 680T Fisherman. Don't count on me to be an objective critic of this boat because I feel more like a proud father. At one time I never would have believed a "perfect" boat could exist for my fishing. Well, now one does.

The Fisherman is basically a grown-up 1600, with a length of 16 feet, 10 inches and a width of 80 inches. The hull is the driest, safest and most comfortable I've run. The interior layout features a *big* livewell and plenty of storage, with a huge rod box. That rod box, in fact, is 7 feet long.

Even better, there is a separate *bait well*, something no other boat has ever had (except some expensive saltwater boats). The transom is designed to carry a trolling motor on either side of the big motor. And unlike some boats that might seem to be in its class, the Fisherman has superb level flotation for the ultimate in safety.

At the time I'm writing this book, I've put in one *hard* season in the new boat. It is not as good as I expected it would be...it is much better! I love it.

Outboards For Control

When I was a kid we thought a 16-horse was worthless as a fishing motor because it "wouldn't troll down slow enough." I can remember when 25- and 35-horse outboards had the same reputation. And now the hot motors for live bait anglers are those in the 45- to 55-horse range. Are we going to be slow trolling with 145-horse motors some day?

Maybe, maybe not. But the improved fishability of outboards just astonishes me.

Most of this improvement has been brought about by hundreds of small design improvements that no angler pays much attention to when they are announced as part of the yearly press releases from the outboard companies. A certain motor may not change much in appearance for five or ten years at a stretch, yet all those little annual changes add up. They make that motor much more reliable, economical, smooth and powerful.

It's true: "They don't make outboards like they used to." And that's a darn good thing!

Live bait anglers make some special demands on an outboard. *Always* there is the requirement that the motor troll smoothly at very slow speeds. I want to be able to back the throttle down all the way it physically will go...and still not have the motor die. At the same time, today's fishing boats are very heavy, so we need a motor with enough guts to punch a big payload through the waves as we run to our fishing spot. Live bait anglers also require good controls on their outboards, and that's where things often break down.

When you are backtrolling, it often is desirable to slip in and out of gear to hover in place or move slower. So the logical place for the gearshift knob is on the front of the motor right near the tiller handle, where it will fall quickly and naturally to hand. That's where it is on some motors, such as the Mariners I use. But on many boats the shifter is way back low and on the starboard side of the motor. That's a dumb place for it, and I've been amazed that such a bad design feature has persisted so long.

There used to be an accessory (once made by Gilco) you could add to some motors to put the shifter where it ought to be. It was a little cheesey, but it worked. Now, I'm not sure it is still on the market. Check with a big marine store to see if any of their catalogs list these accessory kits.

Smoothness at slow speeds is achieved in many ways with today's motors. Just a few years ago we got fouled plugs at slow trolling speeds because one plug or another would gunk up with oil. Now many new outboards run the leaner 100:1 gas:oil mix. That helps. Metered oil injection helps even more, as oil is introduced precisely when it is needed. So do many little engineering changes, as I've mentioned. And it helps to have enough cylinders to make smooth running possible.

My favorite motor has been the Mariner 45, the only motor in its class with four cylinders. It trolls down to extremely slow speeds and offers incredible smoothness.

There's something new from Mariner. They now have a three-cylinder 50 and 60. These motors don't actually come with a tiller, but there is a tiller kit that modifies them very easily to tiller operation. At the time of this writing, the 60 is the most powerful tiller motor available, and I can think of a lot of boats that could use that kind of power. Some outboard engineers argue that three cylinders is the ideal number for two-cycle engines.

Friends have run the 50 and 60, and report they are amazingly smooth and fully capable of trolling slowly. Both are oil-injection motors, so they avoid plug-fouling and smoking.

Fishermen used to have to choose between electric start motors *or* tiller motors with rope starts. A lot of bigger motors are a pain to start by hand. The companies have wised up and now offer electric start on tiller motors. The electric start motors are much more convenient. You'll fish better, too, because you'll be quicker to fire up the motor to move to a new location when you should. Guys with big rope-start

Today's larger outboards perform rings around yesterday's models. Motors like the Mariner 45 have plenty of top-end speed and power, yet troll down beautifully.

motors tend to hang on unproductive spots too long because they're reluctant to start yanking on the pull cord to change locations.

With motors from about 40 horses on up, you'll want power tilt/trim. Motors that big are hard to lift by hand. At the same time, if you have power tilt/trim you can make an outboard troll slower by angling the lower unit up. It won't pull you as fast that way.

Smart boaters pick a propeller with care. The aluminum props that come standard on most outboards are less efficient and far less strong than a stainless steel prop. The steel props are more expensive, but it's money well spent.

Every prop has a certain *pitch*, which is a (theoretical) measure of how much water the prop travels through in one turn. Consider getting a prop that is one or two steps lower (slower) in pitch than the standard prop. For example, if a 50-horse is usually shipped from the factory with a 17-inch prop, consider fitting it with a 15-inch prop.

Why? Two reasons. The slower prop will give you more power at slower speeds, and that's necessary for many fishing boats. A boat whose hull weighs around 800 pounds "dry" will be pretty heavy with a full livewell and gas and all the other things you put in it. If you are

One accessory few fishermen think about is their prop. A stainless steel prop, although expensive, is a wise investment.

trying to move that boat with a 50-horse, you probably need a prop with more torque but less top end speed. As an important bonus, the lower pitched prop will also troll slower. A good marine dealer will be able to advise you on this.

If your outboard won't run smoothly at idle speed, you can't control a boat as well as you should. But the problem could come from lack of maintenance. Even the best motors can't purr like a kitten when they're out of tune. Change the plugs if any of them are fouled. Be careful when buying new plugs because sometimes the plugs recommended by the owner's manual aren't the best plugs for slow trolling. A good outboard dealership will have a repair specialist who can recommend the right plugs.

Check all filters, gas lines and gas line connection. Be *sure* your gas is not the problem. Bad gas will make any outboard run sick, and many boaters are having problems these days because of the alcohol being put in gas by some refiners. Gas with water or too much oil in it will also run badly.

If everything checks out and your motor is still running sick, have it looked over by a good repairman, someone who has been recommended by a friend. Some obscure carburetion and electronics problems can only be spotted by a skilled specialist.

Rigging For Control

To control a boat properly, you need to know exactly how deep the water is beneath you. There is no boat control without absolutely precise knowledge of the water depth.

Beyond that, you want to know the big picture—whether the bottom is sloping, how steeply it is dropping, how firm it is, what cover it holds, etc. You can't control your boat unless you can visualize the bottom and know how it lies. That means good sonar is absolutely necessary for good boat control.

And just one sonar won't do, not if you are serious about things. You need a sonar easily visible from every location where you run the boat.

That means, at a minimum, you'll need a sonar up front for running the bow trolling motor and another unit where you can see it when backtrolling.

If you are running the boat from a console, you will want another sonar on the console.

Then, if you want to run a paper graph in addition to the LCD (liquid crystal display) or flasher units most of us use in moment-to-moment fishing, you'll want one of those units installed where it will do the most good.

For one boat, then, you're looking at anywhere from two to three sonar units.

And two trolling motors. I want to have the option of using quiet electric power from either end of my boat, which means I need two trolling motors.

Is that it? Not quite.

For total boat control, you'll need an anchor and a long line, plus a second anchor and line. Now add one or two sea anchors, and you're getting there. Don't forget the splash guards.

And that's it.

That's a lot of gear, but that's what I use. *It all has a purpose.*

Splash Guards

If you backtroll much, you'll need splash guards. Splash guards keep boats and fishermen dry even when they backtroll into waves. Some boats are better than others at keeping waves out without splash guards, but splash guards are required if you mean to fish in all kinds of weather.

I used to make my own splash guards out of conveyer belt material or truck mudflaps. While those guards worked well, they cut down on my vision as I steered backward.

Today, I like clear plexiglass splash guards that let me see what's behind the boat. The best splash guards come up off the transom and then bend back. They turn waves well, but don't stick up too high and get in the way. Several small companies make splash guards of this sort, and you can buy them custom fitted to about any boat.

Even better, some boat manufacturers are making splash guards you can buy as an option with the boat. Ranger, for example, now sells a great set of splash guards to fit the new Fisherman boat I use so much of the time.

Fishing Sonar

There are three basic types of sonar for serious anglers. They operate on the same principles but differ in the nature of the display. The original fishing sonar, the *flasher*, is still popular and effective. *Chart recording graph* units give you the most detailed and easily understood pictures of what's under the boat.

The original fishing sonar, the flasher, is still the workhorse. But graphs give the easiest readout to interpret, and the new generation of liquid crystals are creating excitement about the detail of their readouts.

These days, however, much of the excitement is about the new *LCD* graph units. The LCD units might eventually replace flashers and graphs altogether, though that day is some time off in the future.

I'm not going to go into a fully detailed discussion of fishing sonar here. It is a *big* topic. If you want more detailed information, check at the back of this book for a form that will let you order my course, the "Comprehensive Guide to Fish Locators." It is a unique combination of text, diagrams and audio tapes.

The Guide presents the complexities of fishing sonar in a clear and detailed fashion. Unless you already understand sonar thoroughly, you will benefit a great deal from this in-depth treatment of sonar.

I can give a quick troubleshooting list for the most common problems people have. First, many fishermen buy cheap units (or even expensive units that are badly designed). But if you've got a good unit, like an Eagle or Lowrance, and it isn't performing well, look at these things first:

- Are all power connections solid? All wires sound, with no shorts?
- Is the transducer mounted in a place where air bubbles run across it? That's a no-no. Make sure the transducer installation satisfies all requirements listed in the owner's manual.
- Do you have the power ("gain" or "sensitivity") set high enough? Many, many guys run their power too low to show anything but the bottom. Dial it up and see what you've been missing!
- Is the suppressor turned *all the way off* when you are fishing? It should be.
- If your paper graph isn't working right, are you sure the stylus is fresh and making good contact all the way across the paper?
- Is some motor or other electronic device giving your sonar interference? Watch out. Try running your sonar with various other aids turned on and off (trolling motors, big motor, other sonar, radios, etc.).

Let me go into a little detail on that last problem, the interference problem. Just lately, many trolling motors have been changed to include *pulse width modulation* power control. This new electronic feature is built into some motors or added on to others, as with the Minn Kota Maximizer.

Unfortunately, these new units can interfere with fishing sonar in some applications.

Which applications? It's a tricky, unpredictable problem, but some boats have problems when the transducer is installed directly against the head of a trolling motor with the new pulse width modulation power control.

What problems? In effect, the pulse width modulation controls create "static" or false signals which can be received by the sonar. When the sonar power is set high, the sonar can pick up this interference from the trolling motor. Suddenly your flasher dial or graph screen fills up with false signals.

What to do about it? First, carefully follow the manufacturer's instructions when installing both the sonar and the trolling motor. Second, if you get interference, rewire the units so your sonar is not running on the same battery as your trolling motor (which is a good idea, even if you don't get interference). If you still have problems, look for a another place to install the transducer than on the trolling motor (with glass boats, you can glass in the transducer to shoot through the hull in the bow area).

Let's get back to considering which sonar you need to buy to get total boat control.

The average angler is confused by all the competing claims made by fishing sonar makers. I'll say one thing that can't be stressed too much: the *type* of sonar you buy is far less important than the *quality* of its manufacture. A good flasher is *far* better than a mediocre graph...and there are a lot of mediocre graphs being sold these days!

I'm like a lot of experienced anglers because I do most of my *fishing* with a flasher. There is an important exception: when fishing deep water, I run my graph all the time.

If you take the time to learn to read a flasher, it will tell you a great deal about what is under the boat. Yes, it *will* show fish. A good flasher even shows baitfish, and that's often a tipoff to the presence of predator fish. A flasher gives a different signal for fish, weeds, timber, muck and rocks. I'd feel blind fishing without a flasher. My favorite flashers are made by Eagle.

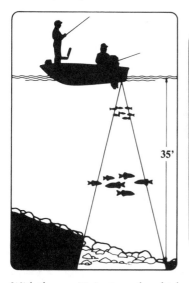 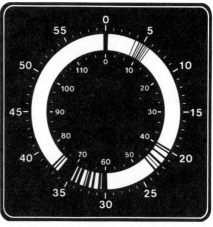

With the sensitivity turned up high enough, a flasher can display a wealth of information. In this case, you are positioned over a sharp rocky drop-off, and there is a school of gamefish 5 or 6 feet up off the bottom. The gamefish are positioned directly under a school of baitfish that is suspended near the surface. Wow! That is the kind of information you need to pattern fish quickly.

Since I fish from two locations in my boat, I've got two flashers. No matter how I'm running my boat, I always know my true depth, within inches. I don't have to crane around to see my flashers—they're right where I can read every little detail on them.

I've got a Silent Sixty in the stern where I can watch it as I run the Mariner or my rear trolling motor. This is my main fishing sonar unit. But I also get a lot of use from the flasher in the bow, a Silent Thirty.

With a transducer clamped to my front trolling motor, I know the depth of water right under *that* end of the boat (which, if I'm on steep structure, is much more important to me than what the depth is back at the transom). The bow flasher is what I watch to keep in position for much of my jig fishing.

Of course, flashers don't use up graph paper and they don't burn much battery power. I'll likely go on using flashers forever because I'm so tuned in to reading them. I doubt more than one or two percent of all anglers see *everything* they could see on their flasher dials. For more details on this, I again recommend my Comprehensive Guide to Fish Locators.

I also use a graph, a chart recording unit. At the time of this writing, paper graphs are unsurpassed at printing out detailed pictures of what is in the water, including fish. As I mentioned earlier, I like to have my graph on when I'm fishing live bait in deeper water. I can't tell you how many times it has paid off for me.

In a sense, graphs don't show anything that flashers don't, but they are far easier to read. Little signals that come and go quickly are permanently marked on paper, while you have to have your eyes glued to the flasher dial to see them. It's just easier to get the whole picture of what's below you with a paper graph—to see the little baitfish, to study the behavior of predator fish, to see subtle changes in the bottom.

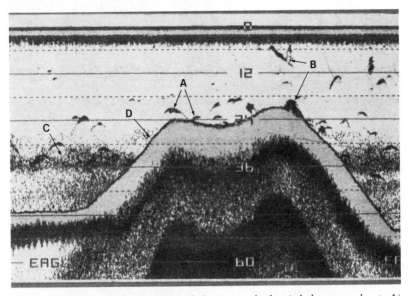

A good graph can show you a detailed picture of what is below your boat: A) fish, B) baitfish, C) thermocline, and of course, D) the bottom and depth.

I'm not content just seeing the depth and whether or not there are fish below me...I want to see *everything*. I want to see all the little details of the bottom, plus I really want to see how the fish are behaving. That is, I want to know exactly how high off bottom they are, whether they are moving and how tightly grouped they are. If there are baitfish, I want to see them. If there is a thermocline, I want to see it. Man, I want to see it *all*!

My paper graph is the Eagle Z-15. It is a *computer* sonar with all kinds of advanced features, including a full choice of upper and lower ranges. I can zoom in on a small band of water and get extremely detailed pictures of what is there. With this graph I have total control over its functions. I can tune it so I can see the backs of walleyes that have their bellies buried in the mud. That is the "state of the art" in fishing sonar!

The LCD graphs are an "in between" type of sonar. Like flashers, they are simple to use and require very little battery power. In fact, LCD graphs drain less power than flashers. With the better units, you just turn them on and go fishing, though you can change settings as needed from time to time. There's no need to change paper, which is a big plus for most people. LCD graphs even take up less space in your boat and less power than flashers.

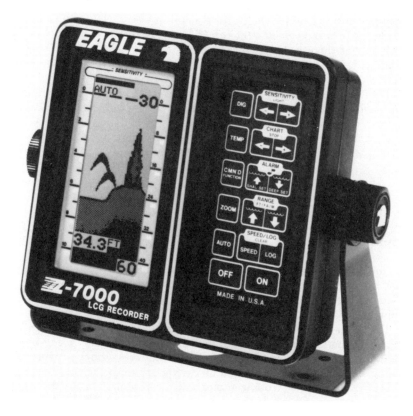

Progress has been made sooner than expected with liquid crystal sonar technology. Eagle makes a unit, the Z-7000, that is the first thing that can truly be called a liquid crystal graph. Its features, and the detail of its readout, are really impressive.

At the same time, the LCD units function as graphs by displaying pictures of what's beneath you, and most people who buy them are looking for that feature. To tell the truth, these graphs are often bought by people who don't know how to read a flasher but figure they can read the graph.

Many fishermen are disappointed with what they get. There are several problem areas. Heck, these machines are pretty much in their infancy, and they're going to get a lot better. They already have.

It's a long story, but many LCD graphs now being sold are less useful than the average flasher. In a nutshell, the main problem is that they have *too few pixels* to show fish and other objects in detail. A pixel is one of those little square dots on the display. A graph without enough pixels will make crude, unreadable displays. Talk to guys who have fished with them. Most units do little more than show how deep the bottom is...and a good flasher does far more than that.

Progress is coming fast. Eagle makes three units I feel good about recommending. The Z-500 is a pretty basic unit, but a good one. In its portable version it is superb for ice fishermen. The Z-6100 has more features and is a better choice for general use.

The Z-7000, however, is the top LCD unit for serious anglers, and is the first of these units to approach the quality level of many paper graphs. It has a number of advanced features, like a surface temperature read-out and optional speed gauge.

But it's the quality of its display that interests me. It is precise enough in its display to have the important "white line" feature that separates targets from the bottom. This is a LCD *graph* that truly shows the underwater world in detail. I've been extremely impressed with the Z-7000. It is an amazingly detailed but easy-to-use unit.

Trolling Motors

You often can catch more fish with silent electric power than with the gas outboard running. Spooky fish in shallow water will ignore an electric motor at times when the sound of a gas motor might put them down.

I've already mentioned that a bow-mounted trolling motor can be extremely useful for the live bait angler. If you have a big, heavy boat, you might find a bow trolling motor is the only way you can maneuver along a contour when working a Lindy Rig or some other live bait rig.

Above all, a bow trolling motor will keep your boat at the right depth when you are working a shoreline or weedline with jigs. Remember, though, a bow trolling motor is just about useless unless you also have a good sonar unit mounted up there where you can watch it while you fish.

Bow mounted electric motors move you forward quietly and with control, and they do it with the lowest possible drain on battery power. Boats are designed to move forward, and bow electrics take advantage of that. You can run into two problems, though, in high waves. The bow may rise and fall so much that the motor's prop comes out of the water...and you get *no* power that way. And the seating position— usually high up in the bow—can be pretty uncomfortable when the lake is tossing badly.

My book, *Bass Patterns*, presents arguments for and against remote control bow trolling motor units. Remote controls allow you to fish continuously without using your hands. But I used to prefer the simplicity of manual units.

No more. A while back, I had the chance to use the modern Minn Kota remote control units, and I immediately realized I'd been missing fish by using the manual motors all these years. Since I've been rigging all my boats with manuals for years, I hadn't caught up with all the improvements they've made in remote control units. They are now perfectly reliable and smooth, though that didn't use to be the case.

More to the point, I now appreciate being able to fish without having my hands ever tied up with the trolling motor. Casting and working a jig is a two-handed job. With a good, modern remote control unit, you've got those hands free for what is most important.

Suit yourself. Most people end up fishing the type they learn to use first. If you're like me, and haven't tried the remote units in a while, give them a second look.

Because most modern fishing boats are heavy, you can hardly buy too much trolling motor power. I've written before that it is extremely rare to talk to a fisherman who believes he bought too much electric power, while most guys are quick to say they'd like more power.

To get enough power it used to be necessary to buy 24-volt units, although the problems of wiring and recharging them were not fun to deal with. The introduction of big geared-down 12-volt motors with oversized propellers changed that overnight. These days, those are the motors that dominate the market.

Minn Kota recently looked at all their motors to see if they were losing power anywhere. As a result, beefed-up wiring and a new speed switch have been incorporated in every motor. A motor can't add to the power coming out of a battery, but an efficient motor makes full use of every bit of power there.

I've got super-powerful 12-volt motors on both ends of my Ranger Fisherman. The bow unit is a Minn Kota 595. I've got the 95 (same motor, different mount) on the transom. These motors are extremely powerful and yet quiet. You can add a Maximizer, which is Minn Kota's pulse width modulator, a device that greatly extends battery life.

Or, on the revolutionary 765, the Maximizer is built-in. And the 765 has another feature that may change the trolling motor world: its remote control is motor driven. In other words, this is a "power steering" version of remote steering, controlled by a very compact foot-operated pedestal. So far, the built-in Maximizer and PowerDrive control are only available on the 65 motor, which has 28 pounds of thrust.

The 95 motors use oversized props. Scuba divers have noted that such geared-down electrics with big props will spook fish less than traditional motors which really scream along at high speeds. To my ear, the 95s are the quietest motor with enough power, so that's what I use.

As I said, I've got a transom-mounted Minn Kota 95 at the stern of my boat. I *could* get by without this motor by doing all my electric fishing with the bow unit, but it is very nice to have quiet electric power at the back. I'd rather fish with electric power whenever possible, even when the lake is fairly rough.

In the stern of the boat I can sit comfortably down in the boat, out of the wind, and fish with total control. I've got not only my flasher but my graph right in front of me. If I have to, I can fire up the big motor without running back from the front of the boat.

But perhaps the biggest advantage of a transom trolling motor is that these motors don't have limits set on their arc, unlike bigger gas outboards. So I can really turn in and out to hug a complicated contour line with the rear trolling motor.

It may seem frivolous to have an electric motor on the back end of a tiller-controlled boat, but the added maneuverability and quietness it gives you make it a valuable fishing aid.

It comes down to this: with an electric trolling motor, I have more *control* over the boat and I have *silent* power that won't scare fish. Every chance I get, I'll fish with electric power if I possibly can! Every year I fish I am more and more impressed with the number of fish we spook. I fish electrically whenever conditions permit.

You really need power to move a heavy boat with a stern-mounted trolling motor. The boat is moving against that flat stern. You should buy a motor with plenty of power, but that isn't enough.

You probably need to rotate the power head. Most transom-mount trolling motors are configured to run efficiently when pushing a boat forward, not when pulling it backward (as you do when backtrolling). When you use these units to backtroll, the motor wastes much of its power by directing power against its own lower unit. Electric motors are efficient when they drive water *away* from their lower units, not *against* their lower units.

To make these motors more efficient for backtrolling, you can reconfigure the motor by reversing the head (see photos).

Revising the head on a MinnKota electric motor is easy. 1) remove the white cover, 2) hold the nut on the inside of the housing with a wrench while removing the bolt running through the shaft on the outside, 3) carefully turn the head 180° and replace the hardware you previously removed. Never attempt to rotate the lower unit on any electric motor, you may damage the important water seals.

Most fishermen now understand they can't run trolling motors off regular "crank" batteries and get satisfactory service. You have to use special "deep cycle" batteries built especially for trolling motors, golf carts and wheelchairs. These rugged batteries are designed to take the harsh use typical of that kind of use.

A new "dual purpose" battery promises to work for running all equipment in the boat—the trolling motor as well as the electric start and all other electronics. Until now, trolling motors had to run off separate batteries. I've run these GNB Stowaway batteries now for two seasons, and I love them. They're tough.

There is no substitute, ultimately, for lots of lead and acid if you want a lot of power. A popular rig now involves two 6-volt batteries wired in series to produce 12 volts. The twin batteries simply have more lead and acid than any single 12- volt model now sold; with them you can fish almost a week between charges.

If your batteries are in the stern, electric power has to get to your bow trolling motor by running through several feet of cable. On many boats—on *most* boats, in fact—that cable is too thin. Thin cables rob your motor of power, like a gas line that is crimped or blocked. Be sure your boat has 4- or 6-gauge cable, and be sure the electric connections pass along the full load of power.

Chapter 5
The Art of Boat Control

Don't trust anyone who tells you it's possible to learn boat control while you sit in your easy chair.

Boat control is like riding a bike. Once you learn it you don't forget, but the only good way to learn is by doing it...with your butt in the boat seat. I can offer tips that might help, but you have to put in your time on the water.

Some day I might produce an instructional video that would *show* people the fine points of boat control. Until then, I present the following advice and pointers...plus the advice that you really need to get out there and practice these skills.

The Backtrolling System

Backtrolling is not simply a matter of running a boat backward. Think of it as a total set of boat control techniques that can be combined in various ways to give you complete control over your boat's position, course and speed.

A good example of this broader concept is *hovering*. If you backtroll slowly enough into the waves and wind, you will not move at all but hover in place while you fish. You can do this with the gas outboard or either of your trolling motors.

But why hover? Why not *anchor*, since what you are doing is fishing a single spot?

Well, if you know you will want to fish a certain spot for a length of time, anchoring is easier and appropriate. But let's say this is one spot of 14 you want to check out as you hunt for fish. You want to throw 10 or 15 casts into a spot to see if there are any active fish there. Then anchoring would be a nuisance, plus you'd probably be tempted to stay too long because lifting an anchor is not especially fun.

So you hover. You might have been working along a shoreline with a Lindy Rig when you had a pickup, and now you think there might be a congregation of fish in that spot. By shifting boat control techniques from slow trolling to hovering, you can switch to jigging to check the area out for more fish. And no need to waste time dropping an anchor and, later on, lifting it again. The hovering angler is always free to move along to fishier pastures.

There are other reasons you might prefer to hover rather than dropping the anchor.

Let's say the wind is pretty fresh, coming off the shore toward you, and you are sure a school of walleyes is hugging a weedline in front of you. You want to throw a jig/minnow combo at them. To anchor, you will have to run way up into the weeds, drop the anchor and then feed out line until your boat blows down to the right position to let you make a cast downwind to where the school is sitting. Hey, that's not easy to do! You can easily get the boat too far from the fish or right on top of them, which can be a big mistake. And all that time you are messing around with the anchor is time lost from fishing.

Even if you do it just right, you end up in the position of casting into the open water then pulling the jig up *toward* the weedline. That might be just the way to catch those fish...but it might not be. You might catch more of them by hovering in deeper water in front of the weeds, throwing your bait up into the weeds and working it slowly back toward you, letting it drop off the weed tops down the front of the weedline.

Either technique might be good, or one might be much better than the other. That's not the point right now. This *is* the point: you want to be ready to do what promises to work best for each circumstance. You have to be able to hold your position by anchoring *or* hovering. And you should have your choice of hovering with either the ready power of the gas outboard or the silent power of your electric.

Being ready to do what's required depends on both equipment and technique. The end result is total boat control.

That kind of versatility and continuous control are at the heart of the backtrolling system. If you can't put the boat where you want it and keep it there, either your equipment or your techniques are not what they should be.

Here's another example of the versatility of backtrolling. Let's say you're working with nightcrawlers on floating Lindy Rigs along a 21-foot contour. On your flasher you spot several fish at 19 feet, right below the boat. By popping out of gear for a moment or two, you can stop the boat long enough to send your floating crawlers rising slowly up through those fish. They'll find *that* hard to resist.

If you don't get them, though, you can spin the boat 180 degrees and bring the bait back at them from the other side while you never lose sight of the fish in your sonar. Tight turns are especially easy with a transom-mounted electric motor. When those fish see the bait again but from a new direction, one of them will probably go for it.

The beauty of backtrolling is the way it lets you adopt the right tactic instantly. Two things are usually running constantly when you back-troll: your gas outboard and your sonar. That way you know your depth and you have power at your fingertips. All options are available to you.

Backtrolling has a precision and flexibility not possible with any other boat control technique. If you're good (and the wind isn't too high), you should be able to write your name on the lake bottom with your Lindy sinker.

Even if your name is Babe Winkelman!

Controlling For Jigging

Before we get into backtrolling, let's look at what is needed to run a boat properly for jigging.

You can guide the boat from the back or the front, with gas or electric power.

Much of the time, when I'm jigging I'm up front with the electric trolling motor running the boat. I am higher, I can see well and I'm running the boat with maximum efficiency because the hull slips forward so easily.

But sometimes in rough weather, the elevated bow deck is not the most comfortable place to be running a boat. Then I'll sit in back. If I can, I'll maneuver the boat with the stern electric motor. Sometimes it's so rough I end up using the gas outboard. You do what you have to do.

The real challenge in controlling a boat for jigging is visualizing the structure. You can't hold the boat directly on the contour you are fishing, the way you so often do when trolling rigs.

Say the fish are in 13 feet of water. You'll want your boat out in something like 18, so you can cast up to 10 feet and pull the jig back through the best water.

Sounds simple.

But it isn't. The contour rarely holds constant. As you work around a structure, you will find that sometimes you need to be sitting in 20 or 21 feet, not 18, because the bottom drops off more quickly. Or, if the dropoff becomes less sharp, holding the boat in 18 might put you out of casting range from the fish at 13.

Unlike backtrolling with rigs, jigging boat control forces you to keep two depths in mind—the depth your are in and the depth you are fishing to. The relationship between them keeps changing, so you have to constantly be picturing the shape of the underwater world.

Structure is rarely as simple as it is pictured in fishing books or magazines. You will find classic reefs, humps, saddles and points, but the more usual thing is to encounter lopsided saddles, reefs that sit in funny shapes or points that basically point one way but have little bumps trailing off in different directions.

Let's take, for example, a small hump that comes up out of 29 feet and tops off at 16. A spot like this, particularly if it is small and there are other humps near it, is wonderful mid-summer structure. If you can find such a hump, great. If it isn't on the contour maps so every other guy knows about it, you have a potential gold mine in front of you.

But it isn't enough to fish to the hump. In almost all cases, the hump will not be perfectly symmetrical, but will have a steeper side and a side that drops off more slowly. The weeds might be better on one side or another, or maybe they are only on top. You've got to figure these things out.

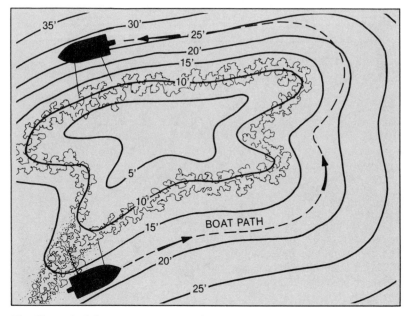

To effectively fish a structure, proper boat positioning is important. You must first learn to visualize the shape of the structure and then compensate for depth changes with your boat.

115

When you work the boat along for jig fishing, the easiest way to maintain the right pace is to step on and off the power button. That's the *easiest* way, not the best way. You'll spook fish less if you set the power right and keep on the button so the motor isn't always turning on and off.

A refined level of boat control for jigging is running the boat so your partners get good fishing, not just the guy running the boat. In a wind, it is really tricky to keep the boat doing what it should be doing without "back-ending" everybody else.

The Basics of Backtrolling

Backtrolling works best when you are moving backward into wind and waves. Wind and waves help slow down the boat and give you a force to work against. By adjusting the throttle or possibly slipping in and out of reverse, you'll be able to find the amount of power to set against the wind and waves to let you troll where you want at the speed you prefer.

All this time, your eyes should rarely leave your sonar. You will have a certain depth—say it is 19 feet—where you expect to find fish. No matter whether you are working a dropoff, a point, a reef, a hump or some other structure, there will be a deep and a shallow side of the structure. When your sonar shows you are going into 20 or 21 feet of water, turn the motor toward shallower water. If the bottom starts coming up, angle the motor out toward the deeper stuff. You can fish with one hand while controlling the boat with the other, keeping your bait always in prime water.

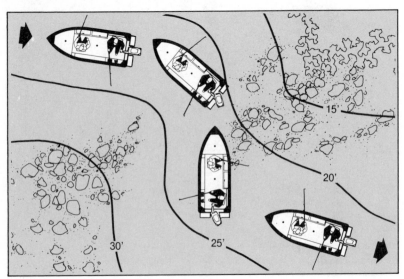

Backtrolling is an excellent method for following tricky contours. By carefully watching your sonar, you can keep your boat at a precise depth. Moving along backwards allows you to make instant corrections in your course.

It's amazing how easily this can come to reasonably coordinated people. I've seen lots of guys do a decent job of backtrolling the very first time they tried it. After a few tries, you will be running the boat well *without thinking about what you are doing.*

Later, with experience, you will be able to move downwind with almost as much control. But I'll admit it: it is harder to control a boat along a curving contour when going with the wind. If you can't hack it, just run below the stretch you want to fish and come at it into the wind. That's certainly better than coming downwind out of control.

Basically, to move with the wind, you usually let the motor idle out of gear as long as the wind is pushing you the right way at the right speed. But that is rarely the case for long. Soon enough, you'll need to put the motor in gear to correct the speed and/or direction of the drift with bursts of power.

As I've said, this is harder than trolling into the wind. Sometimes you might be able to stay right on the contour but to do it you zig and zag in ways that tangle lines. Don't be too proud to make a run downwind and come back through the fishy water by trolling into the wind.

I keep talking about wind for a reason. People who can't control boats in wind will usually hide from a wind by fishing the protected areas. They are usually *hiding from the fish* as well. As I've explained in my other books, the shore being hit by waves and wind is almost always the best shore to fish (with shallow water bass being the most common exception). Wave action reduces light penetration, stirs up general activity and knocks baitfish around. Waves light a fire under such predator fish as muskies, northerns, walleyes and bass.

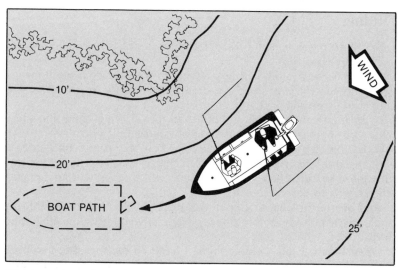

Slipping, *lake style. Although a slightly different version of the technique was originally designed for fishing rivers, it also works well on lakes. It is most effective when high winds make it tough to backtroll. Simply let the wind blow you along, making adjustments in direction by aiming your motor (in reverse) the direction you want to go. The motor also helps you slow your drift speed.*

The answer to wind is not to run away from it but to handle it. With the right equipment, it is just as easy to backtroll into wind as to troll on a dead calm day.

Hovering

I've already mentioned hovering. Here's a short description of how to do it.

If you keep your power low enough as you backtroll into the wind, you will go so slow you are not moving at all. You are holding in place...hovering.

If the wind is heavy, hover with the gas outboard with a low power setting. If the wind is not so heavy, pop the motor in and out of gear with the gear shifter.

You can also hover with bursts of power from the bow trolling motor or transom-mount motor (which is my favorite). You have to decide which motor to use depending on the circumstances—how much battery power you have, how windy it is, how spooky the fish might be, etc. I'll always use the electric if I can.

How can you tell you are staying right on the same spot? By watching the sonar, you can keep from changing depth, but that might not be precise enough. If the guy running the boat is fishing right on bottom (like with a Lindy Rig), he can tell by when his line goes slack whether or not the boat is moving.

The best way of all is to use a marker buoy for a reference point. I'll talk about them in a moment.

Drifting

Drifting is a classic boat control technique that has special limitations and advantages.

On the negative side, letting the wind move your boat often means giving up control over your speed and location. Or at least it is, the way a lot of people drift.

In fishing seminars I talk about "*controlled* drifting," and that's just what you should aim for: drifts that are under full control.

If the wind isn't blowing too hard, the best way to correct a drift is with the transom trolling motor. Remember, that electric motor can turn more sharply than your outboard, which gives you advantages when trying to correct a drift.

And one of the biggest advantages of drifting is that it is silent. So that's all the more reason to prefer electric power when adjusting your drift.

When I drift, I like to have my left hand on the top of my trolling motor while my eyes are on the sonar. I prefer drifting with the transom toward the wind. That makes it easier to correct the drift with backwards bursts of power.

How much power? In what direction? There just isn't any point in my trying to tell you, because every situation is a little different. You have to apply enough power and in the right direction to get the right

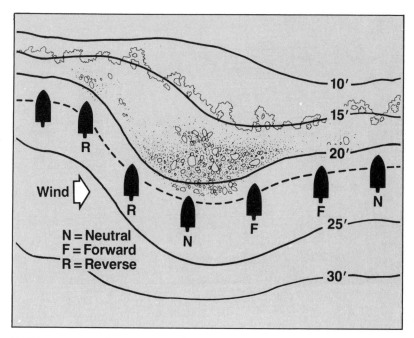

Drifting is an excellent way to follow a contour, if you remember to use the motor to keep you on course. This is known as a controlled drift. By putting the motor in forward, neutral or reverse, it's possible to hug the contour while letting the wind do most of the work.

effect. The correction needed for a 15-mph wind will be different than for a 20-mph wind. And everything depends on the angle of the wind.

There are other ways of controlling drifts. You can affect the attitude of a drifting boat by leaving the lower unit of your gas outboard down in the water or pulling it up. Even the angle of the lower unit can cause the boat to drift differently. With the motor cocked a certain way, a boat might drift forward with all anglers casting over each other to reach the same spot of water. By angling the motor a little, you might be able to set the drift so the boat moves sideways and everyone has an equal shot at the best water.

For advanced drifting, get Boat Brakes. Boat Brakes are special *fishing* sea anchors. They drag in the water like parachutes, slowing your drift. They are made by Blue Harbor Manufacturing, Hopkins, MN 55343.

Boat Brakes are adjustable, so you can get more or less drag from them. I'll most often throw out a Boat Brake from the bow of my boat, though I might put out sea anchors at both ends of my boat and really go slowly with the boat positioned at right angles to the wind. Sometimes I'll use an electric motor or the outboard in conjunction with a Boat Brake to get just the right drift.

In some states, like Wisconsin, you might have to drift a lot because motorized trolling is banned on certain lakes. That's where something like a Boat Brake is especially useful.

Most sea anchors are a pain to use, but they can be the only good way to slow your fishing speed in really high winds. Boat Brakes is by far the best I've seen. They are easy to set out and adjust, and very easy to bring back in.

Drifting, with or without sea anchors, is particularly deadly when you fish over the top of a big reef for walleyes. At times the wind and waves might be so high that everybody thinks fishing is impossible, yet if you get out on a shallow reef and drift over it at the right speed you might find tremendous numbers of walleyes feeding under the choppy water. If the wind is blowing hard, fish over the reef with a Lindy Rig or a baited jig worked right below the boat. If it is calm, set up a slip bobber rig so your minnow or leech is held right above the top of the reef.

After you have completed a drift, power up the big motor and run back upwind for another drift. If the reef is shallow enough and the day calm enough, running the gas outboard over the fish might spook them. Then it's smart to run around the reef before shutting off the motor to make another downwind drift over a slightly different section of the reef.

I remember one day of drifting. I was fishing Bigstone Lake with my wife. It was a tough opening day, but we found a nice bunch of good fish schooled up tightly on a break. It took a while to work out the pattern, but I finally realized I could only catch fish by drifting downwind on this little break. We had to be at 12 or 13 feet. At 11 or 14 feet we got nothing. And we only got fish going one way, downwind. I have to believe the walleyes were all lined up with their faces toward the current.

Anyway, we really began to put fish in the boat, while other boats around us got nothing. Mostly, their boat control wasn't good enough. Pretty soon we were looking for big fish only. But I'll never forget a couple of boats. They were getting kinda upset and rowdy, and when my wife began throwing back 4 and 5 pound walleyes, those guys said a few things I can't put into print here!

Trolling Forward

Trolling forward with the gas outboard or an electric motor (front or rear) is less useful than backtrolling, but still important. Since boats move more efficiently and with less splashing when going forward, that is sometimes the only way to go.

Trolling forward with a transom-mounted motor is clumsy, since the steering is from the "wrong" end of the boat. If the contour line you want to follow does much curving, you're going to wander on and off the right depth. It helps to know your shoreline well enough that you can anticipate course changes.

It is harder to troll *slowly* going forward than backward, but it's not impossible. As in backtrolling, you can slip in and out of gear if your lowest outboard speed is too fast. Some fishermen use little "kicker" outboards for slower forward trolling, while others use the bow electric trolling motor. I'll use the electric motor for slowly trolling shallow water at night when I know the fish are up close enough to the top of the water to be bothered by a gas outboard. Minn Kota now makes a 3- and 4-horse electric motors that are meant to substitute for gas outboards; you should definitely check them out for these sorts of uses.

When fishing rivers, trolling slowly into the current is sometimes called *slipping*. The right amount of power will just keep you in place— another way of hovering—or letting you move up- or down-current slowly. Slipping is used heavily on rivers, with the boat pointed into the current, by guys who are casting jigs to little pockets. This does not work on lakes in any kind of wind, as your nose gets blown all over the place.

Anchoring

Anchoring is an important boat control technique. Rather than seeing it as an alternative to running a boat, I view anchoring as one of the many elements of the total boat control system.

Beginners often anchor for the wrong reasons. The two most common speeds for beginning walleye anglers are "too fast" or "anchored," and they'll often anchor because they lack the equipment or skill to move a boat with control.

I'm probably like a lot of skilled anglers. When we learned to hover, we looked down on anchoring as a beginner's crutch. We always wanted to fish on the fly, using our great skill to put the boat where it belonged.

Well, like a lot of guys, I grew up a little. Hovering is slick, but it isn't not always better than anchoring. Sometimes you just can't beat anchoring. It's efficient, doesn't burn up battery power or gas and anchoring lets you fish with both hands. You can anchor and try one bait for several casts, then switch baits or presentatons...which is tough to do if you're constantly working with the motor with one hand.

For serious fishermen, anchoring is a serious form of boat control. Here, Ted Peck lets out rope as we slide into position to fish catfish in the Rock River.

Anchoring makes sense any time you know you want to fish a certain area carefully. In really high seas, anchoring sometimes is the only way of holding on a spot and fishing. You might be able to hover in high waves, but at a bad price—like getting wet and burning up lots of gas or electric battery power. Sometimes fishing is very, very slow, but you know where a pocket of fish is holding. That's another time to anchor.

Usually there is some kind of wind, and so you have to place the anchor well upwind of where you'll fish. Anchors won't usually hold unless you let out three times as much rope as is needed to touch bottom. It takes experience to judge how far away from the fish you should place the anchor. It shouldn't take much thought, however, to realize that you *must* be quiet when lowering an anchor and feeding out line so you drift back down to where the fish are. Before dropping the anchor, it makes sense to throw out a buoy as a reference point so you can anchor, feed out anchor line and end up in the right position to cover your fish. I'll talk about throwing marker buoys a bit later.

A boat on a single anchor will swing in the wind like a pendulum. That can be good. If you are fishing alone and you want to cover a lot of water because the fish might be spread out, swinging on a single anchor is sure one way to do it. Fishing from a swinging boat is best saved for times you are fishing solo. It gets pretty awkward if you have two or three anglers fishing at a time because the swinging boat tangles lines, plus everybody is trying to cast into the same water.

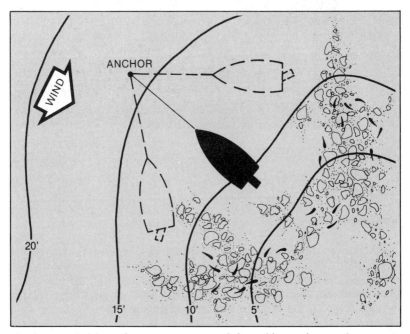

Anchor upwind from the spot you want to fish, and let out line until you are in casting range. Then, if you feel the fish won't be spooked by your motor, slide back and forth by aiming it in either direction. Electric motors also work well for this.

Sometimes the swinging takes you away from the fish or screws up your sense of touch. Then you want to peg the back of the boat in place with a second anchor. This second anchor can be quite a bit lighter than the main anchor that holds the boat in place.

Always anchor from the *bow* if you use a single anchor, as anchoring from the side or stern is unsafe in waves. That is true of sea anchors, as well. The bow is designed to meet and rise above waves, whereas the rest of the boat is not. Anchoring reduces your boat's ability to meet waves anyway, so always anchor off the bow.

I don't like those winch systems that some people use for holding, dropping and raising anchors. I mostly keep my anchors stowed out of sight in the boat until I need them. Then I snub the anchor rope on a handy metal gadget called The Gripper. In a second or two, I can lace the rope through the fingers of the Gripper and have it fixed in place. I have Grippers mounted in front and on both sides of the back of my boat.

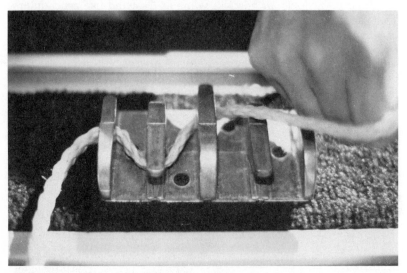

The Gripper is a great gadget for quickly tying off an anchor rope or floating minnow bucket.

Marker Buoys

When I was getting into the new "structure fishing," some experts said we shouldn't fish a point or reef until we'd spent some time carefully mapping it out and then marking the shape of the thing with a dozen marker buoys. Well, that's so boring that a lot of guys who tried it decided they'd never touch a marker buoy again.

But marker buoys are extremely useful. You just have to use them right.

Without mapping out a whole point, you can throw one marker on its tip. Be sure to throw the marker into a depth you won't be fishing. If the fish are at 12, throw the marker up into 8 feet or back out at 18. If

you are working a big reef, you might throw a marker on each end or on any prominent finger coming off the reef.

Those markers let you operate efficiently. Water just looks like water unless you have something to orient yourself with, and that's what a marker or two will do for you. You need reference points. For example, fish holding on a steeply sloping break are easy to find again, but if you locate a school on a broad, featureless flat, a reference marker is helpful.

I'll sometimes throw out a marker when I catch a fish. You have to be careful about this, as you don't want to mark a hot spot for the other boats in the area. One trick is to throw the marker *way* shallow from where the fish are. Some fishermen throw markers both in shallow and off to the side of where they hit fish, always throwing the marker off the target in the same direction. Then when other boats congregate around your marker up in the weeds you can come by outside, catching fish.

It isn't smart to throw a marker whenever you find a school of fish. If you've been paying attention, you should know just where you are anyway. You should *always* know the exact depth, if nothing else. I only drop a marker if I'm not expecting trouble from other boats and when I've got a school located far from shore where it's harder to return to the spot without a marker.

Beginners want to mark a spot where they caught fish, but I more often mark places as reference points or places that just look good to me. If I'm chugging around on a reef and I see a pretty little rock pile or a finger point on the reef, I'm likely to heave a marker at it. Little spots like that often hold fish. If I don't get a fish there right away, maybe I'll sneak back later and try the spot again. Fish are often moving around.

Much of the time, you have to put your bait *right in front of the fish's face*. Pinpoint accuracy is critically important! Marker buoys really help sharpen up your presentation by letting you keep track of where you are.

Spinning

Oh boy, how do I start with this? This technique is definitely in the "advanced" category.

This is a very exacting technique. You have to be entirely on top of boat control and sonar interpretation, or there's no point trying.

But spinning will turn a fish that just otherwise wouldn't hit. I've used it to catch walleyes, northern pike, smallmouth, suspended crappies and many other species of fish. It has paid off several times by giving me some *big* fish.

Not that I do this all the time. In fact, I don't resort to spinning unless it's necessary to catch fish. If I'm in a bunch of fish, I'll probably not spin because I expect one fish in the school to bang my bait.

But spinning makes sense when I see a big fish, a single fish, on the graph.

Spinning basically involves fishing vertically, directly below the boat. What you try to do is to walk your Lindy Rig or jig in a 360-degree circle around the fish, keeping that bait right in front of the fish.

On one hand, you're giving the fish a bunch of different looks at the bait, coming at it in a variety of ways. On the other hand, you're being like a pushy salesman who won't be denied a sale. You are pestering the fish, nagging it.

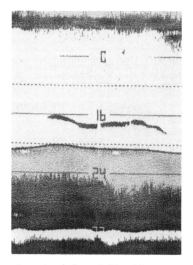 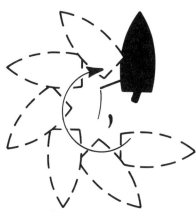

An extended mark like this on your graph readout tells you that a fish is either following your boat path, or you are staying over the top of it. In order to pinpoint presentation to a single fish, you must first learn to stay with them.

This technique only works if you can read your sonar well enough to have a firm idea of where the fish is. You have to watch for motion all the time, so if the fish drifts to the side of your sonar cone you can move to keep on top of it.

Obviously, this is only possible with the top sonar units. For one thing, you absolutely need a sonar with a tightly focussed cone, or you won't have the precision needed to spin over a fish.

Spinning isn't easy and doesn't always work. But it works well enough on big fish that I really wanted to mention it. I won't often work this hard for an ordinary fish. When a fish is big, though, I'm glad to have this trick to try. It often pays off.

Interpreting Your Sonar

Does it seem odd to talk about reading your sonar in a chapter on boat control? It shouldn't. Reading the sonar and running the boat right are inseparable. You can't guide a boat unless you know where it should go, and the sonar is your best way of knowing where you should be.

I can't get into this topic in true detail because it's such a complicated story. Again, this is just the sort of thing I go into in the *Comprehensive Guide to Fishing Sonar*. On the other hand, I can't put out a live bait rigging and jigging book that totally skips the issue of understanding what your sonar is telling you.

So let's compromise. I'll put a few details on sonar interpretation in here. Understand, though, that there is much more to know.

At the *very least*, your sonar has to tell you how deep the water is! That isn't asking much, but if you know that you're still vastly ahead of fishermen 25 years ago.

But any decent sonar unit should *show fish*, though you might have heard the opposite. Small fish, fish in weeds and fish that are moving quickly are all hard to see on some sonar units. But a gamefish in relatively open water that isn't going anywhere in a hurry...*that's a fish you should see every time* with a graph *or* a flasher. If you can't, buy a better sonar or troubleshoot the one you've got.

Hard Bottom, Soft Bottom

You absolutely need to know how *hard* the bottom is if you're going to catch fish like walleyes and smallmouth. Those fish don't usually hang out over soft, silty bottoms. Sometimes, but not usually. Detecting hard bottoms is a different story with each kind of sonar.

Flashers show hard bottoms by getting such a strong signal that a second or third echo appears. In other words, if you get a bottom signal at 11 feet, *and* 22, you're probably over a hard bottom. If the signal shows up at 33 feet as well, you obviously are getting so much signal back that the bottom is hard. As you move from area to area, you'll see those second and third echoes come and go. Those echoes are talking to you, telling you where the bottom is soft and hard. (This only works if you set your unit to put out enough power; for details, see the Comprehensive Guide to Fish Locators.)

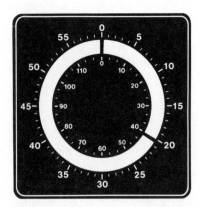 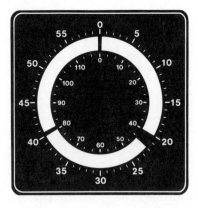

This shows the difference between what soft (left) and hard (right) bottoms look like on a flasher. The sensitivity was set the same for both readings. Notice how thin and weak the left reading is, indicating a soft bottom. The harder bottom will display as a wider, brighter reading, with a second echo appearing at twice the bottom depth, about 40 feet.

With *paper chart recording graphs*, the story is different. Your bottom is displayed at the bottom of the chart, so you can't see a second echo. But if you have a *Grayline* feature, as Eagle and Lowrance graphs do, you can see hard bottoms. This feature causes the bottom to print light, so you can distinguish between low fish and the bottom. A bottom won't print gray unless it is giving back a strong signal. So if you are over a mucky bottom where the returning signal will be weak, the bottom will print dark. Over a hard bottom, the bottom will print with Grayline effect. You'll easily see this.

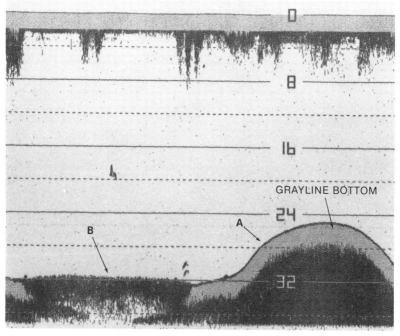

The Grayline *feature on Eagle and Lowrance graphs clearly shows hard (A) and soft bottom (B).*

It's different again with *LCD graphs*. On these, there is a bar graph that runs from left to right at the top of the unit, and this indicates how much power the unit is putting out in order to get a good echo. If that bar is way over to the right, you are over a soft bottom and the unit is beating out its brains just to get any kind of echo back from the silt. If the bar is way to the left, a weak signal is enough to get back a strong signal, so you are over a hard bottom.

One LCD graph, the Eagle Z-7000; is refined enough to have a Grayline feature. If you have one of these units and it is showing a Grayline bottom, that's a firm bottom.

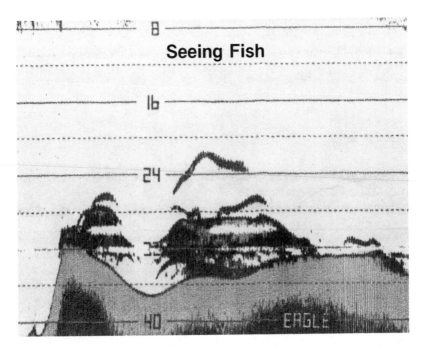

Seeing Fish

Let's get some priorities straight. You can catch fish in places where you do *not* see them. You can see fish and *not* catch them. And I'll tell you, a school of suckers looks mighty good on a graph! So there is no automatic relationship between seeing fish and putting them in the livewell.

But you should be able to see fish if they are below the boat, almost always, and seeing them is a big positive indication. If I see them below my boat I obviously know the fish are there, which is a big advantage for me.

Many times I've been running the boat at half speed when I've seen some fish signals right off bottom. This has often happened in areas where I wasn't necessarily expecting them...maybe I was running around scouting out the shape of some structure. But there the fish were, so I caught them!

How skilled are you at angling? If you are learning to catch fish, concentrate on reading bottom and getting a feel for the way the lake lies. As you get more experienced, you will have an almost unconscious sense of the bottom and then you will want to watch fish closely. Don't make a big deal of watching for fish until you have mastered the main concepts of fishing sonar and you understand structure.

You can learn a lot by the fish signals you see, too.

It is generally a better thing to see a cluster of fish signals near bottom than one here and one there. A school of fish together is more apt to feed competively than a single fish or two. The more fish there are in the area, the better your chances of nagging one into making a mistake. Then the mood of the whole school can turn positive. If it does, fish fast and fish smart! Those moments are pretty special.

It is a good sign when you see baitfish signals in the same area as gamefish signals. When predators are lying right close to baitfish, something is afoot. Get your bait down there so you can take advantage of some active fish.

The height of the fish from bottom is another indication of how catchable they are. Fish with their bellies buried in the mud are very negative and hard to catch. Ditto for fish suspended *way* off bottom, halway to the surface. But fish that are up 2 to 6 or 7 feet from bottom—they're much easier to catch. If the fish have been hugging bottom all day and then lift up a little, expect good things.

It is also a very positive indication if you see fish that are moving. Most inexperienced graph users are extremely pleased when they get beautiful, symmetrical fish arches. Well, that's nice I guess, but I'd rather see a squiggly line. The symmetrical arch is a fish that is going nowhere, whereas the shaky, squiggly mark is a moving fish. Moving fish bite better.

Let's put those pointers together. A single or pair of fish sitting near bottom, not moving, are not good candidates to spend much time on. But if you see a bunch of fish, moving around, not tight to bottom, you really should be catching fish. Those fish are asking for it! If you aren't doing business, switch baits and presentations quickly to give them what they want.

You should also be able to make accurate judgements about the size of the fish you're looking at, though this is harder with a flasher than with a good graph. The size of a fish can be judged by the *height* of its signal. On a flasher, little fish like baitfish make thin lines while big fish make fatter lines. With graphs, the height of the fish arch is the tipoff to size of the fish.

To make that more clear, you should *not* judge a fish by the *length* of its signal. With a flasher, the length of time you see a fish signal is a measure of the length of time a fish is in your sonar cone.

It's similar with graphs. A long fish signal is just that—a long fish signal. Some people think they've got the Loch Ness Monster below their boat when they see a long fish signal. All that means is that the fish is under the boat a long time. A perch that gets under your boat and swims the same way you are moving will leave a fish signal longer than the next world record musky. It is how thick the signal is, not its length, that shows size.

I can illustrate these points with the story of a fish I caught on Gull Lake, near my home, during the 1986 Minnesota season opener. Gull has a reputation for kicking out big fish, though it is very heavily fished. I only had two pickups that whole day. Things were tough.

I was not on classic opening day shallow structure. Instead, I was working a leech on a Lindy Rig on a little bit of structure in fairly deep water. It was the kind of place that might be used by fish coming out of the deep water into the shallows. I was hoping for a bigger fish, knowing I would settle for less action in the gamble to get a good one.

When I'm working deep water like that I like to have my graph on, and I spotted a big fish below me. If you have worked with a graph long enough you can tell when a fish is centered in the cone— which means the fish is right below the boat—or a little off-center. You can also tell whether or not it is a big fish, as I just explained.

This fish looked good to me, and I wanted it. I kept spinning the boat around with the rear trolling motor so I could keep the boat over the fish and keep the bait coming at it from different angles. The fish didn't grab my leech the first or second or third time, but it finally hit. That fish went just ounces less than 11 pounds, which is a fish of a lifetime for just about any angler in my country.

It would sound modest to claim I was *lucky* that day, and I'm tempted to do it. But I don't honestly figure that fish was the result of "luck" to any great degree. I was in a place that was likely to produce big fish. I was looking for big fish. My equipment—all of it, from the boat to my rod, reel and line—was as good as is made. I recognized a big fish below me because my graph was capable of printing a sharp and detailed picture, and I knew how to read it. Once I knew I had a big fish near me I went after it with boat control and a variety of presentations until that fish lost her cool and bit.

Luck? Well, if you refine your boat control and sonar reading skills, your "luck" will improve too! I guarantee it.

You don't think boat control is important? This 10-pound-plus walleye came on an opening day when very few fish were caught, by following it around with a graph and keeping the bait in front of its nose.

Chapter 6
Understanding and Learning Jig Fishing

"The magic bait"

It is the night before the opening day of fishing season. A young boy lies in the top bunk of an ancient resort cabin, or "rustic" as it said in the brochure. Through the crack of the cloth curtain that serves as his bedroom door, he can see and hear everything that matters at the moment.

By the light of a kerosene lantern, the boy can see into the main room of the cabin, where an enormous knotty pine picnic table has become headquarters for his father and his fishing buddies. There are cigars everywhere, and the men have rods and reels and tackle boxes strewn throughout the room. When the laughter and fishing stories die for a second, the boy can hear the klink of glasses, and the sound of waves rushing onto the shoreline of the lake, which is very near the cabin door.

He wants to stay awake all night to watch and listen, but eventually he falls asleep.

Sometime in the night, after all the men have also fallen asleep, he begins dreaming. In his dream, it is the next day, and he is out in the boat with his dad. They have been fishing for a long time, but have not caught anything.

Suddenly, a stranger rides into view in a shiny fishing boat that reminds the boy of race cars he has seen on television on Sunday afternoons. The stranger's boat comes alongside theirs, and the stranger asks how they are doing.

"Nothin" his father says, expecting the same answer in return.

"That's too bad, guys," the stranger says. "I'll tell you what. I've got a magic bait here, and since you are having so much trouble, I'll let you have a couple."

The stranger approached close enough to lean into their boat, and in his hand are six strange-looking concoctions, with a head made of lead and a plastic body with feathers sticking out like a tail. He offers them to the boy and his father.

"But what do you do with them?" the boy asks.

"You'll know," the stranger says, disappearing as quickly as he had come. "It'll take you some time to learn, but you'll know."

His father tied on one of the magic baits to each of their lines, and with great hope they lower them overboard. But sadly, all they do is sink to the bottom and sit there. The boy waits and waits, but no fish come to bite on the magic bait.

Just when he is giving up hope, the stranger reappears in his dream, but this time, he is seated right beside the boy. "It doesn't exactly work magic all by itself, does it?" the stranger says, with a slight chuckle. "It took me years to learn to catch fish with it. Let me show you a trick or two..."

"*Come on, Jimmy, let's go get 'em.*" His father's voice pierces the dream, just at exactly the wrong time. He tries to pretend he is still asleep, but it is hopeless. He can smell coffee and bacon cooking in the main room of the cabin.

It is beginning to get light down at the lakeshore. But all Jimmy can think about is that he might never know the secret of the magic bait.

• • •

That dream has in it a lot of truth about jigs. They are, indeed, a magical bait. For all types of fishing, the jig is unquestionably the best single lure ever invented. But there is no magic in the jig itself. It can do almost nothing without the help of a fisherman.

But in the hands of someone who knows how to fish with it, a jig is like a hand tool in the hands of a master craftsman.

You can't pick up the secrets of jig fishing in a dream. A fisherman must learn to be good with a jig, and there is much to learn. But if you take up jig fishing seriously, you will realize why most truly good fishermen say that it is the one lure they would take with them if they could take only one.

Becoming a Master Jig Fisherman: The Mental Aspects

It takes exactly the same thing to become a good jig fisherman as it does to become a more proficient overall angler: you need to learn to better understand the underwater world of the fish, to train yourself to look for and feel the "little" things, the details that unlock the secrets for catching fish on any given day.

Every time I go jig fishing, I'm looking for the best way to do the job before me. Am I presenting the jig in the most effective way? Would a slightly heavier jig help me stay down in the current? Would lighter line allow the jig to swim more naturally? If I could keep the line more vertical would I be able to feel more of the subtle strikes? These are the kinds of questions you should be asking yourself as you fish a jig.

One of the most important lessons an aspiring jig fisherman must learn is that *many* times the hit from a fish is a scoop or a swallow, or the jig is just inhaled and the fisherman feels almost nothing. Get it out of your mind that you are going to be getting a lot of smashing, jarring strikes! Don't even think about those; you'll feel them even if you're half asleep, or staring at the seagulls overhead.

As a matter of fact, I really feel that you get more subtle-feeling strikes when fishing with jigs than you do with live bait rigs. With a Lindy Rig, for example, you are normally in constant contact with your bait because you are dragging or pumping it along, on or near the bottom. It becomes easier, then, to detect minute changes in the pressure exerted on the bait (not that it is easy!). With live bait rigs, there is a fairly even amount of stretch in the line as opposed to the many times you are swimming a jig up off the bottom, or free-falling a jig down a rock ledge, or whatever the situation calls for.

You'll never get good at it until you have done it an awful lot and practiced with it and taught yourself to concentrate at it. In fishing, you have to be your own coach much of the time, and that takes discipline; I realize that. But that's flat what it takes to get good, and if you want to get good, you'll find a way to pay that price.

To begin with, teach yourself to look for the little *tiny* differences in feel. You have got to convince yourself that many times "it's not going to feel like anything" when a fish hits; it's not always a freight train strike. In fact, it's very rare that you will feel a solid "thunk" when a fish hits a jig. For those strikes, you don't need this book or graphite rods or even most of your senses. For the most part, though, to catch fish on most of the other days, you need a fine-tuned, ever-alert mental approach to what your jig is doing down there. The sense of rhythm your jig has as it is raised and then falls might change *slightly* when you haven't changed anything (is that a fish? probably!)

When I'm out there jig fishing, I am not always actively involved in a conversation. I'm after it very hard. I'm swimming that bait, picturing it in my mind (hint hint: this is a very big part of feeling light strikes), feeling it, nudging it along, I'm touching bottom, trying to figure out if it's a rock or sand or whatever bottom, and that's the key.

I'm asking myself questions all the time, such as "what do I have to do in order to work my jig through this kind of cover?" or "along this kind of bottom?" I am constantly seeing in my mind's eye a picture of a fish coming up off the bottom, about to take my jig. I am always expecting a fish to hit, and always wanting a fish to hit. You must learn to do this as well.

I have to compare this to, say, a shortstop on a baseball team. As the pitcher gets ready to throw every pitch, the shortstop has to get ready; and I don't just mean crouched down with his knees bent and his glove open. I mean he has to expect and *want* every pitch to be hit at him. Imagine that! There are usually well over 100 pitches in a game, and he has to be ready to act on every one. How does he know which ones will get hit to him? He doesn't. So how do you know when a fish is going to hit? You don't, either. You have to expect and want a fish to hit the entire time, as you are fishing along a structure. Then, you will be ready more often than not when one does.

I'm not saying that you have to go out there and put all thoughts of having fun out of your mind in the name of being a deadly fish catcher. I'm telling you what it takes to learn to "see" and feel more strikes. Don't think I never get caught napping, or sitting there watching a young loon riding along on its mother's back while a fish comes up and steals my leech. It happens all the time. If it didn't, I'd start getting worried about my sense of priorities.

As you learn the fine points of jig fishing, much of the time you have to be your own coach. But hey, even that can be part of the fun!

Concentrating as hard as you can at all times makes a lot of difference, because there are a lot of times the hits are very hard to detect. Tennis players and golfers always talk about being "tournament tough." To them, that means that even though the mechanics of their game, the strokes, might be about the same any day of the week, there is a difference in them when they are performing at the level it takes to win major competitions. Their concentration is peaking and they are doing all the *little* things right.

That's the way I feel about fishing. When I'm having a good day, when I'm concentrating well, I can actually swim a jig down the face of a sharp rocky dropoff and hardly ever get hung up, by just barely letting the jig tick the tops of the rocks as it falls. At the same time, I am feeling every inch of the way for something "different" that might tell me a fish has picked up the jig. Also, I am watching the way my line is falling with the rhythm of the jig I am using, looking constantly for any slowing or twitching of the line.

I rely on line twitch as well as feel for detecting strikes, and I'm concentrating on both of them all the time that I'm jig fishing. You can't just rely on one, because you sometimes miss things that way. You shouldn't learn to be an expert line watcher, for example, by ignoring the aspect of trying to feel what your jig is doing in the water. By concentrating on both aspects, you not only have a better chance of catching fish. You also have a better chance of understanding what the fish are doing that day—how hard they are hitting, whether they want the jig dragged slowly right along the bottom, swimming a foot off the bottom, moving faster or slower, etc.

Under those conditions, if you get a good bite, it feels like you've stuck your fingers into an electrical socket! You are so ready that your mind and your fingers are picking up everything that jig is doing, and picturing the type of bottom the bait is going over. You are totally prepared for the time when a fish takes your jig.

Teaching Yourself to "Visualize" a Jig

We have a saying around our office, that it's alright for the employees and myself to get excited about a new segment for the TV show, or a new product, or any new project, but that the time comes when you have to "stop jumping around" and actually do something about it. It's like that with jig fishing. I can sit here all day and tell you about the "syrupy" feeling you might encounter when a fish softly mouths your jig, but until you get out there and settle your butt over a rocky point and have it happen to you, you won't have learned about it.

But still, there's a lot we *can* talk about. And, of course, in most cases it's impossible for you to bring an experienced jig fisherman out with you as your personal teacher. That would be great, but I realize that the world doesn't always work the way we want it to.

So, the next time you go out to fish, take some time to begin teaching yourself. It's a good idea to go up into shallower, fairly clear water, and cast a jig up along a jagged rocky area, or some boulders, or some weeds. Watch how the jig reacts when you give it a good, healthy sweep of the rod. How high does it come off bottom? How fast does it fall back to the bottom? Try different weight jigs, to see and feel the differences. See how well certain jig styles work their way through weeds, and along sand. Learn what various bottoms feel like, by watching your jig as you drag it along them. Shut your eyes and feel it, and then open them again and watch some more. Teach yourself. Coach yourself. That's how you develop a winning sense of feel with jigs. That's how many of the world's best jig fishermen did it.

Oh boy, can I remember the early days of my jig fishing. My dad taught me how to fish walleyes in the early 1960s, with a Little Joe jig called the Bluetail Canadian Jig Fly (which is still available and popular in some areas, by the way). We would drift the deepest holes of the lake with the Jig Fly and a sucker minnow. Most of the fish we caught back then really slammed our jigs, and so that was how I thought fish hit jigs.

Those hard strikes weren't the only ones we were getting, of course. As I know now, for every hard strike, I probably had ten or more "mouthers" that I couldn't feel. I didn't know what to feel for. There wasn't anybody around to teach you in those days.

Eventually, I started going into the shallow water and casting the weed edges and rocky points with a jig and minnow. I can remember long days, and even years, of trial and error, of not knowing what my jig was bumping into. I was desperately trying to detect the difference between a weed and a rock and a fish, etc.

I used to go through a mental exercise, asking myself, "was that a fish picking it up? Is he coming toward me? Is he going sideways? Did I drop into a weed? Have I bounced over a rock?

Certainly, I have learned to distinguish many of these differences by feel. But today's fishermen have a huge advantage over what we had back then: good equipment. I can't tell you what a difference a good-quality, graphite or boron rod makes in the amount of subtle feelings you can pick up. We couldn't have the sensitivity back in those days, with our relatively clumsy fiberglass rods. Thank goodness the fish bit a little harder and there was a few more of them around!

Sure, you might be fairly new to this jig fishing game, but you have better tools to work with. Lately, I have been fishing with Shimano's equipment, and it is beautiful. Their rods are fast-action, which means they have a lot of backbone in the meat of the rod, but the tips are light and ultra-sensitive. For jigging, I have never found a better piece of equipment than their XL Fightin' Rods. Or, I should say, I *had* never found a better piece of equipment until just recently when they introduced their new Speedmaster Fightin' Rods.

They have taken a rod that was already the finest of its type, and advanced it one step further—a step I couldn't believe they could take. The new rods feel like magic wands in your hands! You have got to handle one; you owe it to yourself to pick one up and feel what today's finest fishing rod feels like. I'll talk about the details of what sort of rod-and-reel combination to use for specific jig fishing situations in the jigging methods chapter.

Today, you can detect things that we couldn't have dreamed of back then. But fishing is like every other sport in that it takes practice and practice and practice and practice. A wrestling coach shows a wrestler a hold once, but he tells him to practice it a thousand times until it is fluid. Why should it be any different with fishing? Can you see why a fisherman who fishes every day for a month, or every weekend all summer, will probably have a better sense of feel for light strikes than the guy who fishes three times a year?

Please, for your own development as a fisherman, read over this section again. Go over it every once in a while as a refresher, a sort of pep talk. It's very tough to find a private jig fishing coach, so this might be the best kind of help you ever find. From here on, it's all in your hands. Start thinking of yourself as a fisherman, and go out fishing with a purpose, to better develop your skills and to start catching a few more fish. Now, take your new attitude out on the water and have some fun finding the master jig fisherman inside of you.

Oh, and when you start getting better at catching all those light biters, please think about the future and release some of them!

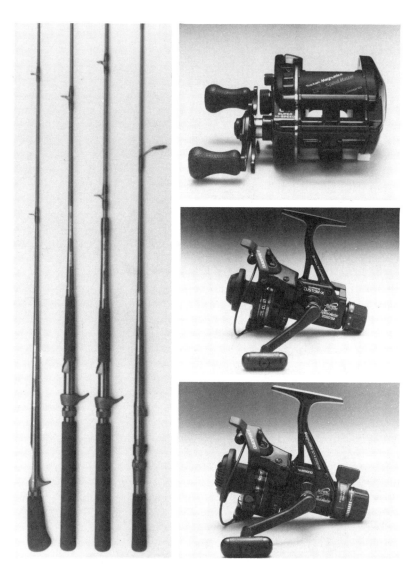

Today's jig fishermen have a tremendous equipment advantage over yesterday's. Modern graphite and boron rods, smooth reels and premium monofilament lines all contribute to a superior sense of feel and control.

There is a growing legion of anglers that pinches off the barb on their jig hooks with a pliers, giving them a barbless hook. That makes it a ton easier to release fish without even having to bring them into the boat. All you have to do is reach over and twist the jig out of a fish's mouth at boatside. It works great and it's a great idea, for when you get to that point that release becomes a bigger and bigger part of your fishing.

Setting the Hook
With a Jig

Setting the hook with a jig can be a tricky proposition. In many cases, you want to set as lightning quick as possible, because fish often mouth a jig, spit it out, mouth it, spit it out, etc., eventually leaving you with a chewed-up bait and "nothing but the memories," unless you can catch the fish with its mouth around your jig and drive the hook home before it can spit the jig.

Other times, you may need to play with the fish, either giving it time to get the hook positioned in its mouth or actually teasing or coaxing it to take the jig deeper into its mouth, giving you a chance to get a good hook-set.

The mechanics of setting the hook, at least with fish that have tough mouths, are built on a quick snap of the wrists. (With some species like crappies, though, you *don't* want to set the hook hard, or you are likely to tear the jig right through the fish's mouth.)

Basically, what I do is set the hook with a snap of the wrists. In most cases, I try to fish a jig with my rod sitting at somewhere between the 8 to 11 o'clock position. When I feel a strike, I instinctively snap my wrists while at the same time driving the rod butt down. That drives the rod tip straight up in the air behind your head and loads the rod up (hopefully) with a fighting fish. It's a quick snap of the wrists, and a very hard one.

This differs quite a bit from the type of hook-set you normally use when live bait rigging in deep water, for example. There, you would want a little longer rod that you could use to sweep-set the hook after you have fed the fish some line.

When do You Set the hook?

Knowing when to set the hook when fishing a jig can make all the difference between catching and missing fish that strike. I will go over some specific situations where you should set the hook right away or hold off, but for now let me give you a good general rule to follow:

"The more aggressive the fish are striking your jig, the more reason you have to set the hook right away. The less aggressive the fish are, the more you should hold off."

One general rule to *always* follow is this: use common sense in determining when to set the hook with a jig. If you are particularly sharp one day and are setting the instant you detect a strike but still not hooking any fish, try giving them more time. If you are giving them some time and missing fish, try setting right away, and so forth.

It is so tough to generalize about all the different species of fish, and that's one of the things that makes writing a book of this nature so difficult. But another *general* rule that we can talk about is that fish you catch in weeds tend to be aggressive and feeding fish. In many cases, strikes from "weed fish" will be hard, and you can pretty much set the hook right away on them. (Watch out for the exceptions to this, though. If you are missing fish, try giving them more time.)

Another "semi hard-and-fast" rule is that fish like northern pike, muskies, and largemouth bass tend to really take a jig in good on the first strike. Largemouth bass, especially, have such a massive mouth, and tremendous capacity for sucking in a bait by wooshing water through their gills, that a jig disappears well into their mouth much faster than you can follow it with your eye. There are times you should pause before setting a largemouth, such as when you are using a plastic worm, or some of the weedless baits like plastic frogs or Johnson Silver

I try to fish with my rod between the 8 to 11 o'clock position (1), when I feel a strike (2), I instinctively snap my wrists (3), while driving the rod butt down (4).

Minnows, but in general, I set the hook right away if I'm pretty sure it's a largemouth at the other end.

I want to also point out that an awful lot of fishermen make a disasterous mistake when a fish comes up and hits their jig and then immediately drops it. They try to set the hook, but almost fall out the other side of the boat, because the fish isn't on anymore. Dejected, they reel in, having long stopped working their jig, to see if there are any teeth marks in the bait.

"Sure enough, dang it," they say, "there was one there all right." It's probably still down there, wondering how the hell a leech swam straight up out of the water after being hit so hard. When that happens to you, don't stop working the jig, and for crying out loud, don't reel up and check your bait right away. Keep working the jig; twitch it, jiggle it, whatever. Many times, the fish has just backed up a few inches after the initial strike, and is about to come back and really grab on for good. Let the fish do its thing, and then set the hook.

Then, you will have a *real* reason to reel up.

Fish, unfortunately, don't always take a jig deep enough to allow you to set right away. In the early season, when the water is cold and the fish are just not as aggressive as they will be later, I often let the fish have the jig for a count of 2 or 3 or 4, so they can mouth the jig and get it into their mouths. This can make a big difference in how well you are able to "seat" the hook when you go to set it.

You'll often feel a little bump on your jig, and a little bit of movement. If you set the hook right away under those conditions, you'll often pull the bait away from the fish before it has it. (This is a condition, by the way, where the Lindy Fuzz-E-Grub really shines. The maribou tail gives a much more lifelike swimming action than other tails in the cold water, and fish have a tendency to hang onto that soft plastic body longer than they will a bare jighead or even a bucktail jig.) In this situation, it often works great to sort of "hold" the jig with a slight bit of resistance. This can cause the fish to clamp down harder on the bait, thinking it is trying to get away. Then, set the hook.

There are other situations where you don't want to set the hook immediately with a jig. One is when you're using a bigger-than-normal live bait such as a big minnow. I often use 5- to 8-inch minnows like suckers or redtail chubs on the back of a Fuzz-E-Grub for big walleyes in the fall. Sometimes, if the minnow is big and the fish aren't really hitting hard, I'll actually let the fish run with the bait like I would with a Lindy Rig. (You might wonder why I don't just use a Lindy Rig in these situations. Actually, with the Fuzz-E-Grub, I can impart a totally different action on the minnow, jumping and dancing and bouncing it around rocks, giving the minnow an appearance it just doesn't have when it is swimming around by itself hooked to a Lindy Rig. Sometimes, I can draw more strikes that way.)

Spence Petros, managing editor of Fishing Facts magazine, is one of the best fishermen I know. "Spencer" as I call him, is a good friend. I'm sure you've seen me fishing with him on television. He and I think a lot alike, and we're both hardcore fishermen. When we get in the boat together to do a show, in fact, we completely forget the camera is rolling.

We've had to "beep" out little phrases that sneak out when one of us has a big fish on, and Larry Sletten, my cameraman and producer, constantly has to stop us and have us start over again because we forget what we were supposed to do.

Spence has a little tip on how and when he sets the hook with a jig.

Spence Petros:

"When I feel that 'tap', or 'tap-tap' on my jig, I don't set the hook right away. I drop my rod back and point it at the jig. Then, I reel up the slack and set the hook. I'd say it takes about two or three seconds, but it gives me a high percentage of fish, so I use it. It's different when I'm using a jig without any live bait; then, I set the hook right away when I sense anything different. But when I fish with a jig and bait, that's what I do."

But many times, walleyes and most other fish will take the entire jig, or at least enough of it to get hooked, on the first bite. Even when the hit is light, as many of your strikes are, the fish *has* the jig deep enough for you to set the hook right away and get him! Many times, in fact, fish come from behind a jig, inhale it and swim toward you. All you will feel is slack line. Believe me, that fish has your bait halfway down to its stomach, and it's time to do something about it. In a whisper, the fish can expel your jig and you will have caught nothing.

The key to getting a good quick hook-set is to put a slight bit of pressure on the fish (or at least tighten the line) by quickly reeling in any slack and raising your rod tip slightly and then...bam!...set the hook with a quick, firm snap of the wrists as I described.

Spence Petros has had good success with this method of setting the hook with a jig. When you feel a distinct 'tap' (1) Drop your rod back and point it at the jig. (2) Then, quickly reel up the slack line created (3) And set the hook firmly. (4) It should take just a few seconds for the entire process. Experiment with how long to wait before setting, if you are missing fish.

It takes years, or at least it took me years, of trial-and-error to learn a lot of the clues that tell you how the fish has taken your jig and whether you should set the hook right away or not, and how you should set it when you do. Sometimes, it's just gut feelings that guide you. Listen to them; many times they are right on the money.

I don't want this discussion to be misleading. I still miss a lot of strikes when I'm jig fishing, and I'm sure I get a lot of bites I don't feel. That's just fishing, and that's how complex jig fishing is. You can't learn it overnight, and you can't learn it by reading about it. You need to get out there and apply these rules on the water.

There are differences, too, in the gusto with which fish take different live baits. Although I hate to make rules, in general fish just plain inhale a leech better than they do a minnow or nightcrawler. So, in general, I set the hook more quickly when I'm using a leech on the back of my jig than I do with almost any other live bait. Again, you will have to do some experimenting each day to know whether this is holding true or not. It's just a place to start.

And finally, I can say with certainty that the time to set the hook when you are using an untipped jig, such as a plain Fuzz-E-Grub, or a jig head with a swirl tail on it, or a plain Quiver Jig for crappies or smallmouth, is right now! Fish can only be fooled for so long *after* they take a purely artificial bait into their mouths, and they will quickly spit an untipped jig most of the time.

Adding a good scent product, such as Chummin' Rub, to a jig can help for maybe another split second, but that's about it. You need to react and set the hook immediately in most cases.

The Bite of a Jig Hook: It Can be Important

One of the most overlooked aspects of a jig's makeup is the bite, or clearance from the body, of a jig hook. Next time you're in a sporting goods store, take a good look at the various kinds of jigs. Some of the hooks offer plenty of clearance between the hook point and the body, and some not nearly as much.

How well the point of the hook aligns with the fish's mouth when the fish grabs it and you go to set the hook is everything. There are a lot of opportunities, unfortunately, for things to get screwed up in this department.

In some cases, the jig you buy doesn't have a generous enough hook bite. Most of the time, though, the clearance gets reduced by something happening to the jig, such as when you unhook a fish you've caught, and the hook gets bent partway shut, or too far open. With any of these situations going against you, there can be many missed opportunities before you take a close enough look at the jig to figure out what is going wrong.

Gary Roach, who is practically my neighbor, is a Merrifield, Minnesota fisherman known throughout the land as one of the best fishermen around. He told me that he has been watching this carefully for years.

"I always check that," Gary said. "I always make sure that a jig hook is opened enough so that when you lay the jig sideways in the open palm of your hand and pull it across your palm, it just barely starts digging into your hand. About the only time I don't open them a little bit is when I'm fishing Dingo Jigs in the heavy weeds for bass.

"But you want to be careful about opening it too much. If it's too wide open, the hook will just scratch a fish's mouth when you try to set him, and won't dig in enough. You'll miss fish that way, too."

So, be careful of this aspect. Examine the hook on your jig after it has gotten caught in the boat carpeting and you've ripped it free, after you unhook a fish, and yes, even when you go to use a new jig for the first time. If the clearance isn't what it should be, bend it out a bit with a pliers or your hand. It'll be a few seconds well invested.

Sometimes, opening the 'bite' of a jig hook slightly can help you get the hook set into a fish's mouth. Check the hook bite from time to time when you are fishing, as it can get closed or opened too far in a number of ways.

Another Key: Sharp Hooks

Now that you have a better understanding of how fish will mouth, touch, and grab jigs in various positions, you can easily understand the importance of having sharp hooks on your jig. When you get a split-second to sink the hook home, there better be an edge there to do it with.

Sharpen all your jigs, even the little 1/8 ouncers! Take a fine metal file, like the one sold by Luhr Jensen, and first sharpen both sides of the outer surface of the hook point. (Hint: if you've tried sharpening hooks before, using a stone, and had little success, don't worry. These little files really work.) Always stroke *toward* the point. That way, you don't get burrs off the very tip, which can nullify your sharpening efforts.

Actually take a bit of metal off both sides of the hook point, and then make a few strokes along the inside of the hook point, too, giving you a roughly triangular-shaped hook (see illustration).

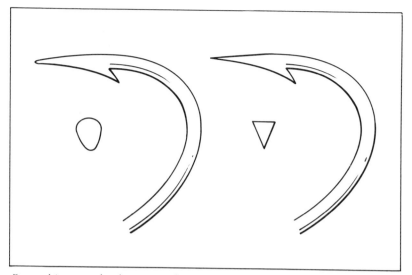

By working your hooks over with a good quality file, you will greatly increase your chances of hooking fish. By sharpening the hook on three sides, you give it extra cutting edges.

If you do nothing but stroke a few times along the outer edges, you've already increased your chances of getting a good hook-set. Believe me, it's worth the time it takes.

Rods and Reels and Lines For Jigging

Is there an all-around outfit for the jig fisherman? What if I want to fish lighter jigs, say 1/8 or 1/16 ounce? Can I use the same rod for that that I do for jigging deep water with 1/4- or 3/8-ounce jigs?

I get questions like that by the pile at seminars all the time.

I used to try to find one certain type of rod and reel that would handle most people's jig fishing situations most of the time. I guess I sort of gave up on that idea.

There are a few things I will say, however.

•The best *type* of rod and reel for jigging is open-faced spinning equipment. The way the line comes off the spool, you can comfortably lay the line right on your finger while fishing, to help you feel strikes. Also, with the line coming out of the guides underneath the rod, it seems easier for me to see my line twitch, and to detect light strikes, as compared to having the line come off the top of the rod.

I'm not saying that you *can't* jig with other kinds of equipment. For some heavy jigging, baitcasting rods can be nice, especially a good-quality, sensitive graphite rod.

•The ideal length for a jigging rod, for most situations, is 5 feet, 6 inches. A few inches either way doesn't matter much, and there are situations where a little longer rod is nice, but that is what I consider the overall best.

Because there are so many different kinds of jigging, you almost need to get at least three good outfits: an ultra light for fishing tiny (1/32- 1/16- and 1/8-ounce) jigs; a light weight outfit for fishing 1/16- 1/8- and even 1/4-ounce jigs with light lines; and a medium-weight outfit for fishing 1/8- 1/4- 3/8- 1/2-ounce, and sometimes even slightly heavier jigs, especially in deeper water and around cover such as heavy weeds and brush.

I can't stress strongly enough the importance of *balancing* your tackle to the fishing it will be used for. Don't put a 3/8-ounce jig on an ultra light rod and 4-pound line and expect it to be a good match. Za Za Gabor has had more perfect marriages than that.

A common mistake made by beginning jig fishermen is using too heavy a line for the jig they're using. If your line is too heavy, such as trying to use a 1/16- or 1/8-ounce jig with 10- or 12-pound line, you will have a hard time fishing even moderately deep. Your line will get a built-in bow in it, because the light jig just can't pull it down very well.

How about the action of the rod? Does that make any difference in successful jigging? You bet it does.

The *action* of a rod refers to the way in which the rod bends when you put a load on it. A *fast*-action rod has a lot of backbone over most of its length, and bends primarily at the tip. This, without a doubt, is the most desireable action in a jigging rod. The strong guts in the meat of the rod help you set the hook well and fight fish, and actually contribute to the sensitivity of the entire rod, by not giving you that "mushy" overall feeling of a *slow*- or even *medium*-action rod. The strong main section of the rod also helps you maintain good contact with your jig in deeper water and on days when waves tend to toss you up and down.

The tip section of a fast-action rod is the section that bends when you "load it up." The tip is lively and sensitive, especially on better graphite and boron rods, and really transmits those little vibrations and differences that you need to feel in order to catch fish.

Of all the rods on the market today, none are better than the Shimano Fightin' Rods. I have been using them for some time now, and have never seen a better jigging rod.

After using their XL series Fightin' Rods, I couldn't see how they could make a much better rod. But they did it! They took it one step further when they came up with the Speedmaster Fightin' Rods, which I mentioned briefly earlier.

They make two 5 1/2-footers, the SM 2551 and the SM 2552. Both are one-piece rods, and they just plain feel like a magic wand in your hands! If you can't feel bites with these rods, you need an operation.

If you can only afford one rod, pick one of these two.

They also have a beautiful little ultra light in the XL line, the XL 2501, that I find myself fishing with constantly. It's got the guts to fight fish, and the lightness to fish the tiniest jigs. It's a wonderful tool for catching everything from perch to sunfish to catfish. For a light weight spinning rod, I like the XL 2551, a 5'6" beauty for working shallow water, or lighter jigs in deeper water. The XL 2532, a one-piece, 5'3" rod, and the XL 2602, a 6' two-piece, are both excellent medium-weight rods.

For heavier jigging, such as using heavy jigs in very deep water for walleyes or a jig-and-worm around heavy cover for bass, it's hard to beat Shimano's XL 2593, a special 5'9" medium-heavy weight rod designed for bigger fish and tough situations, or the XL 2532, a 5'3" rod.

I have gone more and more in recent years to lighter rods and reels and line. It's just plain more fun. I'm not claiming that I can feel everything with a lighter rod that I could with a little heavier one, but you can sure do more things with lighter baits and lighter lines.

I'm convinced that with lighter lines and lighter jigs, you get a bait with a more natural presentation, a more enticing action, that draws more strikes from more fish. One guy that I know agrees with me on this is Gary Roach. Here are his feelings on the subject:

Gary Roach:

"Fishing line magnifies underwater. We don't know exactly if the fish see the same way we do, but I know that 8-pound line underwater looks bigger than it does out of the water, especially in clear water and when you are fishing slow. You should try to use the thinnest, lightest line you can get by with. Everything works better on lighter line; your jigs fall better and work better, they just look better to the fish.

"For the average guy, 6-pound test line is the best all-around line. And today's rods are getting lighter and better all the time, and hooks are getting better and sharper, so you can go to a lighter line and lighter rod and get an outfit that really works. Even on line as light as 4-pound test, you can set the hook as hard as you want in most cases without breaking the line, because the lighter rods have some give in them, while still having the backbone to fight fish.

"The one thing you have to remember to do, though, is check your line and re-tie those first few feet a lot more often than you do with heavier line. The lake bottom, and the fish's mouths, will chew up that little line really easy. Even with fish like crappies, their mouths will dig into the line and maybe cause it to break."

Before we go any further into the subject of lines for jigging, let me make a point that might be obvious to many fishermen, but is worth making.

The only connection you should make from your line to a jig is a knot. No snaps, no snap swivels, or anything of the sort. I prefer the Improved Clinch knot, although knots such as the Palomar and some other good fishing knots will do just fine. It might seem like a small point, but I just wanted to make sure we mentioned it.

Since fish started falling for jigs, it seems, the accepted line, the only line anybody who was serious about it used, was a premium monofilament such as Stren. It was, is, and probably always will be the choice for most people.

But there is a new choice that I think more folks should take a serious look at: a cofilament line made by Du Pont called Prime line. Prime is a fine product for the right purpose, and for sensitive work like jig fishing, I've use it a lot and will continue to use it a lot. Most people, I don't think, realize how much stretch is in regular monofilament, and how much all of that stretch saps their feel for light strikes, and robs much of their hook-setting ability. Prime is by far the best line available for minimizing those two problems.

This summer, I was fishing walleyes on Lake of the Prairies in Manitoba with Hart Chesik, a member of the Lindy-Little Joe Fishing Team, and Mark Strand, a member of my staff. It was anything but ideal conditions: rainy, very windy and cold.

Still, we were able to get over some nice points that were holding fish. It was very difficult to control the boat and watch the depth finder and still try to fish, but I was doing all three out of the bow of the boat.

The line I was using was Prime, and it very definitely contributed to the crisp sense of contact I had with my bait. Even though I was constantly bouncing over waves and trying to keep the boat positioned, I could feel the bottom and feel fish hitting.

In about three hours, we caught over 100 walleyes in those conditions! That says a lot about the fish population on that lake, but it also says a lot about a line like Prime for tough jigging situations.

Prime is a plus anytime you are jigging in deep water, or using lighter rods or longer rods. It very definitely helps you set the hook better, and gives you better sensitivity, better feel "at the bait." Sure, it can get kinky in cold weather, and it's got more spool memory than monofilament, but those are minor tradeoffs for the distinct advantages it gives you.

If you just can't get used to it, a premium monofilament like regular Stren will always perform well, but just realize you are giving up something, in the form of more stretch, when you gain the extra limpness.

You don't want to skimp when it comes to buying line. Buy a good premium line and change it often. Match your line choice to the conditions you face.

In many cases, a fluorescent line is superior to clear line for jigging. It's easier to see, so you can detect slight line twitches, etc. much easier.

I love the color of Prime, but maybe my favorite color fluorescent line is Stren Class line. It is a blue color that blends in with the color of water very well, helping make it less visible to the fish, while still giving you fluorescence.

I do use clear monofilament quite a bit, especially in very, very clear water. In ultra clear water, you can bet the farm that fish can see fluorescent line easily, and in these kinds of waters fish tend to shy away from anything that doesn't look natural to them. Fish in clear water are probably just more used to eyeing things up before striking them. This is especially true in many situations that call for light line and a delicate presentation of a smaller jig.

All About Jigs

What About Jig Styles and Types: How Many do You Need?

There is hardly an industry as full of inventors as the fishing industry. I don't know if it's because fishermen spend so much time out in the boat waiting for fish to bite, that they have hours to design a better lure in their minds or what, but there is a constant flow of new-fangled inventions being "offered" to the fisherman.

The major head styles and types of jigs. Clockwise, from top, are the mushroom jig head, round (ball) head, stand-up head, banana head, slider head, stand-up with custom steel leader and reaper tail, round head with plastic swirl tail, and bullet head.

That is certainly true when it comes to jigs. There are many head styles, body types, sizes, colors and textures to choose from. It gets mind boggling, to sort through it all at the tackle racks.

There are even regional tendencies, favorites that are popular in different locales. That is expected, I guess; something gets hot and everybody has to have some. Pretty soon, a certain colored jig of some type is a standard at a certain lake or area.

The photo shows you the major head styles, and some of the most popular jig types. It gives you a close look at the most important ones.

As you might expect, I have been through the tackle racks a time or two. I have fished with just about every jig, in just about every size and color, that man has come up with. Through it all, I have come to some very definite decisions on which are the most deadly, and on which ones you need and don't need.

One of the most important conclusions I've ever come to was that a *round*, or *ball*, head is the most versatile head style available. If the ball head has a specialty, it's bouncing along the bottom while being back-trolled or drifted along. But it does so many things well. It has been proven the fastest sinking head style, and it does almost anything as well as some of the specialty heads do what they were designed for. Every jig fisherman's arsenal should include many round heads.

Because the round head is so versatile, there are many jigs available in that style. But, as I have for the past 10 years or so, let me tell you about the one that I feel is, without a doubt, the finest all-around jig you can get your hands on.

Lindy-Little Joe makes a jig called the Fuzz-E-Grub that is now a legend in jig fishing circles. It has a round head, a soft plastic body and a maribou tail. The head design speaks for itself. The soft body encourages fish to hang onto it longer than they would, say, a bucktail or plain jig, because it feels natural to them. And the maribou tail swims and pulsates in back of the whole package, to present the fishiest-looking combination I have ever used. I have said that many times in the past, I know, but I say it again with good reason: I truly believe it can't be beaten, day in and day out, for catching anything that swims.

Another important head style is the *stand-up* head. It is designed to keep the hook, jig dressing (if any) and live bait up, as the jig is worked over a variety of lake bottoms. It helps keep snagging to a minimum. Also, in most cases, stand-up heads are perfect river fishing jigs. Current will catch on the head and actually force the jig downward, allowing you to fish a lighter jig than you normally would have to, to stay down in the current. An attractive feature of stand-up heads, especially those with a narrow front nose that tapers back to the flange, is that they usually cut through weeds better than ball heads.

Of all the stand-up head jigs I've fished, none compares to the Flat Foot jig by Lindy. It is, you guessed it, a Fuzz-E-Grub with a stand-up head. It has the same soft plastic body and maribou tail, and it catches fish just like the "Fuzzy" does. These jigs also work well as swimming jigs, when you want a jig head that keeps your bait up as it goes over the bottom.

The Lindy Fuzz-E-Grub and Flat Foot jigs have become legends in fishing circles for a very good reason: they are unequalled as fish getters.

Banana heads are popular in some areas, especially around the rocky lakes of the Canadian Shield. The theory behind their effectiveness is that they slide across the snag-infested rocks better than other head styles, although I don't feel they actually work any better for this than a round head does.

The problem with banana heads is that the lead head is elongated, taking up so much of the hook that not much of the shank is exposed. The result is that you have less hook-setting ability with these heads, and you also have a very hard time adding any dressing such as plastic or hair bodies. I guess I just can't see a drastic need for this type of head.

If you're looking for a really slow-sinking jig, you might want to try a *slider* head, also known as the *swimming* head. There are certain times when fish really go for a jig that just barely settles toward the bottom (although a heavily-dressed jig will do much the same thing, as will a lighter head weight). These heads do have a fish-tempting action, though, and should be considered. They are good for swimming along in mid-water for suspended fish, and for fishing over the tops of weeds.

Jigs with a *bullet*-shaped head, such as Lindy's Quiver Jig, are excellent swimming heads. The Quiver Jig, with its floss body, is the ideal light-line jig for species like crappies, sunfish and smallmouth bass. The light line really brings out the pulsating qualities in the floss.

Mushroom-style jig heads, such as the one pictured made by Gopher Tackle Company of Aitkin, Minnesota, are specialty heads designed to hold plastic worms and swimming tails better than other heads. They do a good job of what they are meant for, and many serious tournament bass fishermen use them.

One great application for these heads is taking a light one, say 1/8 ounce, and putting a plastic worm on it. The worm will stay tight to the head even when you cast it hard, so it works well for skipping worms up under boat docks for bass. Just make a cast at an angle that will cause the worm to skip deep under the dock, and then let it flutter to the bottom, keeping your line tight and feeling for strikes. Then, work the worm out from under the dock.

Mushroom-style jig heads really hold plastic baits well. One great way to use them; rig up with a plastic worm, and skip it up under a dock. The worm will stay tight to the head, and there just might be a waiting largemouth bass under there.

"Jig-and-pig" jigs such as the Lindy Legs are used primarily for bass fishing, along weedlines, in heavy cover, etc. They are often used with heavy flippin' sticks on baitcasting gear, but are also used on medium to heavy action spinning equipment. They are normally tipped with some type of pork or plastic trailer.

One of the best ways to use them is to cast near the outside edge of a weed bed, but still up in the weeds a few feet. Gently pull the jig off the weeds until it falls down to the base, then slowly *crawl* it along to deeper water. Fish it very slowly. These jigs are not really meant for swimming in mid-water; other baits do a better job of that. Strikes are usually pretty definite "thunks" and fish tend to hold onto these jigs almost as if they were live bait. These are very much a big fish bait, for bass and northerns, and occasionally muskies.

Plastic "twister" and "reaper" type tails are intended mainly for fishing without any live bait. They have an action of their own, which a minnow, leech or whatever just nullifies.

They certainly have their place, which is mainly for "un-finicky" species like bass, northerns and panfish. Muskies are also suckers for a big plastic tail fished on a big stand-up head along deep weedlines.

Plain or Dressed: Which is Best?

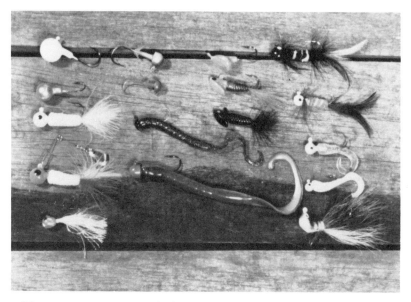

There are times, particularly in post-spawn periods, and sometimes in clear water situations, when I will favor plain jig heads. They can actually be effective over a jig with a lot of body dressing anytime you think the fish are acting a little more spooky than they normally do. I know that a "sparser" fly, for example, will often catch more stream trout in heavily-fished populations on the more popular trout streams in the East, and I think maybe some of the same reasoning applies here. When fish are jumpy, such as when I'm trying my best to scrounge up a few straggler male walleyes along a spawning bed, it sometimes pays to go to a plain jig head.

Gary Roach's rule for this is that when he is fishing in clear water and tipping the jig with "enough bait to fill the hook" he goes with a plain jig head, "just enough color and size to act as an attractor." In dirtier water, he goes more to the fullness of a jig with some sort of body. Again, he doesn't stick to rules all the time any more than I do: he just offers that as food for thought.

For most of the season, especially for walleyes, I fish an awful lot with Lindy's Fuzz-E-Grub and Flat Foot jigs. There is absolutely no doubt in my mind that these jigs, with their soft plastic bodies that fish hold onto longer than other types, will take fish when they are "off the feed," as well as when they are biting good.

Spence Petros likes to use a plain jig head when he is fishing fairly deep water and having some trouble getting down easily, such as when he wants to use a light jig weight but wants it to sink as fast as possible.

"But I don't do that unless it's a pretty extreme case," Spence said. "Most of the time, I think dressings give you a good color contrast. But another thing I'll do when I'm using a big live bait, like a big minnow, is cut the body dressing in half and then put it back on. I think I can get a better, a deeper, hook-set that way. Most of the time, the color that the body dressing gives you is worth any trouble you might have getting the jig to sink. In some cases, in fact, it's nice if it sinks slow."

One addition to a jig that we haven't yet discussed is a safety-pin type spinner, such as what you find on a Beetle-spin.

These spinners are fairly inexpensive, and normally considered an add-on accessory. Some jigs, including the Fuzz-E-Grub, are available with them attached. Fishing wizard Bill Binkelman has been using them more and more in recent years, and is more than a little fired up about the results they give him.

He begins his jig fishing with a jig-and-spinner combination, in fact, up to *80* percent of the time, he says, and if he had to guess he figures he uses them overall about half the time!

Bill Binkelman:

"These spinners create positive vibrations in the water that alert fish to the presence of your bait. They act as a flashy attractant, and go through the weeds nicely. They are extremely effective for all species of fish; these things will catch anything!

"About the only time I don't use them is when fish are striking short and it seems hard to get the (hook) set, or when I am using heavy jigs."

Although Bill is known widely as the man who popularized the use of fluorescent jigs, he doesn't necessarily favor fluorescent spinner blades. His favorite, in fact, is a hammered nickel, #2 Colorado blade.

Ever-thorough, he goes to the trouble of modifying the spinners, taking them apart and replacing the swivel they come with, with a ball-bearing swivel. This, he said, helps the blade work more freely on both the rise and fall. You don't necessarily have to do this, but it might be worth your time to experiment some with something he believes so deeply in!

Another excellent use of safety-pin spinners as an add-on to jigs is in early, cold-water fishing. When pre-spawn, springtime fish are first coming into shallower, warmer water to feed, they are still very sluggish. They can't chase fast for a bait, and they don't seem interested in hitting anything very big.

This is when a smaller spinner, fished slowly in a straight retrieve can take a lot of fish. Try a 1/8 or maybe 1/4 ouncer for bigger fish like northerns, and 1/16 ouncers for fish like crappies. The offering sends out vibration and flash, making it attractive to the fish, but it is fished slowly enough that they can catch and hit it. This combination will work sometimes when nothing else will.

How Heavy a Jig Should You Use?

There is no answer to this question. It all depends on the situation you are fishing in, what species you are after, how badly you want the jig to stay vertical, what type of action you want the jig to have, etc.

The variables go on and on.

It really blows me away, in fact, when I see tidy little charts in magazines and books, telling me how heavy a jig to use, based on how deep the water is, how heavy the current is, and the like. I flip past those things faster than I set the hook on a good strike.

The only rule-maker in this department is resting on your neck, right under your fishing cap: your brain. I do have some ideas and suggestions to get you started, though.

Bill Binkelman says that fish see size, not weight, and he is absolutely right. He contends that even a 1 1/2-ounce jig is still smaller than the average crankbait, and he's right again. He is a nut about fishing vertically most of the time, and tends to use jigs as heavy as 3/4 ounce for fishing in the 15-25 foot depth range.

Remember, this, though. Even though fish don't see weight per se, they can certainly see that a jig falls past them in one millisecond, or just barely glides past them like a ballerina in mid-air. Fish can certainly see the way jigs *behave* in the water, so if you are trying to impart a slow, tantalizing action on your jig, even in deep water don't use any heavier a jig than you need to get down.

For years, Gary Roach has used a neat little trick when he wanted to slow down how fast his jig was falling through the water. He simply uses too big a body for the jig head size. For example, he takes the body off a 1/4-ounce Fuzz-E-Grub and puts it on a 1/8-ounce jig head.

That's using *his* head, and it's all part of the common sense approach he has to fishing, and why he catches so many fish.

Deliberately putting the "wrong" size body on a jig head can help you control the way the jig behaves in the water. Putting on a body that is too big for the head will make the jig sink slower, and the opposite is true when you put on a body that is too small.

There are other ideas, but I think the point has been made. No matter how deep you are fishing for crappies, for example, you don't want to use a big jig. Anything over 1/8-ounce is starting to get too big to interest most crappies. You will catch more panfish on smaller jigs, no matter how much more patience you need to have in waiting for them to get down into the fish zone.

Here, for what they are worth, are some loose "rules" for selection a jig weight to fit a particular fishing situation:

- Lighter jigs, in general, are better for swimming retrieves than heavier ones are.
- Light jigs fished on light line can be a big positive when you are trying to trigger neutral to negative fish, especially in clear water and after the passage of a cold front.
- If I had to pick one jig size as the overall champ at doing the most things well, it would be the 1/4 ounce. You can cast it in shallow and deep water, troll it, drift it, just about anything, and it seems to be an intermediate size that appeals to almost all fish at one time or another.

What About Stinger Hooks?

Most of the time, I find stinger hooks a chore to use. Because I am working a jig so close to the bottom most of the time, there are already enough obstacles to avoid. By adding another treble hook to the back of my jig, that just becomes another dragnet to gather up algae, weeds, catch on rocks, etc. They can make your offering look unnatural to a fish, and so I avoid them unless I absolutely have to go to them.

About the only time I use them extensively is during the very early pre-spawn, say in river fishing situations in February and March, when the fish are so sluggish that they tend to be just coming up behind and nipping at the tail end of the bait.

There have been numerous times when I have used stingers to catch walleyes and saugers in early river fishing on the Mississippi in southeastern Minnesota. Some days, we might catch 75 walleyes, and all but a few of them would be hooked *only* by the stinger hook, not by the jig hook. When the water is cold like that, fish sometimes just grab at the tail of the minnow as it comes by.

Sometimes, this can be the case in late fall as well. I remember a day in early November when I fished the Mississippi River near Brainerd, Minnesota with Gary Korsgaden. We were casting a jig-and-minnow to a school of walleyes holding along the edge of an eddy. When you got a strike, it would just be a little tick, nothing heavy, and barely noticeable compared to what the river current was doing to your jig.

The fish, again, were just barely nipping the end of the minnow, and most of them got hooked on the stinger. In that case, the stinger hooks saved the day for us; we caught a nice bunch of fish.

Any time, really, regardless of the time of year, when fish are just nipping at your jig, it might be time to try a stinger. Let's say you get a strike and miss the fish, and reel up to check your bait. If you can see teeth marks on the end of your leech, or the skin is peeled back on your minnow, but the fish probably didn't bite deep enough to get to the hook, a stinger might work wonders.

But in almost all situations, you don't need a stinger hook. If you work the jig right once the fish hits it, you can catch them without the stinger.

Color in Jigs: Critically Important

Color in Jigs: Critically Important

Anybody who has fished any amount has come to realize that color can make an awful lot of difference in your success. I think every fisherman has found himself asking, "am I using the right color for this situation?" If the fish are really biting, it can make no difference. But some days, just one color or a few colors will be the ticket.

When I first started fishing walleyes, it was all with the Little Joe Bluetail Canadian Jig Fly. It had a blue-and-white wrapped chenille body, a blue-and-white feather tail, and a white head. That was all I used. But a neighbor of ours on Hay Lake, Orland Juelleum, was using something different.

He was also using a Little Joe jig, but his was the Bumblebee color, a black and yellow. He told me he also used the Bluetail, but he liked the Bumblebee better.

Well, it took me about two seconds to get down to the store and get a few black-and-yellows, and after that I began seeing situations where I could only catch walleyes on the Bumblebee jig. After a while, it became my favorite jig. I saw more situations, in fact, where I could catch fish on the bumblebee than on the blue-and-white, although both were good.

The Bee (left) and Bluetail Canadian Jig Fly, the color variations that started me realizing how important color can be.

My early northern pike fishing also showed me the importance of color. We started out catching fish only on the old red-and-white Daredevils, then on orange-and-white, and black-and-white, and green-and-white. We found that the only times the blacks, and the greens, would work well was during very cloudy days. The shinier colors worked far better on very bright days.

Those were my first big experiences with color, things that proved to me that it can really make a big difference. They were very basic experiences, I know, but I think every fisherman needs to do that.

When you are over a school of fish, you are going to know very quickly if you're doing the right thing. You'll get a response, a bite, from a fish, as a rule, if you're going to. The longer you stay on top of that fish, even if you're sneaking with the electric motor or just drifting over the top, the more aware of your presence it becomes and the more cautious because of it, even if you're over fairly deep water.

The point of this is, that if you don't get a strike within a reasonable amount of time, do something. Switch colors, or retrieves, or even switch from a jig to a live bait rig. Whatever you do, it's time to experiment.

The fish are down there dealing with "exacts," exact color combinations, among other things, that trip their trigger. We, as humans, are up there on the surface, peering down, floundering around trying to figure out their exact rules. We probably will never learn the fish's exact rules, but every time we learn something about color and its affect, we get another piece of that big puzzle put together.

I've seen the information on what colors look like at certain depths in water of different clarities, but all of that information has been gathered through human eyes. We don't understand color as a fish does, and probably never will. I've seen times when slightly different shades of the same color have made all the difference in 55 or 60 feet of water!

I'm not sure why it is, but I know that fish very definitely show color preferences. Maybe the amount of sunlight coming through the water at ever-changing angles causes certain colors to appear a certain way to the fish. Maybe the atmosphere is thicker and thinner on different days, and that causes shades of color to appear certain ways to the fish. I don't know; I don't think we'll ever really know.

Also, for whatever reason, those color preferences change throughout the day. By hitting the right color at the right time, you can catch a bunch more fish than if you are fishing with the "wrong" color. In fact, I am firmly convinced that in many situations you will catch nothing until you find the color the fish want at that particular time.

Even as recently as two years ago, I don't think I would have been as adamant about that point. But I've been doing a lot more work with color lately, and have found too many situations where color is a big influence on a given school of fish. I'll sit and change colors, for example, once I've caught a few walleyes or bass in an area, and see whether I can still catch them, doing the same things I have been doing with the retrieve, on other colors. Sometimes it makes absolutely no difference what color I throw, the fish are determined to commit suicide. But in many, many cases, there are only a few, or even just one, color the fish are willing to bite on.

Another thing that really hammered the importance of color into my head was spending a lot of time on Pipestone Lake in Ontario. It's a very clear oligotrophic lake that has very little prime shallow water feeding area. On the little there is, you can slowly motor with your electric, peer into the water and physically see whole schools of walleyes, up feeding.

In many cases, you can actually back off those fish, cast back into them and catch them. Well, for years I didn't realize that as simple a thing as color would be enough to trigger reluctant fish. I can remember sitting by and watching big walleyes up on those shelfs, obviously up there for only one reason, and not being able to catch them, or being able to catch only a few, on my "favorite" colors. Man, is that frustrating!

Finally, out of sheer frustration, I really *began* to experiment with color. I knew those fish wouldn't be up in clear, shallow water in the middle of the day to get a suntan. They were up there, out of the deep water, to feed. They were doing something that I was missing out on.

I started trying every kind of a bait, in every color combination I could think of, and realized that on certain days, color combinations were critical. Later, I'll give you some of the "rules" I now go by, but don't get stuck on using them, either. Keep experimenting with color on your own, especially if you are reasonably certain you are over fish and can't get them to bite.

The biggest single mistake we make all the time as fishermen is to lock *our* little pea-sized brains into our little tunnel-visioned "rules" on how fish are always going to behave, whether it comes to what color they are going to hit, where they are going to be, or whatever.

One of the most obvious instances I've ever come across happened one early summer day on "Pipe." There were four boats of us, just plain up there to have a good time and catch some fish. On the second morning of the trip, all of us split up and went on a search for walleyes.

My wife, Charlie, and I were in my big Ranger 372 running from spot to spot, checking out everything on the locator and graph, and watching for any sign of life. It took us about two hours, but we finally found a school of nice walleyes working on a shallow flat that dropped off into the deeper water of a bay.

The flat sat in about 8-12 feet. There were maybe a dozen great big boulders on one end of it, then it turned to gravel and finally had a section of grassy bottom. You could actually see the walleyes down there, moving around.

We backed off, and cast in with a fluorescent green Fuzz-E-Grub and a leech. Boom, boom, boom, I smack a bunch of nice walleyes from about 2 to 6 pounds. Needless to say, Charlie and I were a big hit at the shore lunch. We were all to meet at 11:30 a.m., and ours were the only walleyes caught.

After lunch, the two of us laid down for a little nap, and when I woke up, everybody else was gone. I had told them about these fish, so I knew where to go find those little crooks! Sure enough, when I came driving up to the spot, there they sat, casting right on top of *my* fish. But nobody had caught anything yet.

Now, these guys are all good fishermen. So I asked them what they were using. They had tried green, hot yellow, and even white Fuzz-E-Grubs, had tried taking the body off the jigs and everything else they could think of, to no avail. Naturally, I assumed I could still catch them, so I baited up with a green Fuzz-E-Grub and started working them. Nothing.

I decided to try something completely different. I found an old Bill Binkelman jig head in fluorescent orange laying around, and grabbed a root beer body off a 1/8-ounce Fuzz-E-Grub. In my first five casts, I caught three walleyes! They hit it hard, not reluctantly as you might expect from fish that were beginning to get spooky from all the activity around them. In fact, I had two good strikes on the plain jig, after my leech flew off on a long cast.

We tried some other colors, but found nothing else the fish would take. David, who had been casting for over an hour to these fish, started catching them as soon as he talked me out of my only other orange Binkelman head. We couldn't believe how much difference changing color made in that instance.

Spending a lot of time on Pipestone Lake in Ontario, observing schools of shallow-feeding walleyes, taught me a lot about the subtleties of a fish's color preferences.

Color, without a doubt, was the single factor that triggered those fish. The entire time, we were working the jig in exactly the same manner. You would cast it up onto the grassy portion of the flat, and count it down until it reached near the bottom. Then, you would swim the jig along the grass until you reached the rocks. At that point, you bounced the jig up and down, ticking the top of the gravel and boulders hoping to draw a strike. We did the exact same thing every cast, and only when we switched jig colors did we catch any fish.

That's not an isolated case, either. I have seen it so many times, that I have learned to switch colors as I fish, until the fish tell me what they want. It's a good lesson for everybody to learn.

Fluorescence: The Beginning of the Color Revolution

Up until the time Bill Binkelman began heavily using and promoting fluorescent jigs, fishermen used to talk about colors in jig fishing, but never to a great extent. I know it broadened my horizons when it comes to jig colors. I had been following the things Bill was writing, about his early experiments with fluorescent jig heads. He got me so excited about them that I drove over to Milwaukee and bought a bunch of his jig heads in the fluorescent colors and started working with them.

This took my color awareness another big step. I found times when oranges, and reds, and yellows and limes were extremely good.

Fluorescent colors have been demonstrated to hold their true color, even under conditions where there is little light. In fact, they can show their actual color when there is no light of that color underwater!

The result, in plain English, is that a fluorescent jig is normally more visible than a non-fluorescent jig, and will even "shine" its true color when very little other light is present underwater, such as in stained water and during low light conditions.

This is all in human terms, of course, and I want you to realize that we still don't know what color a fish sees, and whether a fish can detect differences in even non-fluorescent jigs down deeper than humans can. For that reason, I don't necessarily view fluorescent jigs as a complete cure-all, or as the only colors you should carry.

But, they sure catch fish! And, as usual, we fishermen owe a debt of gratitude to Bill Binkelman for bringing us the first evidence that this fluorescent thing worked.

Bill Binkelman:

"The idea (for using fluorescent paints) kind of came from our experiments using the glass-bottomed boat and divers. We had a glass-bottomed boat, you know, made of fiberglass. We put a viewer in front of the glass, and he worked with the divers. The viewer could see a lot, and what he saw was a big help, he could probably see down to 20 feet sometimes, depending on how clear the water was.

"Anyways, when we tested jigs painted with regular paints, the divers would come up to the surface and tell me 'what's the use of painting anything except black and grey, because the colors are lost down there anyway?'

"We went to see a local paint supplier about it, and he got us some fluorescent paint to try. This was in 1972. The next time we went fishing, I was fishing with Bob Reimer, and he used the fluorescent jigs and I used regular ones, and son-of-a-gun he outfished me 9 to 1 on my favorite fishing spots. That convinced me.

Here's Bill Binkleman in the early days of his basement jig operation. The things he wrote, and the jigs he produced, have changed fishing forever.

Photo courtesy of Bill Binkelman.

"I spent the next six months just testing various fluorescent paints and colors, and my catches really went up. We also studied, actually watched, fish taking jigs. We saw how, with regular colors fish would come up from behind to take it. We'd watch fish come up behind the jig and climb up the crawler, literally swallowing it from behind.

"As a rule, when we were using fluorescent ones, they would attack the head instead of the worm. The same thing applies to minnows. We had one place where we could watch them, and there was a school of minnows down there, and when we would drop a minnow down there with a fluorescent jig hooked into him, the other minnows would try to take it away from him."

The rest, as they say, is history. Bill began publishing his findings, first writing about them in his book "Catching Walleyes," and then he began selling fluorescent jig heads. His favorite colors out of those early experiments were chartreuse, fire orange and "real" orange, a lighter orange with little red in it.

These remain good colors today, although we have now begun to take the color concept another step further, into the idea of contrasting colors.

Contrasts: Taking Color a Step Further

As I started to get more into studying the affect of color on fish, and got heavily into bass tournaments, I found, for example, that a blue-and-chartreuse skirt on a spinnerbait was absolutely deadly. Another good combination was lime-and-white.

Prior to that, a charteuse spinnerbait with a hammered copper blade was unquestionably my favorite. But then along came this blue-and-chartreuse. I did a lot of my own testing, and there was without a doubt, times when the blue-and-chartreuse would kick the socks off a straight chartreuse. Both were identical, with hammered copper blades, except for the color of the skirts.

I did some work with plastic worms for bass, too. Back in those days, everybody was really becoming adept with plastic worms, and guys used to say things like "I'll use any color worm as long as it's purple." We were actually thinking, just because we could catch bass most of the time with our favorite colored worms, that color was important with spinnerbaits but not worms! We later learned that there are times when even slight changes of color with plastic worms can be critical, too.

For a few years there, I did most of my work on bass, because I was so wrapped up in the hardcore bass tournament scene. But I was still fishing walleyes some, and in the mid 1970s, when the Fuzz-E-Grubs first came out, they became by far my favorite jig. Because I had come to feel that contrast colors were so important in bass fishing, I started working with them a bit with jigs for walleyes and other fish as well.

I started taking some of Binkelman's jig heads and putting them on Fuzz-E-Grub bodies, because almost all the colors Lindy was making back then were straight colors.

Those contrast color jigs really caught fish! I shouldn't have been surprised, but I felt like I'd really discovered something.

The more you learn, the more you start to realize about the way Nature works. When you look around in Nature, you don't see things that are one color. You see things that are in contrast. If you look at baitfish, you see that they're in contrast; their backs are different colors than their bellies. If you look at any kind of game fish, and most types of forage, they are not just one color. So it just makes sense to me that lures, including jigs, are effective when colored in contrasts of some kind.

Back in those days, in the early and mid 70s, color ranges in lures were just beginning to expand. It used to be pretty simple: a company put out three or four colors and that was it, that was what you needed to catch fish. Both as fishermen and as an industry, we didn't understand color and its complexity as well as we do now.

There are times when you can tease and tempt fish into biting by switching colors. Up until the advent of the Color-C-Lector I didn't really realize how often a guy could be on fish that could be caught if the person was simply using the right color, and other colors would hardly trigger any response from the fish.

Now, I am not saying we have the answers yet, but I have come up with a few understandings that I think are "rules," such as:

- The single most important factor with color is visibility. At the same time you are fishing, can the fish see the color you are using?
- The second most important factor is, without question, contrast. And the fact that you have a bait with contrast, in certain cases, might even be more important than the actual colors making it up.

This whole chain of thought, this whole rambling story, everything we have learned about color and the effectiveness of a contrasting color combination, has led to the development of a new line of jigs. The jigs in this line are, without question, the single best jigs a person can buy to catch walleyes, and a lot of other fish as well.

Lindy-Little Joe is introducing a line called the "Master Series" Fuzz-E-Grubs and Flat Foot jigs. They are all of contrasting color schemes, in proven combinations, and are already winners in my book. I have been using them for about a year now, and they have produced consistently for me.

You know by now how I feel about the Fuzz-E-Grub jig. I am saying this without reservation, because I have felt this way for years about the standard Fuzz-E-Grub. Now, with the addition of the contrast colors, there simply is no other jig that I would stake my chances on, day in and day out.

That's not to say that you won't do better on something else on certain days. I'm just saying that for overall consistency, you won't be able to beat them.

Lindy's Master's Series Fuzz-E-Grub and Flat Foot jigs, in their contrasting color schemes, are the end product of many years of researching fish color preferences.

Spence Petros has run some tests on the little contrast-color Fuzz-E-Grubs on a few panfish lakes outside Chicago. In a couple days, running a tandem rig that had a Master Series Fuzz-E-Grub and one of a number of other jigs side by side, the "contrast Fuzzy" out-produced the other jigs nine to one.

The contrast color concept knows no species bounds. It works terrifically well for bass, also. Just this summer, John Christianson and Duane Ryks from our office were on a local lake pre-fishing for a bass tournament. They were over a school of what they were sure were bass, but they couldn't get them to bite "traditional" bass color worms and jigs, like black and purple.

Duane gets to rummaging through his tackle box and puts a chartreuse yellow Fuzz-E-Grub head on a purple worm. Pow-pow, he smacks a couple fish. John puts a plain yellow head on his worm and takes a nice fish.

Later, when they rendezvous with Wayne Ekelund, another good fisherman, they compare notes. Wayne says that earlier, he had been over those same fish, couldn't catch any, and had almost the same idea. He put a pink jig head on a black worm and smack-smack-smack, took three nice bass right in a row.

In that case, you see, it wasn't really the exact colors they were using as much as that they had a *contrasting* color combination on. And it doesn't just work on crappies walleyes and bass, either. It's something to use for any species of fish.

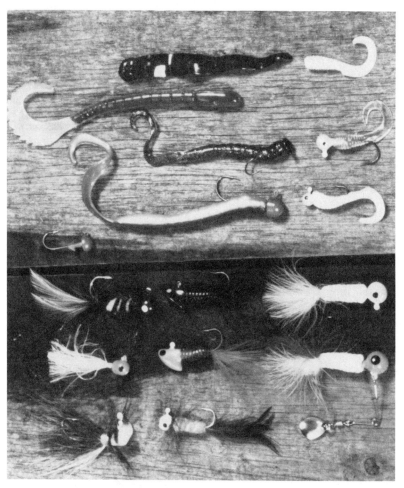

Many times, the fact that your bait exhibits a color contrast is more important than the colors making up the contrast.

To really maximize your efficiency, to really stay on top of fish as the day wears on, as you get cloudy or sunny or rainy or really windy conditions, you have got to play around with colors a whole lot. You can't expect to go out there with just one color jig and catch fish under ever-changing conditions.

Are there situations, or certain lakes, for example, where you can say with some certainty that one color, such as chartreuse yellow, is effective? Sure.

But, I'm convinced that in order to be a consistent jig fisherman, after getting a firm grip on the basic retrieves and learning to detect bites, you need to arm yourself with an arsenal of colors. You'll need a few straight colors, and a number of jigs with contrasting colors.

That doesn't mean you need all the colors for a particular lake. A lot of guys fish one certain lake most of the time, and I realize that. A person who fishes mostly on clear-water lakes is in a very different situation than somebody who fishes tannic acid-stained or very dirty water lakes, or shallow lakes with tremendous algae blooms, etc.

But if you want to be a complete jig fisherman, and you're going to be versatile and travel around and fish all different sorts of lakes, then you need all the colors.

And now, a word of caution before I even start talking about which colors I like best for certain conditions. These are rules of *thumb*, a place for you to begin your search, based on the best information I have and my own experiences. Don't get stuck with these recommendations. Think of them more as guidelines.

This information pertains primarily to walleye fishing, so you will have to play with it a bunch with other species. The colors are also good on bass, northerns, crappies, etc., but they are not as fine-tuned for those fish. Purple, for example, is a color I won't talk a lot about for walleyes, but it is a very important largemouth bass color.

To begin with, let me cover which jig *head* colors you need to handle almost any walleye fishing situation you will encounter. If you have heads in fluorescent red, fluorescent orange, fluorescent yellow (chartreuse), lime green, a dark jade green, fluorescent powder blue, pearl white, and black, I can't think of a time you wouldn't have what you need.

Babe's Jig Color Recommendations

1.   Clear water, bright light, such as mid-afternoon on a sunny day:
I feel that the white bodied, blue headed Fuzz-E-Grub is the hottest single color you can throw. I've proved it to myself enough times. In very cold water, such as early spring, straight white is still a top color. Orange/white, pink/white, red/white, and chartreuse are also good.
2.   Clear water, not as much light penetration (such as early mornings, evenings, overcast days, etc.):
This is a time when you would still want to check the same colors I talked about in #1, but now the brown/orange, purple/white, and lime/black Fuzz-E-Grubs can be dynamite, too.

The "darker" the conditions become, as night falls, or as cloud cover gets heavier, etc., or the "darker" the clear water is, the more you should lean on the lime/black, straight brown, and purple/white combinations.
3.   Still clear water, but during midsummer, when the water is warmer:
Whites become less important now. Straight chartreuse, lime/black, brown/orange, and greens are your primary colors to check. Also, if you are fishing in deep water, blue/white and purple/white are excellent.
4.   Stained water (tannic acid-stained or coffee colored), bright light conditions:
Greens, chartreuse, lime, and orange are your four predominant colors, and can be used as straight colors (green head/green body),

with browns, with white or even each other. Orange/white is good at times. Pure whites are not so good.

5.   Stained water, low light conditions:

Here, brown/brown, brown/orange, black/lime and black/black have been my most consistent performers.

6.   Stained water during heavy algae blooms:

Your two predominant colors in this situation will be chartreuse and orange.

Again, please don't think of these as hard-and-fast rules. I usually start with one of these suggestions, but I proceed to experiment if the fish don't cooperate!

Tipping Jigs With Live Bait

You always hear fishermen talking about "tipping" jigs with various live baits, and how some guy caught a bunch of nice smallmouths on a jig "tipped with a minnow." But rarely does anyone take the time to explain *how* he tips his jig with that minnow, or that leech, or that nightcrawler, or that...

With a minnow, I almost always hook it through the head, from bottom to top, so the minnow rides right side up on the jig hook. That way, I can control the action of the jig. I can make it bounce, twitch, and swim in and around rocks. The minnow follows the bait wherever it goes.

I've always felt that a jig with a minnow running off the back of it represents a small fish that is trying to run off with something in its mouth. If you've ever tossed a bunch of popcorn or Cheerios to a school of small minnows or sunfish, you know what I mean. One grabs a piece of food, and tries to swim away with it, but it's too big for it and the others are all over it trying to take it away. To a big predator fish, I think that the action and appearance of a jig-and-minnow might trigger the instinct to strike a vulnerable prey item.

A different situation comes in, for example, fall, when I might be using very big minnows on a jig. Then, I will hook the minnow the same way, from bottom to top, with the minnow riding right side up, but will only put the hook through the minnow's lips, not the head.

That minnow is big enough to fight the jig and still remain quite lively. Often, that struggling of the minnow against the weight and awkwardness of the jig will be enough of a triggering factor to draw me many more strikes than if I were just dragging a big, dead minnow along behind the jig.

But normally, as I said before, when I'm casting into the shallows or drifting a river, I simply hook the minnow up through the head and impart all the action myself by twitching and dancing the bait around, hoping to draw strikes that way.

You should hook leeches to a jig by inserting the hook up, from underneath, just behind and then through the main sucker, located at the fatter end of the leech.

With nightcrawlers, you have several options. You can hook them once through the nose, hook them on somewhere at a midpoint and let two fairly equal lengths trail off in a "v" fashion, or actually thread the crawler all the way onto the jig. To thread a crawler onto a jig that has a body, such as the Fuzz-E-Grub, you must first remove the plastic body.

One of the situations where a jig-and-nightcrawler combination has proven deadly for me is with smallmouth bass feeding on crayfish along a rocky bank. Here, if you hook the crawler midway and let the two halves trail back in a "v" they seem to undulate in the water almost like a crayfish darting along the rocks. Maybe it's my imagination, but I really think those smallies take that 'crawler to be exactly that. What I do know for sure is that it has worked for me a lot of times.

Normally, I fish a nightcrawler on a jig by simply hooking it through the nose. When the fish are active, though, that extra wiggling from the two tails of a 'crawler hooked at the midpoint can be that intangible ingredient that gets you more fish. With this, like anything else, learn to experiment to keep on top of what the fish want.

Another, less common bait to tip a jig with is a crayfish. They can be absolute dynamite, especially on bass! They can be hopped along the bottom slowly under post-frontal conditions for finicky fish, worked in a swimming motion, fished fairly quickly along boulder-strewn shorelines and humps, etc. The soft-shelled stage of the crayfish is most appealing to the fish.

Hook a crayfish onto your jig through its tail, so it streams off backwards. That's the way a crayfish naturally swims, so it will look "right" to the fish.

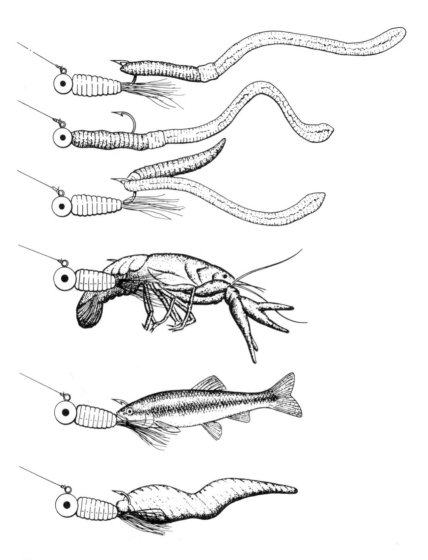

There are various ways to tip a jig with a nightcrawler. You can thread the 'crawler onto the jig head (take the body off first!), hook it midway so it trails off in a "v" fashion, or simply hook it once through the nose. Hook a crayfish through the tail, so it streams off backwards. Normally, a smaller minnow is hooked up through the head (although bigger minnows that can "fight" the weight of the jig can be hooked through the lips). Tip a jig with a leech by hooking it once through the sucker (fat) end.

There are certain situations, and for very specific reasons, where good fishermen will fish with an untipped jig.

That statement comes as close as I can come to saying "you should always tip your jig with some sort of live bait." There's a good reason for that: in *almost* all cases, it is to your advantage to tip your jig.

A lot of times, in order for fish to hit artificial baits, they have to be aggressively feeding. That's not always the case with live baits, and jigs tipped with live baits. I would say that I tip my jigs at least 90 percent of the time. Even some very good fishermen I know who say they fish with untipped jigs more, still use live baits about 80 percent of the time.

Fish just take "meat" better, more of the time, than they do plastic and lead and feathers. Can you catch fish with an untipped jig? Certainly, but usually only the aggressive fish, and keep in mind that most of the time, the most aggressive fish are also the smaller ones. So when you fish an untipped jig, you may be giving up some chance that you'll catch the bigger fish out of a school.

Certain species, like bass and northern pike, are more sight- and sound-oriented feeders, so are more susceptible than others to an untipped jig. But still, live bait on a jig will usually out-produce a plain jig with these fish as well.

There are situations where using live bait is not practical, such as when you are fishing bass in very heavy cover. The toughest leech or minnow will rip off a jig long before a piece of pork rind, so that is what I use in heavy bulrushes, weeds, etc. if necessary.

Certain species like the northern pike, by their nature sight- and sound-oriented feeders, are more susceptible than others to a jig without any live bait on it.

Spence Petros likes to fish an untipped jig at times for early-season smallmouth bass. "If they will hit a plain jig," he said, "I'll use it, because you can really get a nice rhythm going, working a jig without something hanging off the end of it. A live bait can restrict the free fall and the swimming action a little bit. With a plain jig, you can get that rhythm going, and I've really seen it work good sometimes."

Another place where untipped jigs can be more than adequate is where you are fishing "less sophisticated" populations of fish, such as walleyes in northern Canadian lakes. It becomes more important to tip your jig when you are fishing in waters that get more fishing pressure.

Just recently, we were up at Reindeer Lake in northern Saskatchewan, filming a trophy northern pike segment with the winners of our "Fishing Safari Sweepstakes" drawing. The contest winners and I were busy catching northerns right up in the mouth of a river. Just out of camera distance, my brother Dave and Dave Greer, editor of Fins and Feathers magazine, were so busy catching walleyes they couldn't even look over to see how we were doing!

In about two hours, they caught and released all but a few of 47 walleyes from about 2-4 pounds, all on plain Fuzz-E-Grubs with Chummin' Rub smeared on them. They did some experimenting, by the way, and found that the jig with scent on it produced noticeably better than without it. If you are going to fish an untipped jig, I would strongly recommend adding a good commercial scent to it, like Chummin' Rub. If nothing else, it will mask the human odor on the bait, and it could very well act as an attractant.

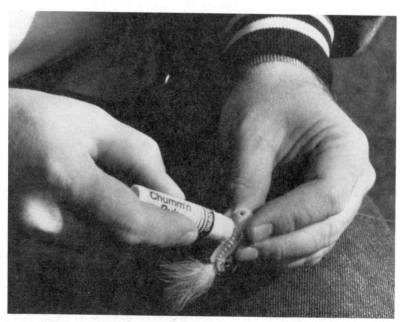

When you do fish an untipped jig, it is a good idea to add a commercial scent product.

Which Bait to Tip With?

When you walk through the door of the bait shop and start staring into the minnow tanks and the guy is standing there with a net in his hand, and there's 50 other people waiting, and 25 people waiting to pay, is not the time to start wondering what you want to get that day.

Know all that ahead of time. Then, buy bait based on what the shop has, and how healthy it looks. I will go into detail on how to pick baits in the chapter on live bait, but for now let's talk a bit about deciding what to tip your jigs with.

In general, in early season, a jig tipped with some sort of minnow is hard to beat. In fact, a jig tipped with some sort of minnow is hard to beat anytime, anyplace, for any kind of fish! It is just plain and simply one of the fish-catchingist combinations ever discovered.

For the bulk of my bass, walleye, northern, etc. early-season jig fishing, I like small to medium-sized (2 1/2 to 4 1/2 inches long) fatheads, shiners, redtail chubs, suckers, etc.

In deciding which type of minnows to buy, take some time to find out about the predominant forage base in the waters you will be fishing. If, for example, the lake you'll be going to has a good population of ciscoes, tulibees, whitefish and that sort of critter, you might do better with golden shiners or some other minnow that closely resembles what the fish are used to feeding on. If in doubt, though, for walleyes it's hard to beat redtail chubs or fatheads early in the year. For northerns, suckers are usually my top pick. The fish haven't really turned onto baits like leeches or nightcrawlers well yet (although these baits do work at times, so it pays to bring them along and try them just in case).

In the case of early-season crappies (and sunfish), I love Lindy's smaller Quiver Jigs, say from 1/32- to 1/16-ounce, tipped with a small fathead minnow, or "crappie minnow" as many bait shops call them. I use the Quiver Jigs without minnows with great success at times, too. They are deadly when fished on a small bobber, and allowed to just bob up and down with the waves along the tops of old weeds or any other cover you can find.

If you're looking for a real good general rule, I would say go primarily with minnows on the back of your jigs in spring and fall (using larger minnows in fall than spring), with leeches and sometimes nightcrawlers in midsummer. But, even this rule is made to be broken. Especially in the case of weed walleyes and bass, you might want to go back to minnows in midsummer.

Chapter 7
Basic and Advanced Jigging Methods

One of the things that makes a jig such a magical bait is its adaptability. Walleyes will succumb to its charms, for sure; but so will largemouth and smallmouth bass, northern pike, muskies, lake trout, sunfish, crappies, perch and anything else that lives in the water.

And, while some folks may think of the jig as a fishing tool to be used in drifting along deep rock piles, and trolling along with an electric motor (and these are important uses), the jig is also at home being cast out and reeled back in.

I've heard people say that there's no such thing as a "wrong" way to fish a jig, that if you keep it hopping, jumping, or even just laying there long enough, a fish will bite it. While that is partly true, I think you know me well enough by now that you and I aren't going to be satisfied with such an easy way around expanding ourselves as fishermen!

There definitely are right ways to fish a jig, and I'd like to take some time now to look at many of them. These have taken years to develop in some cases, and reflect the combined experiences of an awful lot of good jig fishermen. We don't have space or time to go very deeply into specific patterns for specific species of fish. I will point out in some cases how this method or that will work for walleyes or smallmouth bass, but it will be up to you in many instances to try the techniques on your waters, for whatever fish you seek.

In our other books, there are lengthy chapters on specific patterns. Go back and look these over, or look into them if you haven't seen them.

Then, get out there on the water where the real action is, and start seeing how these jigging methods fit into your fishing style. Good jig fishing requires much in the way of ability, both in retrieves and other presentations, and in learning to detect strikes and set the hook. For as simple a device as a jig is, it takes a lot to become a master of it!

Polarized Sunglasses: A Big Jigging Aid

If it were up to me, good polarized sunglasses would be manditory equipment for fishermen, just as certain books are required reading for students who wish to become really good at something.

There are so many reasons they are important for jig fishing. They give you vision down into the water, so many more times acute than you have without them, that you can see things that completely dictate what you do, where you cast, which direction you head, etc.

You can see weed edges, and underwater timber, actually see down *in* there sometimes. In fact, in many shallow-water jigging situations, you can actually spot fish and cast to them, and set the hook when you see them put their mouth around your jig!

For deeper water, you can see your line twitch better. With the exception of some liquid crystal displays, you can see the face of your sonar equipment much better, so you don't have to squint or move as much to see what's "going on down there."

Sometimes, it's more than just the obvious: you can actually see dark spots that indicate you are approaching a drop off, so you can decide whether you want to change course, cast into the deeper water, etc. You can also inspect the shallower portions of a sunken island, or a shoreline where it leads out onto a point, to see what type of bottom is present. Is it boulders? Sand? Weeds? That way, you can at least guess that it might be similar in the nearby deeper sections, and it gives you a headstart in understanding the spot you are fishing.

Glasses are a big safety factor as well. With hooks flying around, bugs banging into your face as you drive the boat, and other obstacles that come with fishing, it's a nice comfort to have your eyes shielded from possible sources of injury.

Also, it is nice to be wearing sunglasses, simply to cut down on the eye strain that bright sun can give you. That's not to say that sunglasses are only for use in sunny conditions, because they are an advantage even in very cloudy weather. But, just as they do for you while driving your car, sunglasses can help you go a lot longer before you feel weariness from eye strain.

For many years, I used glasses with plastic lenses—until I had a doctor explain to me that I had actually lost a portion of my eyesight from the strain the plastic was putting on my eyes. It was at that point that I searched for the ultimate polarized glasses with *glass* lenses.

Because I couldn't find what I needed, I had a company make them for me. I was so impressed with the way they did the job that I began having them made in mass quantities and offering them to sell. And now you know...the *rest* of the story behind my "Fisherman's Favorite" polarized sunglasses. I truly believe they are the best available, and they have all the features a serious fisherman looks for in sunglasses. Ground and polished glass lenses, sturdy, form-fitting frames, a lanyard to keep them on your neck when they're not on, and a floating case that protects the lenses and your glasses if they fall overboard.

We have just come out with a new line of our sunglasses, in fact, in a more stylish frame. I plead to you: don't go out on the water and expect to be the best fisherman you can be, without a good-quality pair of polarized glasses.

A good pair of polarized sunglasses are a tremendous fishing aid, and a safety factor as well.

Casting With Jigs

Casting can be the only effective way to fish jigs in some situations. Particularly in shallow water, where getting right over the top of a school of fish would send them scurrying for the depths, drifting or backtrolling is out of the question. Any time you encounter skittish fish, such as clear water lakes, middle of the day, etc., it's a good idea to back off the fish and cast into them.

Before we make our first cast, though, a word of caution: one thing I'm learning more and more about every year, or at least getting more conscious of, is that we spook a tremendous number of fish away from us while we're fishing. They move off at least a cast's distance away, because of the presence of the boat or because we are making too much noise. If you even think you might be spooking fish, use only an electric motor to position your boat, or let yourself drift in. Or quietly paddle into a spot and wait a minute before beginning to fish.

Trout fishermen are famous for their patience, for slowly working their way into casting shape and then waiting—for half an hour or an hour sometimes—until the fish have begun doing what they were doing, feeding, before he got there. Then, the fisherman makes a cast. We could learn a lot from a strategy like that.

I'm like you, though. I'm too impatient to wait to start fishing. Just learn to be quiet while getting near fish, and keep sudden movements and noise on the bottom of the boat to a minimum. The quieter and calmer it is out on the water, the more critical this becomes.

Every year, I get more aware of how many fish we spook by being careless. Sneaking along with the electric motor, especially when fishing calm, shallow water, is one way to cut down on noise.

Casting is a great way to cover a lot of ground, and that is a pleasant coincidence. Because when fish are found along shallower structure, or in weedbeds and other places that casting is the ticket, they are often more scattered. That makes a pinpoint presentation almost impossible, because a group of fish is tough to nail down.

Don't get the wrong impression. I am not saying that shallow fish will forgive *sloppy* presentations, or that they are easier to catch. For although they are normally a bit more aggressive, and moving around more, they are also in water that is clearer, with more light penetration, where they can see your bait better and give it a more discriminating look.

And, don't get the impression that casting is only a shallow-water method. It works well for covering mid-depth humps and flats, or really anywhere you want to fish without driving your boat right over the top of the spot.

While casting can be deadly, it takes care and precision to work right. Much of the time, the fish you are trying to catch will be in a neutral to negative mood, making it important that you put the jig close to them and give them a reason to strike it.

Yes, casting situations call for being thorough, which casting is made for. You can fan-cast an entire area, laying as many casts as you wish into an area you are convinced holds fish.

Casting a jig is a great way to cover a lot of ground when looking for fish, or when faced with scattered fish.

While the *way* you bring the bait back to the boat is going to vary quite a bit (or it should, if you are trying to be a versatile fisherman), it all begins with a very important fundamental that we might call:

The Cast and Fall

There are a few things to be aware of, a few keys to successfully casting a jig. One thing to learn right away is that any live bait you tip the jig with will go flying another direction if you snap your wrists hard. Learn to lob cast a jig that has live bait on the back of it. Try sidearm, or 3/4 overhand, or whatever is most comfortable, but be smooth, easy and gentle as you release the bait at the beginning of the cast.

When your jig hits the water, don't immediately close your reel. That prevents any more line from paying out, and your jig will sink toward the bottom at an angle. If you're in water deeper than 10 feet, your jig might be right under the boat by the time it gets there. That doesn't leave much room to make a retrieve, does it?

Let some line pay out as the jig sinks. Don't let gobs of slack form in the line, though, and don't let it sink all the way to the bottom. Close your reel well before the jig gets to the bottom, so you can maintain constant contact with it as it falls. As the jig nears the bottom, decide whether you are going to let it sit there a while before starting to retrieve it, or begin your retrieve right away.

How do you know your jig is almost to the bottom? Good question. What you need to learn to be conscious of is the drop rate of the jig you are fishing with at the moment. How fast is it really dropping? Don't let it be a matter of guessing any more.

186

The only way I know of to get good at it, is to take the jig you are going to fish with into clear, fairly shallow water. Check the exact depth on your depth finder. Then, cast your jig out and count it down, watching it the whole time, one-thousand one, one-thousand two, etc. until the bait hits the bottom. (Make sure you attach any live bait you plan to fish with before doing this test.)

This way, you can figure out just about exactly how fast the jig drops. Then, if you should want to begin your retrieve while the jig is still about a foot from the bottom, for example, you can be pretty accurate about it.

There is also another very good reason for learning to do this. I use this practice to my advantage all the time. If I know, for example, that the 1/4-ounce jig and 3-inch minnow I'm using sinks at about one foot per second, and I'm casting up onto a rock pile that is about 12 feet deep, I automatically begin counting it down as soon as the jig hits the water. If my line goes slack at a count of six, or eight, or anything before 12, I know that it happened for a reason: a fish has probably got my jig. It's time to set the hook!

If you don't pay attention to these types of little details, you would have no idea the line went slack sooner than it should have. You would have no idea you might have a fish on.

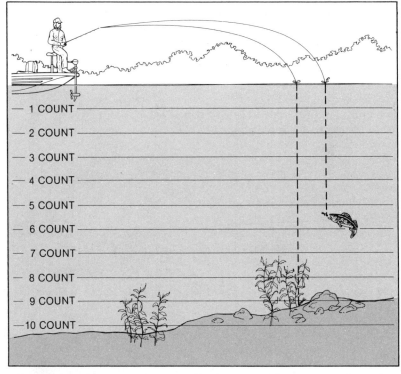

Always count down your jig as it sinks after a cast. That way, you know how long it should take to get to the bottom. Then, if you aren't done counting and the line twitches or goes slack, you better set the hook!

Early one morning a number of years back, I was fishing Fishtrap Lake in northern Minnesota with a good friend of mine named Kevin Flansberg.

We were fishing bass on a big weed flat. We were backed off, in about 20 feet of water, throwing crankbaits up onto the flat. We didn't catch any bass, but all of a sudden I pop a walleye on a crankbait, and then another one.

After I casted a few more times without a strike, you never saw anybody set down the crankbait rod and grab a jig any faster in your life. The flat was a gradually-tapering cabbage bed, with the tops of the weeds at different depths depending on how deep the water was.

Because I knew that break very well, I knew right where the weeds were, and could cast my jig in and let it settle to the tops of the weeds. Then, the only way to fish effectively with a jig was to set up a swimming motion that would take it right along the tops of the weeds.

As the jig got toward the deeper water, I would slow the swimming motion down and let the jig settle down even deeper, always keeping it close to the weed tops. You had to feel for that little "tick" that told you the jig had hit a weed, then quickly snap it off and keep it swimming.

The walleyes I had caught on the crankbait were right up on top of the cabbage flat, in fairly shallow water. But they had moved down into the deeper break, and I *had* to keep the jig following the contour of the deeper weeds in order to catch more fish.

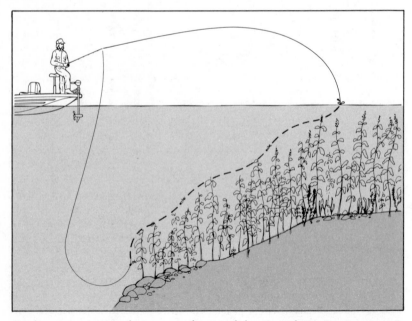

It takes concentration, but you can learn to fish a jig with a swimming motion over the tops of weeds — even if the weed tops are at different depths through the course of the retrieve.

The jig also had to be occasionally ticking the weeds, it seemed, in order to draw hits. We caught more fish after that, but it was a very exacting retrieve, a swimming retrieve, that it took to do it.

That's just one example of a situation where a swimming retrieve, one that doesn't allow the jig to settle to the bottom, was effective. That's not the *only* way to swim a jig, however. You can move it in a steady, rhythmic fashion, or erratically up and down. You can raise and lower it very slowly, or really pump it quickly.

You need to learn to recognize times when you want a swimming instead of a bottom-bumping presentation, and you must also experiment with the fish's moods, every day and even many times during each day.

Bill Binkelman has a stand-by swimming retrieve that he has used to take countless fish. He calls it his "starting" retrieve, and I'll let him tell you how he does it:

Bill Binkelman:
"I can't stress enough the importance of retrieve. Generally, you're going to be fishing for fish that are pretty neutral; that is, they won't go out of their way to chase your jig. You are going to have to get the jig directly in front of them in order to get them to hit it.

"This starting retrieve works in either shallow or deep water. Make sure after you cast out that you let lots of line come off your reel as the jig sinks, so it goes straight down. Once it hits bottom, point your rod tip at the jig and then give it a short—maybe six-inch—flip. Keep giving the jig those short jerks, reeling in slack line as you go, until your rod tip has gotten so high that you might not be able to get a good hook-set should a fish hit. I call that the "danger point." When you get there, lower your rod tip, without pausing your retrieve at all, and quickly reel in the slack that makes. This puts your rod tip back into the beginning position again. Repeat the whole thing over and over, until you get to the boat or catch a fish. That's the starting retrieve."

Bill also has very definite ideas on catching suspended fish, especially walleyes, with a swimming retrieve. "Suspended fish are generally about three feet off the bottom," Binkelman says. "Now, these fish will come up for a bait but they won't go down. This has been proven over and over again.

"The best way I know of to catch them on a jig is to take a lighter jig, about 1/16 or 1/8 ounce, and just do your best to swim the bait slowly as close to that three-feet-off-the-bottom level as you can. It takes a lot of practice to be able to do that, but swimming a jig along from about 2-4 feet off bottom will take a lot of those fish, when fishing right on the bottom won't catch any.

"And there's one other one I try not to forget to try. After you make the cast, let the jig hit bottom and just raise it enough to get it to that three- or four-feet-off-the-bottom level, and retrieve it straight in, no action, just keeping it there at that depth. Those fish will hang there, three or four feet off the bottom, and they will hit a jig worked that way. Some will also come up off the bottom to take one."

Here's how to do Bill Binkelman's "starting retrieve." Cast out and let the jig sink straight to the bottom. Then, work it back to the boat using short, increasingly higher, twitches of the rod tip. Each time your rod gets too high to allow you a good hook-set (the "danger" point), drop the rod and start the process over. This gives you a retrieve as shown, which covers various depths.

Remember what we said about learning to understand the drop rate of the jig you're using? If you take a few minutes to figure out how fast the jig is really dropping, and how deep the water is you're fishing, you should be able to take a shortcut to success with this retrieve.

You might want to give this idea a try, if you are fishing an area you really think should have fish, but can't catch any by fishing along the bottom. It might pay off big!

When you are swimming a jig, line color is less important than in free-falling a jig down the face of a break or even vertical jigging, because you are relying less on watching your line for a twitch and more on just feeling for strikes. You have a constant contact with your bait.

Also, I normally keep my rod at between 8 and 11 o'clock for jig fishing, so I can keep it a little bit to the side, rather than straight on to the fish. That way, I can carefully watch the amount of tension the jig by itself is putting on my rod tip. This is especially effective with a lighter action rod, that can show you small changes in tension clearly. If you watch your rod tip, you can see even a slight change in the amount of pressure on the tip, and that sometimes is signaling a strike from a fish.

More often than not, in fact, when you're swimming a jig along, the fish will come up from behind and take the bait. If they keep coming right at you after taking the bait, there will be a noticeable slackening of the line, but many times it just doesn't feel like anything at all. These are some of the kinds of strikes people tell you feel "syrupy," like your jig just fell into a cup of molasses. There's still drag on your line, there's still pressure, but it's a different kind of pressure and only absolute concentration will allow you to detect the difference.

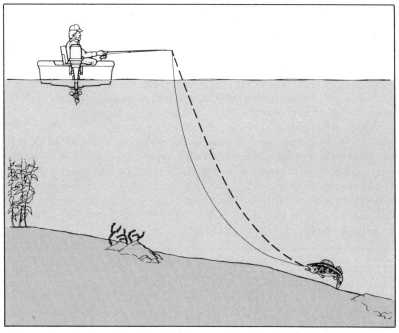

Often, when you're swimming a jig along, a fish will come up from behind, take the bait and either come slowly with you or not move much. You won't really feel a strike as such, you just feel a slightly different type and amount of pressure on the line, or see a slackening of the line. Set the hook!

Believe me, I'm not making this stuff up. It is probably happening to you all the time in your fishing now, and you are merrily reeling in without the slightest hint that a fish has your jig in its mouth.

Wouldn't you like to start catching some of these fish? It's a matter of concentrating hard for those small changes in your jig. Most people, after driving the same car for a year, can tell right away if it's not running quite the same as it usually does. There's not a lot of difference, and someone riding in the passenger side, who hasn't spent the same amount of time you have in the car, won't notice it. You can't even explain it to them, but it's there; you know it's there.

That's the way it is with jig fishing. You need to fish jigs a lot, you need to go a lot of miles with them, until you begin to learn what they *usually* feel like, what they feel like when they run into weeds, over rocks, and yes, into the mouths of fish. You need to learn to detect minute changes in the pressure on them. Once you learn it, you never unlearn it. Of course, you will get rusty over the winter and you will have bad days, but you won't ever totally forget. You will have taken another big step toward becoming a master fisherman.

Free-Falling Jigs Down Breaks

In this situation, you are usually casting up onto a flat that sits off a very steep drop off. You can fish the jig along the flat, and then when you want to fish down the ledge, you must swim the jig, letting it fall on a slack line from a shallower ledge down to the next deeper ledge.

If you try to drop the jig down the break on a tight line (many people do, mistakenly thinking that maintaining a tight line is the most important aspect here), the jig will fall away from the structure pendulum-fashion, and usually waltz right over the tops of the fish, too high for them to see or care about.

When done properly, it can be an extremely effective retrieve for many species of fish. As I discussed, the best way to detect a bite is to watch your line. When you see it twitch, or if it isn't falling even though you can't feel the bottom, set the hook. It could be the fish of a lifetime!

Many species of fish will follow the bait down or up the drop, and scoop it up off the bottom. This often happens while your line is slack, such as when it is falling from one ledge to another. Seeing the line twitch can be the *only* way to detect a bite.

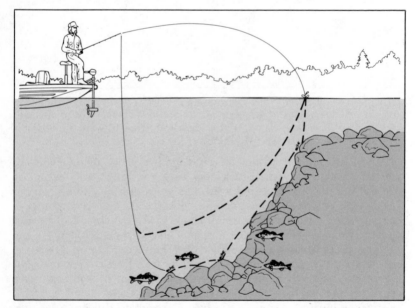

If you try to fish a jig down a steep break on a tight line, it will fall away from the structure — and any fish — pendulum fashion. You must learn to swim the jig, letting it fall on a slack line from ledge to ledge, always watching your line for a twitch that signals a take from a fish.

192

Always pay attention to your line when jig fishing! There are many instances when seeing the line twitch is the only way to detect subtle strikes.

This technique can be used in slightly different situations as well.

Some years back, on Otter Lake in Minnesota, my brother Dave and I used a slow free-falling presentation with plastic worms to easily win a local club bass tournament.

The lake has very clear water, with a pretty good expanse of flat, shallow water off the shoreline. In some places, the bottom then drops straight off into a very deep muck basin. A sort of apron of moss grows over the edge of the drop, creating almost an undercut bank situation.

We found fish sitting tight up under that moss overhang, but we couldn't figure a good way to get to them. We had seen one flash out at a worm as it was dropping down, but the worm was evidently moving too fast. We eventually figured out a way to catch those fish.

You could throw a really light plastic worm right up into the weeds, and let it just slide down over the moss. We had the right idea, but it became obvious that even a 1/8-ounce head was dropping way too fast. They just wouldn't hit it. We had to go to a 1/16-ounce head, so it would very slowly free-fall. A worm on a plain worm hook fell too slowly and was too hard to work.

You'd just let that worm flutter down in front of that moss, and what you'd see was a flash—woom!—a bass would come out from under the moss, grab the worm, and be back underneath before you could blink.

You had to set the hook right away or they would spit out the worm. It all happened so fast that if you weren't constantly watching, you'd miss it. You didn't feel anything; you could just see the flash.

In the underwater world, there are no such things as spectators. Every living creature, every fish, is a potential meal for another creature, unless you happen to be the biggest dude in the lake.

Life goes on day after day in about the same manner. There are no such things as time outs, no such things as breaks for sleep. Every fish is like a fugitive on the run from the reality of death, and instinctively it knows it.

One of the most active arenas where this game of cat-and-mouse is played out is the fully-developed weedbeds of midsummer. Especially after the thermocline sets up in many lakes, the lack of oxygen in the depths forces fish up into the weeds.

Here, in a web of shade and shadows, predators hide and baitfish squirm. Every move could be the last one.

This can be a real "hoppin" spot, and maybe the best place to work a jig with a hopping retrieve.

While there are many patterns that will work in the weeds, this is one of my favorites. What I look for is a good weedgrowth on a big food shelf that offers access to deep water. Look for "edges," places where two types of weeds meet, where there are pockets in the weeds, inside turns and points in the weedline, places where rock, sand or gravel meets the weeds, thicker clumps of weeds, logical places for fish to travel while moving up from or down to deep water, etc. These are all key holding spots for fish—places for predators to be.

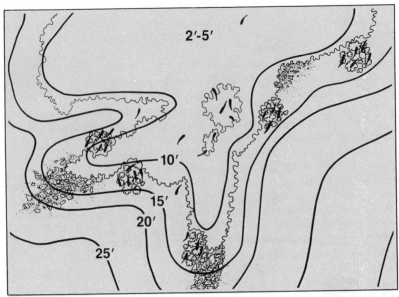

The fish in this illustration are all holding in "edge" habitat. Pockets in weeds, the thickest weed clumps, where two weed types meet, where rock, sand or gravel meet weeds, etc. are key spots that might concentrate fish. Learn to look for and carefully fish these areas.

This pattern will catch many species of fish, so you never know what you might get.

My favorite jig for this pattern is a 1/8- or 1/4-ounce Lindy Flat Foot, tipped with some type of live bait. Cast in and around the types of edges mentioned, and let the jig settle. Occasionally, it will make it all the way to the bottom, but usually not. Often, it just hangs up in the dense weeds, especially when you are fishing in cabbage.

A Flat Foot has a stand-up head, which is good for working and cutting through weeds. As the bait hits bottom or gets hung up on the weeds, give it a quick snap to pop it off. The ripping motion causes commotion, which calls the fish's attention to the bait. It creates a virtual "underwater dust storm" as John Christianson likes to call it.

"And you don't always rip it off the weed right away, either," John says. "The way I do it, and I prefer lighter jigs for this simply because I think they work their way through the weeds better, is cast into the weeds and let the jig stop. I figure when it stops, it's either a fish or a weed. I gently tighten the line and feel. If it's a fish, I set the hook; if it's a weed, I don't immediately rip it off. I yo-yo the jig up and down right there, for anywhere from a second to ten seconds. Fish will really slam that thing as it bobs up and down there.

"If I don't get a strike after a while, I rip it free and swim it until it gets hung up again, and then yo-yo it again. The fish are aggressive, but it doesn't hurt to fish slow."

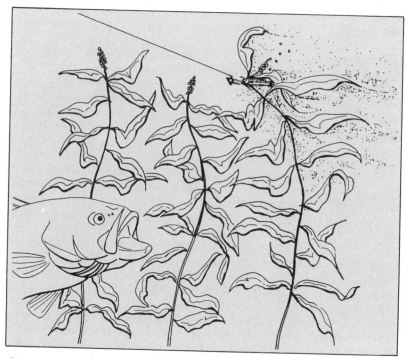

Ripping a jig off cabbage weeds creates an "underwater dust storm" that attracts the attention of fish, and often leads to vicious strikes.

This method can almost seem to be a miracle-worker at times. Big John remembers a day a few years back when it turned a bummer into a bounty.

"We were fishing a series of cabbage points," John recalls, "in about 10-12 feet of water. This was midsummer, when we knew fish would be up in the weeds. We worked the area hard all morning long looking for bass, using everything from plastics to spinnerbaits. The fish just wouldn't hit artificials. We knew there were fish in there, so we went to the dock and drove into town and bought some minnows, and came back out to the same spots and started working the tops of the cabbage with 1/8-ounce Dingo Jigs and minnows.

"Right away, we were *ripping* fish. We caught everything—bass, northerns, walleyes, and some big fish. We just cast into the cabbage and let the jig settle until it hung up, and then ripped it through, creating that underwater dust storm. The fish would really hit hard."

Experiment with how hard and high to hop the jig. When your jig hangs up in the weeds, and it will happen a lot, the same type of snap you use to work the jig will usually tear it free (although it might also tear your bait off). In really dense weeds, a stand-up head with a plastic tail such as Lindy's Swirl Tails, can be a good substitute at times. Cabbage weeds are the best type for this kind of fishing, because it's fairly easy to rip your jig free of the leaves. When you are fishing other weeds, like coontail and sandgrass, you will find it difficult to fish with a conventional jig. Go to something like the Dingo Jig, that has lots of bucktail on it, or a Lindy Legs or similar Jig-and-Pig jig with a weed-guard on it.

There are better live baits than others for this situation, and none surpass the redtail chub. It has an extremely tough skull, so it will stay on the jig hook long after more fragile baits have ripped off.

Normally, as I've said before, fish that are holding in weeds are feeders. They are used to feeding up in the tops of the weeds a lot, too, so don't worry if your bait doesn't make it all the way to the bottom. The fish tend to be pretty aggressive, so you will get a lot of surprisingly hard strikes, even from notoriously light biters like walleyes.

A jig tipped with a minnow, nightcrawler or leech will also work in more open water situations, particularly along underwater rock piles and humps, and along boulder and gravel-strewn shorelines where smallmouth bass are feeding on baitfish and crayfish that scurry along the rocks.

One of my rules of thumb about using this hopping retrieve in open-water is that in spring and fall, when the water's cold, it's usually best to just drag the jig along the bottom, with an occasional quick hop mixed in. In warmer water, short hops off the bottom, with an occasional big jump, work best.

Most fishermen put too much action on their jig, especially in cold-water situations. With this method, as in all jig fishing, it's important to remember that different kinds of retrieves will work under different conditions, and you should try to learn something every time you go fishing. Too many guys have a good day with a certain style of jig

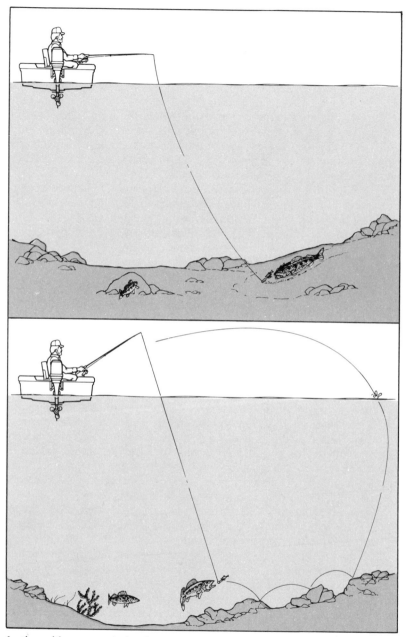

In the cold-water periods of spring and fall, it's usually best to just drag a jig along the bottom, with occasional little hops mixed in (above). In warmer water, a good rule is to work your jig in short hops, with occasional big jumps.

retrieve, and then get stuck in a 50-foot rut with it for years, when a little experimentation would pay off. Don't let yourself get caught in that trap.

The Dead Stick Retrieve

> "This is the single most effective way I know of to work a jig, day in and day out, for all species of fish."

> —John Christianson

You may have gathered by now that what "Big John" Christianson says carries a lot of weight with me. It does—as it does with anybody who has ever fished against him in tournaments, because his walls are covered with plaques and trophies, and his wallet regularly gets thicker with prize money from cash tournaments.

Big John is a good friend, and a close associate. He is the national product sales manager for Babe Winkelman Productions, and he does the same thorough job in that department as he does catching fish. But, because we work out of Brainerd, Minnesota, you don't always see John wearing a tie in the office. Sometimes, in fact, when he arrives for work, his hands still smell like fish he has been out catching early that morning.

He is a *very* knowledgeable and experienced fisherman. Not everything he does to catch fish is what we might call conventional, but as he often says, "I don't care how anybody else fishes. They can fish however they want to. I know how I'm going to fish."

More often than not, when he is working a jig on fish, he uses what he calls the "dead stick" retrieve. I'll let him tell you about it:

John Christianson:
"The way to do the dead stick is to cast out a jig, and as it hits the water, close your bail or click your baitcasting reel, but have your rod held high in the air; very high, as high as you can reach, so you can keep a tight line as you let the jig sink, but can still avoid having it coming at you too much. Keep your line tight all the time, maintaining contact as it falls. If your line goes slack before it gets to the bottom, reel up to feel for a fish, and set the hook if one is there.

"If you get strikes a lot before the jig gets to the bottom, that's a sign you have active fish up off the bottom, and should switch to a lighter jig with a more buoyant dressing, and get a good, slow descent.

"If it does make it to the bottom, or onto a weed, *don't* move the jig. If you are cranking the reel at all, you're moving the jig. If you are moving your rod tip at all, you're moving the jig. Don't move the jig. Let it sit there for about three to five seconds or so, and then gently—and I mean *gently*—lift your rod tip and feel for any resistance. If nothing is there, move the jig to its next resting spot, by making a high sweep with your rod. Make that jig jump high off the bottom and in an arc land about five or six feet from where it was before. Let it sit again like you did before. Maybe every once in a while, slightly quiver your rod tip—not enough to make the jig come up off the bottom, just enough for your jig to create a commotion, to stir up some dust.

"Keep doing that, moving the jig quite a ways with a high sweep of the rod, then letting it rest, until you get back to the boat. At each and every resting spot, and this is important, picture in your mind's eye a big fish, a huge fish, looking at your jig, about to pick it up. That will keep you ready. Don't cast your bait anywhere you don't think a fish is going to be, and don't move it anywhere you don't think a fish is going to be. When you feel any resistance, set it to it.

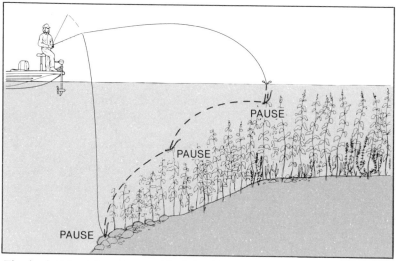

The dead stick retrieve, invented by John Christianson, may be unconventional but boy does it catch fish! You can use it in thick weeds, as shown, or along any bottom type.

"The best way I know of to tell the difference between a fish and a weed is that as you tighten up and feel resistance, if it gives at all, it's a weed. With a fish, there is almost never any give to it. That's not always the case, but it holds true most of the time. If there is a give but you feel a 'tap-tap' that's a fish, too. Although a lot of times, when people feel taps, they are feeling a fish spitting out a jig, that they never felt when it took the jig. They try to set the hook when they feel the tap, but it's already too late. You have to learn to feel earlier than that, and to watch your line for twitches and movement.

"One tournament I was in last year is a good example of how deadly this can be. My partner and I landed 28 1/2 pounds of bass and won the tournament, by dead-sticking a jig-and-plastic worm along a bare rock point that stuck off of a hump with cabbage on it. Now, normally I would fish in the cabbage, but I saw the fish out on the point on my locator and went after them. They wouldn't touch your jig if you moved it, but if you cast it out and let it lay there, eventually you would feel a definite 'bump-bump.' Every once in a while, I would get a fish to hit by gently twitching my rod tip to make the worm dance up and down, but not enough to make the jig move. These fish were anything but active, but still 'kawoom' they'd practically rip the rod out of your hands sometimes."

With deadly accuracy, a minnow attached to a weedless hook is dropped in a tiny hole in a thick carpet of lily pads.

A huge northern pike is resting at the bottom, in the coolness of the shade the pads offer. It sees the minnow come dropping down, and can't resist the temptation of an easy meal. In one deft movement, it inhales the minnow.

Above the water, a young boy's eyes get real big real fast as the weight of the resistance is felt. He tugs and yanks with everything he's got, but the fish is just too big, and finally pulls free.

A big lesson is learned, and in the excitement, a fishing technique is born.

In other places across the country, similar things were happening, and other folks were discovering flipping for big fish.

It was some years later, of course, that people quit using long cane poles and heavy dacron line for flipping; in fact, it was years before a Californian named Dee Thomas would wipe everybody's eyes at a big cash bass tournament and a name would be given to the technique.

Today, there are rods and reels designed for "flippin'." The reels have the ability to be "locked off" so no line can escape from the drag when you want to haul a big fish out of heavy cover. The rods are long and substantial, to give the fisherman a good reach and enough heft to haul a big fish out of heavy cover.

Flippin' isn't just a bass technique. You will catch big bass using it, for sure, but big northerns are a welcome bonus as well.

Modern flippin' has gotten fairly precise, but it remains simple. To be successful at it, you must learn to be accurate with your flippin' technique.

To practice, simply get a jig-and-pig jig of anywhere from 1/8 to 3/8 or even 1/2 ounce. Depending on how heavy the surface clutter is you will be trying to penetrate, you will use a lighter or heavier jig. Put the bait on the end of a flippin' stick and a flippin' reel if you have one, otherwise a good stout baitcasting outfit will do. For most flippin' situations, 17-20 pound-test monofilament is what you need, but in real heavy timber I sometimes go up to 25-pound.

You can practice right in your front yard. First, place a paper cup, small plate, or anything you want as your target, about 10-15 feet from where you will be standing. Hold the rod in your right hand and have enough line out so you are standing with your hand outstretched above your head, rod extended, and the jig is sitting just above the ground. Peel line from the reel with your left hand until it is fully extended out to the side, and you're ready to start.

Begin by practicing the "pendulum swing" while in this position. Just practice swinging the jig to you, back away from you, etc. until you can do it smoothly and have good control of all the line you have all over the place.

When you can do that, try a flip. Get the jig steady, then swing it in to you and back out. As it is swinging out, bring your left hand back toward the rod, and try to land the jig on your target. Missed? No biggy. You've got plenty of time to learn it.

Some fishermen like to let the line go with their left hand, so they can jig up and down with both hands on their reel, but most good fishermen keep hanging on with their left, and learn to fish the jig with their left hand resting against the outside of the reel, so they can immediately go into their next flippin' motion without having to grab the line again with their left hand.

Practice until you can lay that jig just about anywhere you want it, and you're ready for the water. Being good at the technique of flippin', though, is only part of the answer to being a success at it. You must also know *where* on the lake to spend your time.

Flippin' is a shallow-water technique, so the first thing you have to do is pick a lake that has a lot of good shallow-water cover. That may seem obvious, but it is important. If a lake has little to offer fish along the shorelines, and mostly deep-water points and sunken humps, etc. it will not be good flippin' water.

Look for heavy weed cover in back bays, good stands of bulrushes and cattails and lily pads. It is also tailor-made for the brushy back ends of coves on reservoirs.

Okay, so you're out there on the water, and you approach a good-looking stand of bulrushes. But, where do I fish, you say? It all looks so good! Believe me, it's not all the same to the fish. There are always certain prime areas the fish favor. Look for the thickest clumps of weeds, for holes and pockets in thick clumps, for little indentations in stands of bulrushes, for trees and brush that have the thickest trunks and most branches, etc. Those are the ticket.

Also, there should be good depth of water around the cover. Look for about 3-5 feet of water, and look for good access to deep water, so the fish will have an easy way to come in and out of the area.

Once you get started flippin', try to establish a rhythm that allows you to fish continously, getting your bait into as many promising pockets as possible. You may only catch a few fish per hour, but if you don't put your bait into many spots, you won't catch any!

Flip your bait into the first good-looking spot you see, and jig it up and down in the pocket. Give the fish some time to move over to the bait and hit it. Normally, three or four up-and-down movements is enough, unless you see the weeds part, or get some other indication that a fish is present. Pop the jig up out of the pocket, at the same time swinging it toward you. That's the "backcast" for your next flip. You should have your eye on another hole by now, and be able to just send the forward swing of the bait in that direction. Three or four more bobs up and down, and pop it out in one motion and send it into another one.

That's flippin', and it can be a very exciting and fun way to fish.

Accuracy is the name of the game, and that's why I suggested you do some pre-fishing practice. You need to be able to hit some awfully small holes and pockets. Try to drop your jig on the shady side of trees and stumps most of the time.

Another good tip is this: set your jig down with a good heavy splash when you are fishing in good heavy cover, and more softly in thinner, sparser cover. That is not a hard-and-fast rule, but it is a general guide that can help. In dense cover, fish often need a "hint" that your bait has arrived, while in thinner cover, they can get spooked easily from a big splash.

When you get a strike, you'll know it most of the time. You don't normally get a lot of light biters. Be ready to set the hook immediately when your jig hits the water, in fact, because many strikes come right away. Rear back and set the hook and do everything you can to simply yank the fish right up and out of the cover, before it can twist your line around roots, branches, stems, etc.

As John Christianson says, "play with the fish when you get him in the boat."

The fish will be very green, but if you're careful, the smaller ones can easily be released.

Flippin' in action. First (1) peel line off your reel with your left hand, and hold your right hand extended, with the lure resting just off the water's surface. Swing the lure away from you, then toward you, pendulum fashion. As the lure again swings away from you, land it on the spot you have selected, by bringing both hands together, still holding the line in your left (2). Twitch the lure up and down a few times, and if you don't get a strike, move it to the next spot by pulling in the line with your left hand. When you get a strike, horse the fish out of the cover and swing into the boat (3).

Fishing a Bobber With a Jig

A bobber with a jig? Who are you kidding, you say? Hey, it works sometimes.

Probably the most obvious example of when a bobber-and-jig combination is effective is for early-season crappie fishing. A light jig worked along under a small bobber, lets you work shallow, clear water slowly for crappies, and they really respond to that kind of presentation.

Another time you might consider it, says Spence Petros, is when walleyes are in the weeds, or any time they are finicky and want a slow presentation.

Spence Petros:
"Yeah, I use slip-bobbers and jigs sometimes for walleyes in cover. It can be a great way to keep that bait over structure. I can twitch it, let it lay, twitch it, let it lay, until a fish finally grabs it. I've fished them that way, and I think it can be an advantage over a plain hook and sinker, because when you twitch a jig, all the action goes to the jig-and-bait. With a hook-and-sinker, you work it and the action all goes to the sinker. And the jig gives you a color contrast, too."

Trolling and Drifting With a Jig

As yet another testament to the jig's versatility as a lure, it can be dragged or hopped or swum along while your boat drifts on wind power; and it can be effectively trolled, slowly or even quickly.

Many of the actions you put on the jig will be the same as those described in the casting section, and the way you detect strikes will be almost the same. But there are specific reasons for trolling or drifting with a jig instead of casting.

Some people simply prefer to troll or drift, because they are used to it, just as some prefer to cast. But there are also situations where trolling becomes the best way to present a jig, such as working the edges of deeper structure. In deeper water, for example, it takes a long time for a jig to sink to the bottom. If you are constantly casting out, waiting for the jig to sink, reeling it in and starting over again, your bait is not in the "fish zone" very much of the time.

There are times for casting, times for trolling and even times for drifting. Learning to employ all these methods will take you another step toward becoming a master fisherman.

205

Backtrolling With Jigs

How do I decide when I should be backtrolling a jig and when I should be casting, or drifting? How do I decide whether to fish vertically beneath the boat, or allow the jig to trail out behind me?

Some situations are obvious: you don't troll a jig-and-plastic-worm combination under docks and through heavy brush, for example. I use casting primarily to cover expanses of shallow water and to go after fish that are very spooky and sensitive to movement.

There aren't really any depth rules to go by, though. Sometimes, fish in 15 feet of water can be very spooky, especially if the water is clear. But a general rule I have is that I backtroll a jig when I need to be precise with my presentation in deeper water and other times "when I can get away with it" in shallower water.

Sometimes, remember, water that appears clear to us on the surface might have good amounts of algae in it, making it fairly stained and limiting visibility as shallow as four to six feet down. In those situations, fish can be fairly shallow and still not that spooky.

You need to play with the fish you are working, to determine whether you can troll over the top of them and still catch some, or whether you simply have to back off and cast into them in order to score. But in really deep water, say 35 feet and deeper, casting becomes a time-consuming and difficult job. Then, trolling or drifting with the jig either right under the boat or trailing a bit behind, is the best plan you can have. In those circumstances, bring the bait to the fish by moving your boat around.

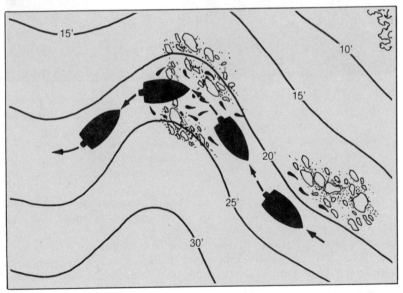

Backtrolling with a jig is an effective method any time you need to follow a tricky contour, as shown, and you can put your boat over the top of the fish without spooking them.

To consistently catch fish, you have to learn to think in terms of "combing" a structure in your search. Always check out the shallower and deeper parts of an area, even if the "rules" say, for example, that fish can't be on the sunny side of the weeds, or up shallow in the middle of the day. You shouldn't assume fish will be at 12-18 feet, just because that's where you caught them last night, or somebody told you that's where they'll be.

Fish move, and they can go a long ways in a short time! Remember that, and learn to hunt for fish. Be on the move, always searching for clues such as baitfish on your locator, or little bumps on your bait that tell you the fish might be sluggish that day, etc.

Vertical Jigging

Vertical jigging, especially while backtrolling slowly along *exactly* the piece of a structure you want to cover, is probably the deadliest way to present a jig in deeper (say, 12-15 feet and deeper) water. Jigging "vertically" simply means that you try to keep the jig as directly beneath you as possible.

Why is that important?

There are many advantages, really. It allows you to keep your jig in the same general area as the cone coverage of your depth finder, for one thing. When you are seeing fish on your flasher, graph or LCD, you can guess that your jig is at least *close* to those fish.

Otherwise, especially when you are dealing with tightly-schooled fish, you might move right past an entire school a number of times and miss *every one*, if your line is trailing too far behind your boat. You can be doing a great job of controlling your boat, putting it right over the fish, but as you twist and turn to make consecutive passes, your bait can be swinging wide of the fish every time.

Also, because there is the minimum amount of line out for the depth you are fishing, your sensitivity, your connection between subtle bites, the bottom, etc. is as good as it can be. Letting out more line behind the boat only deadens your sense of feel.

Thirdly, your hook-setting power is at its best for the same reason. You are setting with a straight lift on the shortest line possible, compared to a long, sagging amount of line trailing out behind the boat.

Also, and this is no small matter, you will have less of a chance of getting hung up when fishing vertically. The farther back your bait goes from the boat, the more of an angle it makes with the bottom, and the better the chance it will catch on something.

Bill Binkelman has always told me he prefers to jig vertically when he is fishing the "sharper" edges of a structure. He tends to cast and swim a jig along flats and gentler tapers.

I agree with him, and when I am seriously working to keep the jig vertical I go to a heavier jig than normal. I'll use a 3/8, 1/2 or sometimes even 3/4-ounce jig in situations where I want to keep my line right under the boat, especially when the waves are rocking me around or a heavy current wants to pull the jig off at an angle.

Another situation where vertical jigging really shines is in fishing deep boulders. Many fish, especially in midsummer, seek the shade of big boulders in midday, when the sun is beaming a lot of light down into the water. Remember, fish won't seek the shade of boulders if there aren't any in the lake, or if all the boulders are in water below the thermocline where there's no oxygen, or if all the baitfish are in weeedbeds and the weeds also provide shade, etc. Whether or not fish use boulders is determined by what else is available to them. One type of lake where they do, though, is the Canadian Shield lake, full of boulders and strewn rock and often short on weeds and other cover types.

The fish have a habit of tucking right tight to the shady side of the rocks. If the boulders are big enough the fish might be quite shallow, but it is most common to find fish along points or sunken islands in 20-30, sometimes as deep as 40 or even 50 feet. How clear the water is, water temperature, how bright and direct the sun is, and other factors will determine how deep the fish go.

These are classic neutral to negative mood fish, and you have to get the jig right in front of them in order to interest them. My favorite way to work fish in these conditions, is to slowly and methodically work an entire boulder area, hopping the jig a few inches at a time, twitching it a bit, and letting it sit in each new spot a few seconds, hoping a fish will take it. Often, they don't want the jig moving too much.

On hot, calm days, many fish will seek the shade of big boulders. These fish can be caught, but you have to go in after them! Get your jig right down in the cracks of the rocks, and fish along slowly. You will lose some jigs, but you will also catch some fish.

Because this is a situation that occurs mostly on hot, calm days, it's a good idea to fish a light, sometimes as light as 1/16 ounce, jig. But when you are trying to fish fairly deep, you will have to go to a little heavier jig, a 1/8 or even 1/4 ouncer. Also, because you are fishing so slowly, light line is a must—no bigger than 6-pound test. I often use 4-pound Stren for this type of fishing. Here's another important thing to consider. This goes for any time you are fishing vertically, but especially when you are trying to work a jig right down into the cracks of boulders, pay close attention to what that jig is doing at all times. Feel it, and try to mentally picture what it is going over, etc. Work it down into cracks, and slowly twitch it there, trying to coax a strike.

These are just a few specific examples of situations where vertical jigging is the best option for presenting a jig to fish. There are countless others, of course. You will find many of them, by just using common sense in approaching a fishing situation. Ask yourself how to best work a given area, and if you are faced with deep water, or think you can get right over shallower fish and they seem to need the jig held right in front of their nose, etc., give it a try.

It works, believe me. It didn't get to be one of my favorite ways to fish by leaving me out there on the water with a lot of time on my hands!

There is one real kicker to fishing a jig vertically, to being right over the top of fish. It places a real premium on being quiet, on keeping boat noise, excessive movements, etc. to a minimum. Not that being quiet isn't important in other situations also, because it is, but here it is absolutely crucial to your success.

Again, I can't give you rock-solid rules of thumb. In fishing, those hard-and-fast rules are hard to come by. I can't say that "once you get into 15 feet of water, it's okay to run your big outboard instead of your electric, or it's okay to make a little noise on the bottom of the boat."

How wary fish are depends on the species, the mood of the fish, the clarity of the water, the amount of sunlight penetrating, to a degree how much boat traffic the fish are used to, etc. This kind of thing varies tremendously from day to day. My best advice is this, though: be more cautious at first than you think you have to. Then, when you start catching fish, somebody is bound to knock a tackle box over, or kick the bottom of the boat or something. If you continue to catch fish, it didn't bother them too much. If not, it probably did.

Vertical Isn't Always the Answer

As much as it is an advantage to fish vertically, there are times when letting the jig trail out behind you a ways will turn the trick. I've talked about this with several good fishermen over the years, and they all seem to think the same thing, that sometimes trailing the jig behind the boat just gives the fish a "different look" at the bait. That can be enough to trigger them sometimes.

There's another trick you might try, that Bill Binkelman suggests. He said he really became convinced of the value of this idea during an outing with noted outdoor writer and fisherman Dan Gapen.

"We were backtrolling with jigs," Binkelman said, "and weren't catching a thing. We decided to try letting some line out behind the boat. Periodically, we would let more line out, so the bait would be just sitting there on the bottom, not moving at all while the boat was still continuing to move. When you stopped letting line out and the slack tightened up, the jig would start off again with a jerk.

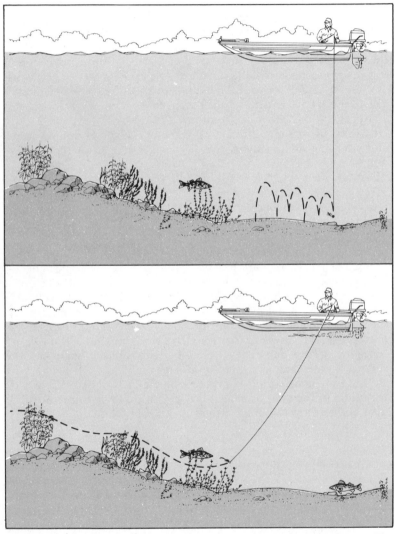

Fishing vertically with a jig (above), you normally get a hopping motion. That can be the ticket with agressive fish, but sometimes letting the jig trail out behind the boat (below), giving you a more gentle motion, will be the action that triggers the fish. Learn to experiment!

If I knew why fish could be so particular at times I could probably tell you when you need to do this! All I can say is, try it if you aren't catching anything by vertically jigging.

It might also be the ticket when trolling over spooky fish, that spread out around the boat as you come over them. If your jig is trailing behind the boat, it might come by the fish after they have re-grouped behind the boat—the same theory as that behind long-line trolling any other bait!

If you think the fish are doing this, try letting the jig out behind the boat, and then slowly trolling in S-curves along the structure you are fishing. As you turn, you will put the jig along a path that isn't following directly behind where you have been with the boat. Sometimes, that can make a big difference—it just might put your jig in front of fish that haven't been spooked by the boat.

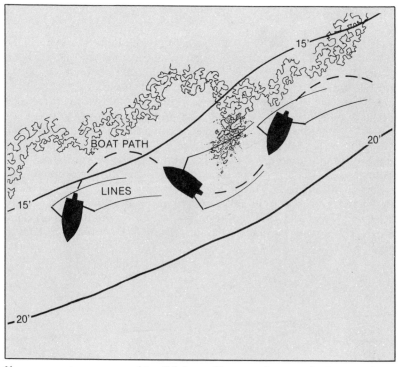

If you suspect you are spooking fish by trolling over them, try letting out a long line and S-trolling. The line will go away from the path of the twisting boat, and you have a better chance of presenting your jig to a fish that hasn't been spooked.

Trailing the jig behind you while you drift or troll slowly puts more of a swimming action on the jig, rather than the "hippety-hop" movements you tend to make with a jig that is fished vertically. That hopping motion is often the best thing you can do for fish that are really biting good, but sometimes more reluctant fish need to be "triggered" by working your jig in more of a sliding fashion.

"Well, there must have been fish down there eyeing it up at times, because, sometimes, when it would start to jerk forward, we would get a strike. Hard strikes, too, not little playful taps. It reminded me of what a cat does when you get him to chase a string or piece of yarn. When the jig was laying there motionless, the fish were probably sitting there looking at it, but when you jerked it along after it laid there a while, they would pounce on it, like a cat. We caught fish that day doing that little thing, when no other way would catch them. Since then, I have repeated that several times. It doesn't always work, but it sure is worth a try if nothing else is working. It's better than sitting there catching nothing, isn't it?"

Boy, it sure is, Bill. Again, that's just a little thing you might do next time you run into fish that won't bite—another of those little things that sometimes add up to being big things under the right circumstances.

Swimming a Trolled Jig

There are also times that call for a trolled jig to be worked off the bottom in a swimming motion, for many of the same reasons you do it while casting. There is no rule that says you have to bounce a jig along the bottom, especially when fish are up off the bottom.

Bass and walleyes are famous for holding up, say two to six feet, off the bottom. When you see fish off bottom on your flasher or graph, or suspect fish are suspended, try just swimming the jig along. Even if fish are right on the bottom, if they are active and feeding, searching for food, they will often come up to hit a jig swimming over them.

To do this, first let your jig hit the bottom, and then troll off, raising your jig with the rod tip. If you work carefully along, it will stay close to where you raised it. To better cover various depths, though, slowly raise and lower your rod tip, keeping pressure on the line so no slack forms. By keeping tension on the line, you will be able to sense takes much better.

Mastering jig fishing techniques will help you produce fish under all conditions no matter what species you fish for.

Chapter 8
Live Bait Rigs

In the next two chapters, I'll talk about several live bait rigs. But I'll emphasize the Lindy Rig, the best and most versatile of all live bait rigs.

The Lindy Rig is not a bait, but a total system that lets you fish for almost anything that swims, in shallow water or deep.

Simple systems are often the most effective. That's sure the case here. The Lindy Rig presents live bait slowly and in a natural manner to fish near bottom *and* allows the fisherman to delay the hook-set until the fish has taken the bait completely. For what it is designed to do, the Lindy Rig is absolutely unbeatable.

The Lindy Rig was invented and popularized by guides whose clients mostly had not polished their skills. It is as close to a *foolproof* fish catching system as you can find. Of course, you can fish with it badly if you try hard enough, but this is a rig that makes good fishing easy.

That does *not* mean the Lindy Rig is a beginner's rig. If you work with it and explore its possibilities, you can work wonders with variations on the original Lindy Rig. Combine the Lindy Rig with a sense of where fish are and the ability to control a boat, and you have a tremendously effective fishing system.

With the *Lindy Rig system*, you can catch almost any kind of fish that swims. The obvious applications are on walleyes, smallmouth, and northern pike. But you can also take crappies, bluegills, perch, muskies, largemoth bass, lake trout and striped bass on Lindy Rigs. I've probably forgotten a few, but you get the point.

This is *not* a narrow, limited piece of gear.

Instead, it is a comprehensive fishing system with interchangeable components. By choosing sinker weight, hook type, leader (snell) length, floats and attractors, you can customize the basic Lindy Rig and make it into many different kinds of rigs.

The Basics of Lindy Rigging

Let's cover the basics...although I'll sneak in a few sophisticated wrinkles for those of you who are already experienced riggers.

Your main idea is to present a bait in the most natural way possible, moving it along the bottom very slowly and with lively action.

Pick a likely depth and area to troll. Tie on an appropriate Lindy Rig with the right sinker weight for the circumstances.

What weight? Pick the *lightest* sinker you can get by with, though the sinker has to be heavy enough to keep you in touch with the bottom at all times. I'll offer more details on this later.

Sometimes the guy running the boat can get by with a lighter sinker because he knows more about what the boat is doing, whereas other guys have to rely strictly on what they feel. The boat operator has another advantage, since his bait gets to the fish first. That's only fair, I guess, since he's doing extra work.

Different rigs are designed for different baits. If you are using a leech or crawler for bait, use a rig tied up with a small hook for those baits. The other most popular Lindy Rig snell has a larger hook for minnow fishing.

A feature of the Lindy Rig is that it allows you to switch snells instantly. You can switch from a spinner rig to a yarn rig or a straight rig. The open end of the Lindy clip is designed to make these snell changes simple. Arrange the rig so the bend in the sinker *points back toward the bait* and is free to slip *up the line* toward your rod.

One tip: to make the rig more secure, don't just pop the leader loop in the clip but *loop* it in. The illustration will make this clear.

Lindy is introducing a new cross-lock swivel that will completely avoid the problem of snells slipping off the swivel. You might look for these, although the traditional swivel works perfectly if you loop around it as I've described.

When you let out your line to drop the sinker, don't just let go and have the rig sink at full speed. If it does, the leader and main line can twist on each other. It's better to have the boat moving a little as you let down the line, and then slow down the line as it passes through your fingers so that the rig drops without tangling.

Troll along slowly at the right depth, with the weight on the bottom *as nearly under the boat as possible.* Fishing with extra line out usually leads to tangles and missed strikes. On tricky contours, if you have a lot of line out your sinker will not move precisely with the boat as it cuts left and right but will take a sloppy "shortcut" route that will often have it out of the right depth.

There are exceptions to this "shortest possible line" rule. When you are fishing in very shallow water in spring, you might want to use a 1/8- or 1/4-ounce sinker and get back behind the boat. How shallow? If you are in 10 feet of water or less, consider getting the line back. You want to present the bait to a fish that isn't looking at your boat right above it at the same moment. But in most situations, you should be fishing right below the boat with the shortest line you can use.

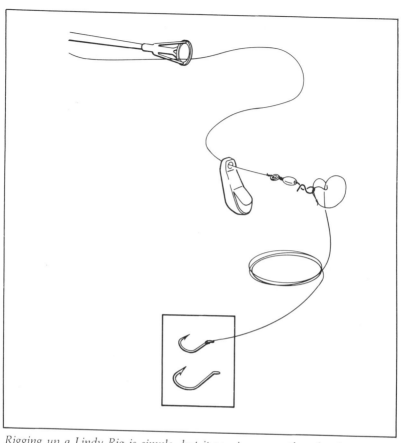

Rigging up a Lindy Rig is simple, but it requires some thought. First (inset), decide what size hook you need. Then, select the proper weight sinker for the situation, and thread it on your line as shown. Tie a Lindy swivel clip to your line with a good knot, then loop the snell onto the clip so it doesn't come off when you're fighting the fish of a lifetime.

Open the bail of your reel and hold the line with your index finger. You can simply drag the sinker along, waiting for a pickup. Or you can pump the sinker with many repeated short sweeps of the rod tip. I find this gives me a *much* better sense of the bottom than just *dragging* the sinker. Keep your rod active and pay close attention to what you feel.

You will usually feel a fish pickup as a *ka- chunk* that definitely has more life to it than the feel of the sinker bumping a weed. Some pickups are soft and spongey, but most have a distinct plucking, lively feel.

If you are in doubt about whether a certain "heavy feeling" on your rig is a fish or a weed, treat it like a fish. Pull *very gently on the line* and see if the weight acts like a fish or weed. If it is a fish, you'll feel the fish shaking its head or chomping. You may have to drop the rod tip back to the fish or even pull off line to keep the right tension without spooking the fish. If you test the rig and all you feel is a mushy dead weight, you're weeded.

At the pickup, open your finger to release the line to the fish. Spill line off the reel with your free hand if you think there is any chance the line will hang up. Don't just dump gobs of line out, but keep track of it. Watch the line moving to get an idea of what the fish is doing.

The two touchiest aspects are deciding *when* to set the hook and then *setting* it properly. I'll talk about the decision to set in detail a little later. But here's the basic rule: the more aggressive and definite the pickup, the quicker you can set. When a fish bangs your bait, drop the rod tip for a second or two and sock it to 'im. When you just feel a soggy "something" hanging on to your bait, you're going to have to be more patient. This has to be worked out each day, as the fish and other factors will always be changing.

Let's turn to the hook-set itself.

Because the fish has been running around with the bait on a loose line, you won't have a tight connection to the fish when you close the bail to set. So close the bail, lean way out toward the fish, then reel quickly but cautiously.

Don't set until you make a tight connection to the fish. If you reel and set quickly, the fish will have no time to let go of the bait before you set the hook. If you reel and find that there was no fish after all, you can let the rig stay on the bottom or bring it on in if there is any chance you have a piece of weed on your hook or that your bait is gone or mangled.

It's no good trying to set a hook when there is a lot of line out, particularly if the line is passing under the boat. You're just asking for trouble if you set then. If the fish runs around a lot with your bait or if you've been forced to fish with the line under the boat, start the set by turning the boat or walking around until you can get a free, straight and short shot at the fish. Use the trolling motor to get the boat near the fish and to free the line. *Then* put the tip down near the water and reel in quickly to start the set.

When you feel the line come tight against the weight of the fish, snap the rod up sharply while you lean back away from the fish. Don't just set with your hands, but put your body into the set. Right after the first set, I often drop the rod several inches and set again as quickly as I can.

Set firmly. Remember, mono stretches a lot. The deeper you are fishing, the more line you have to move on the set before it moves the hook. At 40 feet, for example, it is hard to break 6-pound test line even if you are *trying* to. You also have to pull the hook through the crawler or minnow or whatever before you can get it into the fish. So set hard enough to get that steel planted.

Obviously, with crappies you don't need to try to cross their eyes, but most people have the problem of setting too weakly.

Here are the most common Lindy Rigging mistakes:

- failing to detect a pickup,
- forgetting to reel up the slack before setting, and
- not setting firmly enough.

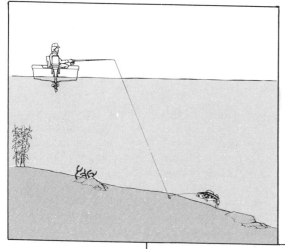

The whole idea behind the Lindy Rigging concept is to allow a fish to pick up your bait, then run with it without feeling any resistance. So, when you get a bite, feed

the fish line in a controlled manner. You have to experiment each day with how long to let the fish run, whether you need to gently pull back on the line to "tease" them into biting harder, etc. This all varies with the mood of the fish, the size and type of bait you are using, and other factors.

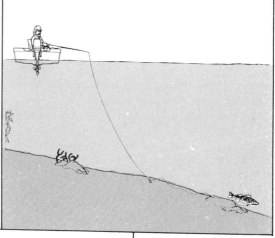

When you think the fish has the bait in its mouth, close the bail on your reel and set the hook. Remember, especially when rigging in deep water, you have to use a long sweeping motion to set the hook, to take up all the slack and stretch.

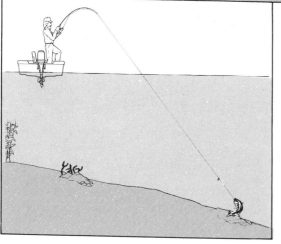

Where and When to Lindy Rig

No system of fishing is best for *all* conditions, places and times. Some situations are better for rigging than others.

The beauty of Lindy Rigging is that it lets you *search* for fish *while you are fishing*. You are always moving, presenting the bait to new water.

The essence of Lindy Rigging is that you fish along bottom through a certain *zone of water*, a certain depth spectrum, while you search for fish schools. When you've got fish located in *spots*, not zones, you might switch from rigging to a form of fishing that intensively targets that spot...like throwing jigs, or using bobbers.

A perfect time to Lindy Rig is when you think you know what depth the fish are using, but you aren't exactly sure exactly *where* they might be. By running rigs along the contours of good structure at the right depths, you can catch fish while you are hunting them.

Let's say you're after early season walleyes and the guy you buy bait from says the fish are mostly coming from 12 feet. By moving your boat along good spring walleye structure at about the 12-foot contour, you can quickly zero in on the spots where walleye schools are holding. Even if you've never seen the lake before, by rigging and covering a lot of water, you are fishing smart and learning the lake. Your sinker will be talking to you about what the bottom is like in different areas, and that goes into your mental computer, too.

You won't always find fish schooled in big numbers. You might find fish staggered in little groups or even singles—one here, one there—all along a certain contour. Once again, trolling a Lindy Rig will be the deadliest way to go after them. You want to keep moving, showing the bait to as many fish as possible.

Rigging is effective even when you don't know the depth of the fish. Simply find promising structure and work it with with a wandering course that presents the bait in a range of depths. When you catch a fish, note that depth. On your next passes you'll be able to pinpoint the exact location of the school. If you don't find a school, you can return to fishing the depth that worked before, still hunting fish.

Lindy Rigging is one of the smartest ways to fish when winds are blowing and it is rough. Your boat can be pitching around so bad that you'd have trouble fishing a jig or crankbait with control, yet a Lindy Rig will go right on sneaking along near bottom in a natural way. That sinker on the bottom is your firm connection to the bait. Even in rough water you will feel pickups.

There are limits to this. If it gets extremely windy, boat control gets to be more of a hassle than it's worth. But a good boat with splash guards can help you catch fish on Lindy Rigs in pretty lousy weather.

Rigging works beautifully at times when fish are in a negative or neutral-negative mood. (And that's *often* the case with walleyes in heavily fished waters!) The natural slow presentation of the bait can trigger a hit, even when fish aren't active. The fact you can let the fish

run and play with the lure means that your chances of hooking a
negative fish are excellent.

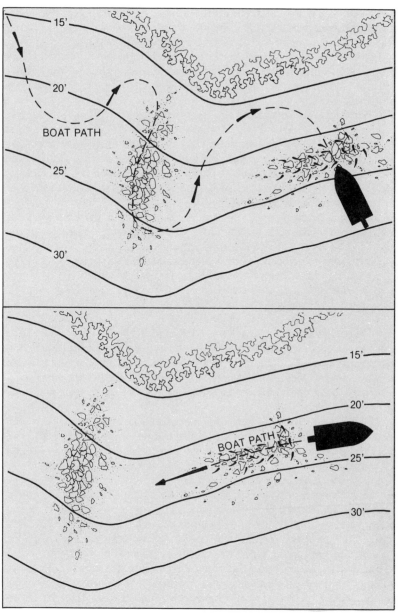

*When searching for fish, it's a good idea to "comb" a contour, roaming up and
down at different depths (above). When you locate fish, you can then concentrate on working the area again, keeping your boat at the depth you found the
fish (below).*

Lindy Rigs work best for fish that are close to bottom. As I've said, that is where a great many fish are most of the time. Lindy Rigs are especially famous for catching walleyes, which are bottom-hugging fish. But you'd be amazed at the numbers of crappies, bluegills, northerns, smallmouth and largemouth bass I've caught while Lindy Rigging. Not to mention catfish and muskies.

Actively feeding fish are very, very often right near bottom. They might be in fairly shallow or deep water, but that zone of water near bottom is where the action is, much of the time. It pays to have your bait low.

When fish are suspended a long way off bottom, trolling a Lindy Rig is usually not the best way to get them. Up to a point, you can get your bait off bottom by using floating rigs and longer snells. But there are limits to how high you can get your bait if you are moving at all. If the fish are suspended way off bottom, you're generally better off cracking out the jigs or bobber rigs to fish *down to* them from the surface than *up to* them from the bottom.

Trolling a Lindy Rig usually requires that you put the boat over the fish. When fish are spooky, they may be bugged by the presence of the boat and be reluctant to hit a bait presented right under a boat.

When are fish spooky? Certain factors make fish spooky:

- they have been harassed by many other boats;
- the water is super-clear;
- the surface is super-smooth;
- the fish are in shallow water; or
- a cold front has just come through.

These factors all work in combination. But, generally, shallow fish in clear water are going to object to a boat right overhead, especially if it is being run by the gas outboard. They won't leave the lake, but they'll drift off to the side, hide in the weeds or just refuse to feed while the boat is too close.

When fish are spooky, you have a choice. You might want to switch to another technique, like jigging or slip-bobber fishing, where you can keep the boat away from the fish. You can run Lindy Rigs way behind the boat, usually with light sinkers. Or you can stick with the Lindy Rig, but use an electric trolling motor.

I often compromise. If I'm trying to find fish, I'll troll a rig until I contact a fish or two. Even when fish are negative and spooky, you can often find one that's aggressive enough to feed. That way I'm catching fish while I hunt for them. Then I'm free to switch to bobbers or jigs, holding the boat away from where I've contacted the fish.

But usually, when you've contacted fish using a Lindy Rig, you can go right on fishing with it. It worked before, so it will very likely work again. Most times of the year, most fish are so deep they'll pay no attention to a boat right over them.

It is hard to troll a Lindy Rig *in* heavy weeds. I've taken limits of walleyes by running my bait *right up to* the front face of weeds to catch fish that were holding in the weeds. I've caught many fish casting Lindy

Rigs with light sinkers over the tops of weeds. I've also caught fish by rigging in short weeds, such as deep water sandgrass.

When trolling rigs in weeds, the standard Lindy Rig works but is not as snag-free as the Weedless Lindy Rig, with its weedless hook and bullet sinker. By and large, trolling a rig right through the middle of thick weeds is hard. Or maybe I should say that fishing that way is less fun and productive than other techniques.

I will never forget one situation where Lindy Rigs worked in weeds. A friend once bought a cabin on a lake. He was unable to find walleyes in summer there, though guys caught some big ones in winter. So, one fall day, I came out to help him. Hey, that's what friends are for.

I finally located the fish in the weeds in shallow. Get this—the school of fish was so close to my friend's dock he could have almost fished to them without using a boat! I found I could catch these fish by casting a Lindy Rig with an inflated crawler and a very light sinker, easing it back over the tops of the weeds. The weeds had fallen over a little by this time. My first fish was just under 10 pounds. In the next two weeks, we caught 15 fish over 7 pounds. If Lindy had invented their floating rigs by then, we would have done even better.

Rigging over snaggy bottoms can also be difficult, but hardly impossible. It all depends on the nature of the snags. You should shorten up your line so you're fishing right under the boat as much as possible. Move slowly and immediately lift the sinker over rocks as you encounter them. If you just drag a rig way behind the boat, you're asking for trouble in rocky lakes. Your sinker gets pulled into the crevices under rocks rather than riding up over the snags.

In snaggy areas, you can also switch sinkers. I'll talk about some sinkers for snaggy waters in the next chapter.

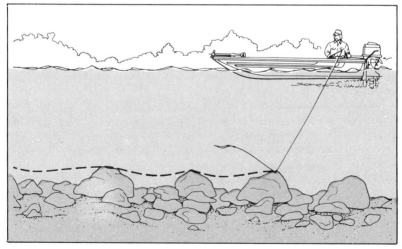

When Lindy Rigging along a snaggy bottom, it's a good idea to shorten your line, use a heavy sinker and fish as vertically as possible. Move slowly, and lift your sinker over rocks as soon as you feel them. This will help keep the sinker from getting hung up in crevices.

Choosing a Weight

When casting a Lindy Rig, you choose a weight that lets you make the cast. The general rule, as with all forms of Lindy Rigging, is to use the lightest sinker you can get by with. In the original Nightcrawler Secrets technique, the predecessor to Lindy Rigging, Bill Binkelman advised using very light weights and long rods (converted fly rod) to allow soft, lob casts that would not whip off the bait.

When trolling, again you want the sinker to be light because heavy sinkers can spook fish. Above all, heavy sinkers interfere with your sense of touch on the light takes.

Yet your sinker shouldn't be too light. The sinker has to keep your bait down and give you a feeling for the bottom as you pump it along. If it is too light, it will float up and feel mushy. Just as in jigging, the more experienced anglers develop the ability to work with lighter weights.

Here are some factors that affect your choice of sinker. The deeper you fish, the heavier your sinker must be. The faster you fish, the heavier your sinker should be. The rougher the wind and waves, the more weight you need to keep in good contact with the bottom.

Conversely, you want a lighter sinker when fishing slowly, when working shallow water and when fishing calm days.

Lindy sinkers are stamped with their weight, so you always know what they weigh, even after the weights get all scrambled together, as they inevitably will do.

Baits

In general, a rigger needs to use live bait. For some fish, especially walleyes, it's often necessary to bring several types of bait. Because you'll be moving at a slow trolling speed, the best place to hook the bait is in the very front. That gives the most natural action.

I talked about baits earlier, and you know how important it is to use high quality, lively bait. What follows is a quick guide for matching baits to different fish. This is not a comprehensive list.

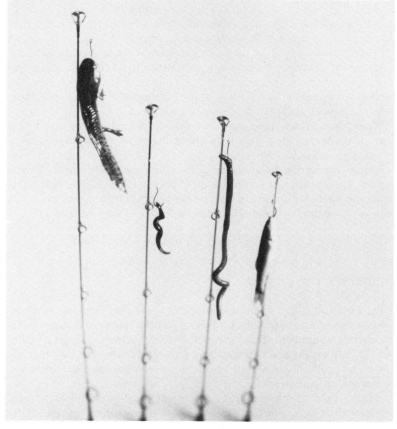

The best baits for northerns are minnows and waterdogs. The best bait for smallmouth is the leech, though smallies *love* crayfish and they'll hit minnows or crawlers very well. Big smallies really go for small waterdogs. For crappies, you can't beat crappie minnows, though worms and grubs will catch them. Bluegills love worms and crawlers, but the big ones go for small leeches. Perch and bluegills both like insects and insect larvae or crawler parts. Catfish (in addition the usual stink baits) prefer minnows, frogs and waterdogs. Walleyes generally go for leeches, crawlers or minnows, though they often will jump at a crayfish, waterdog or frog. Waterdogs are trophy walleye baits.

A common beginning rigger's mistake is failing to check to see what bait the fish want on a given day. This is particularly a problem with walleyes, the fish most often sought by Lindy Riggers.

The three most effective walleye baits, most of the time, are crawlers, leeches and minnows. As you already know, it is *not* true that a "leech is a leech" or a "minnow is a minnow."

There's good bait and bad bait. Walleyes (and other fish) sometimes prefer one species of minnow over another. I've seen times when jumbo leeches filled the boat when little leeches brought in perch...and I've seen it go just the other way, when jumbo leeches weren't much better than a bare hook but little leeches were dynamite.

Friends, there is no way on earth you can go under water and force-feed the fish! If they want crawlers, you better have crawlers along and give 'em crawlers. If they want leeches, you better give 'em leeches. You can't always predict their choice, so the only smart thing is to ask them what they want and then be ready to provide it.

When the fish are "off" one bait and "on" another, they still might bite on the wrong bait. But they'll bite better on the right bait by a factor of, say, six to one.

Anglers go wrong by assuming they know what will work. Maybe leeches tore up the fish yesterday on Winkelman Lake. Are you going to hit the water with nothing but leeches this morning? Don't do it! Do minnows "always" work best on Lac la Roach? Don't believe it!

Equipment For Rigging

For Lindy Rigging, spinning equipment works better than casting or spincasting equipment. Almost always. I know some good riggers who use casting equipment, but I sometimes wonder why they do it. With your thumb on the spool of a casting reel, you *cannot* feel soft pickups as well as you can when your line is on your finger, as it is with open-face spinning equipment.

Is there a place for baitcasting equipment? Yes. Baitcasting equipment works well in such places as the Missouri River reservoirs, especially North Dakota, where they fish with spinner rigs behind big bottom running sinkers, like Lindy's Bottom Cruiser. That is heavy equipment, with the sinkers often weighing 3/4-ounce, and they fish *fast* out there to cover a lot of water. The fish hit like northern pike, too. For all these reasons, the strength of baitcasting equipment makes it a top choice. This is real rock 'em and sock 'em fishing, not the kind of delicate fishing Lindy Rigging usually is. There the best rod is a baitcasting rod of medium or medium-heavy action, about what you'd use for spinner-baits.

If you fish Lindy Rigs with heavy weights a lot or if you're just more comfortable with baitcasting equipment, be sure to use a rod with a grip that doesn't get between your hand and the blank. In the Shimano Fightin' Rods, for example, your hand is not insulated from the graphite or boron by a spongey grip, and these rods work better for rigging. But, day-in-day-out, I'll fish spinning equipment with my finger on the line.

Some spinning reels are better than others at wrapping line so it comes off smoothly. With some reels, the winds get buried in each other and the line sticks. That alerts a wary fish to possible danger. Find a reel that doesn't snag up, and always be ready with your free hand to feed line to the fish without interference.

Some spinning reel bails are a lot harder than others to trip. Avoid them. Some bails can be tripped manually as well as by advancing the handle, and you might prefer them. When you've got a big fish chomping on your minnow, you don't want to be worrying about whether or not your bail is going to trip right.

A new concept in live bait reels from Shimano is a line of "Baitrunner" reels. These actually feed line out to the fish by rotating while the bail is closed. In other words, the line moves freely to the fish even though the bail is closed. You only need to move the handle forward to lock the reel up for the set. I worried at first that the reel wouldn't be smooth enough as it unwound, but I was wrong. This is now the only reel I want to use.

Shimano's new line of Baitrunner reels add a function useable by Lindy riggers. The Baitrunner feature very smoothly feeds line to a fish after it takes your bait.

For rods, riggers usually like fairly short rods with good strength in the butt but some flex in the tip. Rods of six feet or slightly shorter are about right, preferably one-piece. You will feel most of the pickups on your finger, but you still want the most sensitive rod possible.

If the tip is too stiff, you will find it hard to keep in touch with a fish without tipping him off to the fact you are there. A rod with a tip that "works" a little is handy. You can watch it to get an idea of whether a walleye is chomping your bait or moving off steadily with it. At the same time, you want a moderately stiff and strong rod. Sloppy, spongey rods are no good for feeling bites and are weak on hook-sets as well.

The rod I've used most for rigging in recent years is the Shimano 2593, which is 5 feet, 9 inches long. It has just the right balance of qualities.

Every now and then I'll use a longer, lighter rod. Sometimes I cast a 1/8-ounce sinker Lindy Rig with a fat crawler, throwing it way up on a point and pulling it back into deeper water. To make the cast without throwing off the crawler, I need a long rod with a flexible tip. Shimano's 2651 is good for that.

As you know if you've read my other books, I believe strongly in using nothing but the best line. Fortunately, the best costs little more than the cheap lines. By all means, buy a top quality line, inspect it often for nicks and re-spool several times a season with fresh line. If you try to save money on line, the fish it will cost you are the biggest and most exciting fish you hook. Does *that* make sense?

In critical situations, a fluorescent monofilament might be bright enough to spook fish. You can use a fluorescent line on your spool, since what the fish mostly sees is the Lindy Rig leader and it isn't fluorescent. But there isn't really any big reason for using a glowing line when rigging, as this is not a "line-watching" style of fishing. So I'll ordinarily use clear line, not a fluorescent line.

I work with monofilament all the way from 6- to 12- pound test for rigging. Most of the time I like a clear 8-pound line, though I use 10-pound for heavier sinkers. My favorite line has been clear Stren or Stren Class line.

Recently, I've been doing extensive testing of a new DuPont line called Prime. Prime, unlike any other line on the market, is a *cofilament*. It has a nylon sheath around a core of polyester. Making this line is an extremely tricky process, but the results are pretty special. That polyester core has more hooksetting power and sensitivity than any other line ever built. Prime tends to be a little stiffer and kinkier than other monos in the coldest water, but those qualities don't detract from its ability to serve as a Lindy Rigger's line. Do you want to feel those half-hearted pickups in 38 feet of water? Try Prime.

Miscellaneous Gear

Very quickly, here are some other items of equipment that a Lindy Rigger will want in the boat.

Worm blowers are little syringes for putting small bubbles of air in crawlers to make them ride higher off the bottom. Go easy. Over-blown crawlers have terrible action.

Hook files work much better than stones for sharpening hooks. The hooks found on standard Lindy Rigs are as sharp as you can buy, but no factory hook is as sharp as it ought to be. A file, like the one made by Luhr Jensen, will quickly remove excess metal from the sides of a hook point and make your hooking percentage higher.

Sinkers should be carried in a variety of weights. You might have bought Lindy Rigs with 1/4-ounce sinkers for shallow spring fishing, then you find that the fish are in 23 feet. Switch to a 1/2-ounce sinker. Since Lindy sinkers are stamped with their weight, you can always grab the right weight, even after you kick your tackle box and scramble up the weights you had neatly sorted out last winter.

You can use several sinkers as slip sinkers (such as egg or bell sinkers), but I prefer the Lindy walking sinker almost all the time. Bullet "worm" sinkers are tops for slipping through weeds, and the Lindy Bass Rig comes with them. But switching sinker *types* as well as switching weights is not smart. Your sense of feel goes down the drain when you play around with different types of sinkers.

Extra hooks are good for customizing rigs. A well-stocked bait shop will often have hooks sold in Lindy's packaging, and those will be hooks that are top quality for the job they are intended to do. If you have to buy your own hooks, selct a Mustad or other high quality hook and be sure you tie a good knot. Because many bait stores don't stock high quality hooks, Lindy now sells packages of hooks proven for their different rigs.

Attractors can add to the appeal of your presentation. Well-equipped riggers will have a variety of attractors in their rigging tackle box. I'll discuss such attractors as yarn and spinners, etc., in the next chapter.

Snell Holders are simple but useful devices that hold snells neatly in your tackle box. Every serious rigger will want a variety of snells at all times—some with yarn, some with big hooks, some with crawler/leech hooks, etc. It used to be a headache to store these snells after they were taken out of their shrink wrapping. But now Lindy sells a simple plastic snell holder that solves this old problem.

Nets are taken for granted until a fish comes along that won't fit in a net. Most riggers fishing for walleyes like those rubber nets that expand when a fish's weight is in them. They are the fastest net to use because fish and hooks won't get caught in them the way they do in mesh nets.

I know a guy who would have won a major walleye tournament if he'd had a decent net. He had a trophy fish up beside the boat, but couldn't fit it in his little rubber net. Several people who saw it figured that fish went 13 pounds.

I'll use rubber nets at times, but landing big fish is pretty important to me, so I carry a full- sized nylon mesh net whenever I think I might hook good-sized fish.

Casting Lindy Rigs

The classic walleye technique developed in the north central Minnesota region where I now live involves backtrolling with Lindy Rigs. But you need to know that many, many fish are caught by casting Lindy Rigs.

A Lindy Rig with a little hook and a 1/8-ounce sinker is excellent for throwing leeches for smallmouth in shallow water. With this rig, you aren't waiting for the sinker to hit bottom usually, but are slowly reeling to keep the bait swimming along. Since the sinker is far ahead of the bait, the bait won't have a sharp up-down action if you pause and then resume reeling. This even, flowing action is often attractive early in the year.

Some fishermen like to anchor in a specific spot where walleyes will come in to feed in the evening. Then they cast around the boat very quietly, working Lindy Rigs with leeches, minnows or crawlers along the bottom. When a fish strikes, they have the choice of hooking it right away or giving it a little time. The Largemouth Bass Rig is preferred for casting in weeds.

When I was just learning how to fish, I spent many happy hours fishing the Mississippi River near my home. I used two rigs to catch smallmouth there. One was a jig baited with crayfish or crayfish parts. The other was a Lindy Rig (with the 1/8-ounce sinker) baited with a crawler. I'd wade the river in tennis shoes, working the shallow pockets behind rocks where smallmouth held. This was classic river fishing, where you cast upstream of the hole and let your offering drift with the current down to the fish. You walk along, almost like you are hunting, and flip little casts in to drift them by the boulders where the smallies lie.

But I'll tell you, the memory that stands out is of this little spot I found near the home of a friend, Ed Gerchy. There was this little finger of rock sticking out into the river, and it held a wonderful bunch of big smallmouth. I came through there one day and took six smallmouths from 5 to 6 pounds.

Then, like a dummy, I had to tell somebody about how well I was doing. So I told Ed. He told a neighbor. The neighbor went down there and fished that spot the same way I had been...and caught a smallmouth that went 7 pounds, 3 ounces. Can you believe it? A smallie over 7 pounds? And I could have caught that fish—would have caught that fish—if I hadn't opened my big mouth!

Bank fishermen also cast Lindy Rigs. This is one of the most effective ways of catching catfish in all sorts of bank fishing situations. Pier and shore fishermen along the Great Lakes are using Lindy Rigs (with normal or floating rigs) for catching salmon or trout.

Floating Rigs

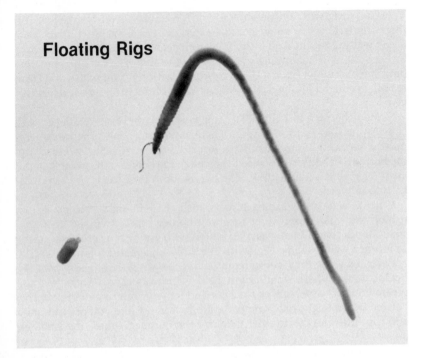

Floating rigs have a variety of uses. They float the bait above snags and weeds. They get it up where suspended fish will see it. And they give your bait another kind of action—dropping as you move forward, then rising slowly to the surface whenever you pause. The floats can be attractors at times, too, and on days when walleyes are picky I often find floaters get them moving.

The Lindy Floating Rig has an adjustable float that can be put near the bait or farther away. That affects both the action and the height of the bait. The closer to the bait the float is, the higher it rides. You'll get the bait higher off bottom if you use a crawler with a bit of air injected in it. You can't inject leeches and minnows.

Don't expect this rig to get up to fish several feet off bottom. In fact, all floating rigs are pretty limited in terms of how high they rise in normal fishing. If I want to get a rig way up, I take the black sponge float off the Lindy Crappie Rig and put that on my snell. I also combine floats on my line with a Lindy Floating Jig Head or Floating Quiver Jig.

When you are moving, any floating bait is pulled by water pressure toward the bottom. So go slow. You can't fish quickly and high above your sinker at the same time. If you really need to fish high, buy the Lindy floats in bulk bags and put several on the snell at a the same time.

I had an experience with this sort of rig. Several years ago I was fishing Mille Lacs in midsummer, out on the mid-lake reefs called the "flats." A stiff breeze was blowing that day. Though I saw fish on my sonar, I couldn't get them to pop. Something was wrong. I began to experiment. Finally I decided the heavy wave action was kicking up so

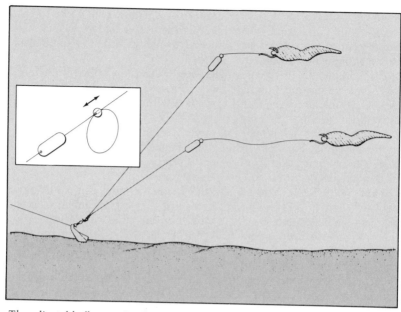

The adjustable float on Lindy's Floating Rig can be moved closer to your bait to make the bait ride higher in the water, or farther away to make it ride closer to bottom. To move the float (inset), loosen the loop holding the bead and slide the bead the desired direction.

much silt at the bottom that the fish couldn't see my bait. I tried a drift where I dropped my rig to bottom, then cranked it up about four feet to get the bait high. And I began banging the walleyes, one after the other.

But I was also bothered by the fact I was missing strikes. It was clear that the fish were running up to the bait, biting it and going right on running toward the boat. I couldn't get a tight line on them. So I tied up a new rig. Lindy, in those days, had a crappie rig with a black bobber on it. I put some of those bobbers on a snell eight feet long. Then I dropped my rig back down...only this time I let the sinker go to bottom so I could feel what was going on.

And that was it. By fishing with my sinker on bottom, my sense of feel was back. And the crappie bobbers kept the bait up where the fish could see it. It took some time, and I had to do it the hard way, but I'd invented the Lindy Floating Rig.

Recently, my Research Team divers have been amazed at the number of areas where silt will lie on the bottom of a lake. This stuff is the same consistency as water, but it is thick enough to obscure a bait trolled in it. The value of floating rigs in such areas should be clear.

At times, when walleyes suspend way off bottom in summer, I'll tie up special snells that are as long as 10 feet, with three, four or more floats on them. To land the fish you might have to climb up on a boat seat and lift your arms high so your partner can net the fish! This is awkward, but at times it's the way you have to fish. This extreme "up-from-the-bottom" fishing has fallen out of favor now that slip bobbers have been shown to be so successful on suspended fish. I like to take Lindy floats in different colors and mix them. I've had good luck with fluorescent red and chartreuse, but you always should have some black floats along if that's what the fish want.

A friend and great walleye angler, South Dakota's Mike McClelland, has some interesting theories about the need for floating rigs. Mike began to think about the fact that walleyes often *inhale* baits by making a cavity in their mouths. He saw that the bait had to be free to move backward, or the fish would fail to get the bait even though it tried as hard as it could. For this reason, Mike began to worry about rigs that have a tight connection from the bait to the weight, as there would not be enough slack for the bait to behave naturally.

That's why Mike likes to use the Lindy Floating Rigs. The float between the bait and the weight gives just that extra element of slack that lets the bait pop in the fish's mouth on the take. Mike's success on the pro walleye tournament trail is legendary, and he's got me convinced to use floating rigs more. I'll come back to Mike's theories a little later, in the next chapter.

A trick that will take suspended fish is to park the boat right over the fish and keep with it, using a floating rig. Of course, you are using your sonar (best is a graph) to do this. When the fish moves, follow it. That pulls your bait toward the bottom. When you stop, the bait will float up to the fish like a mayfly nymph that's escaping from the mud. This is more work than you'd want to put out for a small walleye, but this stunt has accounted for a number of trophy walleyes for me.

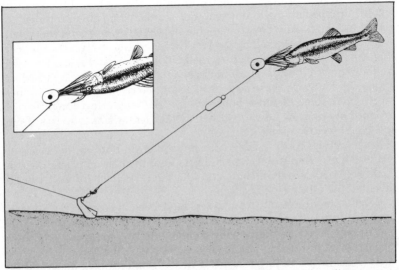

Replacing the hook of a floating rig with a Floating Quiver Jig will give you a package that rides higher in the water, and offers the additional attractions of head color and the floss body action. A neat trick you might try (inset) is hooking a minnow from the bottom up, which is actually upside down for a floating jig head. Hooked that way, the minnow has to constantly struggle to remain upright, presenting a very active bait.

I'll use floats on rivers, too. The float gets the bait up off bottom just a little bit and then the current waves the bait around.

Before the Floating Lindy Rig was invented I really felt the need for it. I remember guiding on the Mississippi River, going after smallmouth in cold fall weather. On one trip we were having a tough day until I finally figured out that the fish were in bends of the river, tucked up tight under floating debris and logs. We were able to get those fish by going upriver, anchoring, and then fishing down to them with Lindy Rigs with pumped up crawlers. We were basically letting our crawlers wash around in the current, getting up under the obstructions. On one trip we took 30 fish doing that, with some of them up to 5 pounds. But the technique we were using would have worked much better with a floating rig.

You can add scent to the float, either Chummin' Rub or (if the weight is flocked) any liquid scent. Some people feel this helps them. When I'm using natural bait, I usually skip other scents, but that doesn't mean you have to do the same.

My family and I have done very well this year with the new Lindy Floating Worm Harness. It has two floats (for greater lift) and a spinner (for attraction). One day my dad caught five species of fish on this rig.

The two floats of the Floating Worm Harness can be arranged so they present contrasting colors. Fishermen often worry what color they should be using when, instead, they need to think in terms of *contrast*. The different colored floats make it certain that this rig will be seen. The new rig works remarkably well...but why wouldn't it? It combines several elements we all know are attractive to fish.

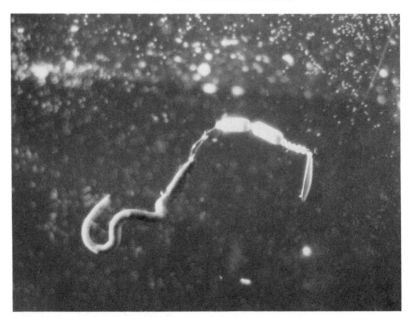

Lindy's new 'crawler harness really gets the bait up where the fish can see it. The fluorescent colors of the floats don't hurt either!

Rigs for Toothy Fish

Northerns and muskies are routinely taken by Lindy Riggers, but many get away by cutting the line with their teeth.

That's not necessary. Lindy's Northern Pike Rig is tied on a wire snell. It isn't fat, stiff wire, and neither muskies nor northerns are put off by wire leaders anyway.

Once I was fishing a big lake for trophy walleyes in the fall, using big redtail chubs on a Lindy Rig. I hit a fish at 18 feet, set the hook and had the rig come up minus the hook...I'd been bitten off. I put down another rig with another chub. The same thing happened again.

Okay, so I finally realized there were northerns down there. The next rig I put down was a Lindy wire snell for northerns, and that had hardly gotten down to 18 feet when it was snarfed up by a pike. In an hour I took three pike from 13 to 17 pounds, and I lost two others.

I've frequently taken big northerns and muskies with sucker minnows on Lindy Rigs. Both these fish have a tendency to get lazy when they get big, and sometimes you have to put a big piece of live minnow right in front of them and let them take their time with it.

When fishing huge baits for huge fish, you often have to wait a l-o-n-g time for the fish to take the bait in his mouth. I'm no longer that patient, and I'd rather hook fish in the outer mouth for easy release. So I rig up a stinger treble hook on a short wire snell and slam the hooks home when you get a pickup. Or I fish the Lindy Big Bait Rig in place of the usual hook.

One of my most exciting experiences with northerns came on Lindy pike rigs. I was fishing with my father in Canada, trying to catch walleyes. We were working a big rock flat which dropped off extremely steeply on two sides. My dad was bringing in a little perch that hit his minnow, when up came this northern and grabbed the perch.

Well, that was the start. We switched to wire snells to avoid bite-offs, and the action was incredible! We could hardly get a minnow down near the bottom before another big pike was running off with it. They were like a pack of piranhas, and in a long lifetime of fishing I have never seen a northern pike feeding frenzy to match that one. Finally a storm came blowing in and we had to run for shelter, but while it lasted it was unbelievable. Now I *always* carry some Lindy Rigs with wire snells for special moments like this.

Chapter 9
The Art of Live Bait Rigging

The art of live bait rigging is something you never quit learning. As long as I've been at it, I learn something new with almost every trip.

To keep learning, you have to pay attention to the fine details. I can't emphasize it enough: little things add up to big differences in your fishing.

Live Baits for Riggers

Remember, you've been told it is important to keep your bait in tip-top condition. Remember, you've been warned to bring a full supply of bait and to experiment to find what the fish want. I'll make some comments about what baits work best at different times, but don't overlook the need to be prepared and then to ask the fish what they want.

Let's look at live baits for riggers in a bit more detail. Note: these comments are geared toward walleyes. Other fish don't show the same kind of seasonal changes in bait preference. Other fish might have bait preferences, but they don't have the cyclical, seasonal quality that walleyes show.

Minnows

Minnows are most effective for walleyes in spring and fall. In early spring, smaller minnows are best, even crappie minnows fished on a "Leech- Nightcrawler" Lindy Rig. In late spring or in an early spring, you might find bigger shiner minnows or chubs are red hot. Shiner minnows are especially good early in the year. They're also touchy about water temperature and oxygen, dying easily in summer.

Although spring is a time when minnows do well, they're hardly the only bait then. I see a lot of walleye anglers who only fish minnows in spring, catching nothing, when I'm having a ball fishing crawlers or leeches.

It isn't enough just to carry "minnows" because at times the fish can be selective about minnows. Shiners, with their silvery sides, will often outfish darker fatheads and chubs, but not always. If you don't like the look of the minnows in one bait store, drive a few miles and check out the next batch. It's worth being fussy when you are going to be spending hours and hours in the boat with the bait.

Minnows lose effectiveness for walleyes when the water warms up. That's a darned good thing, because keeping minnows alive in warm weather is a miserable job. When walleyes feed in weeds heavily, as they often do late in the summer, minnows once again become hot baits. A jig-and- minnow then is a bait that will take fish of all species. Note: other fish than walleyes go right on hitting minnows in summer.

Minnows are deadly in fall, which is convenient because it can be hard to locate good leeches at that time of year. When the water gets cool the leeches are less active and hard to trap. The best fall minnows will be bigger minnows, even great big sucker minnows, because fall fish are looking for a serious meal. If I'm going to freeze my butt fishing on a cold fall day, I'm not looking for pan-sized fish. I'll fish a big bait and know that what I sacrifice in terms of fast action will be worth it in terms of the quality of fish I catch.

For rigging, you want to hook minnows up through the lower jaw and on through the top of the mouth. Check your minnow now and then when fishing to make sure it is still wiggling for you. Don't drag around a minnow with a bunch of weeds around its face, either.

Leeches

Leeches are a super bait for walleyes and smallmouth. At times, fished on a Lindy Rig, they'll also do a number on jumbo bluegills.

My buddy, Spence Petros, was typical of many fishermen who hadn't fished leeches before. He had bait leeches confused with bloodsuckers, which are another critter altogether.

But Spence thought bait leeches would bite him. One reason he was confused was another friend of mine, Gary Roach. Gary did quite a number on Spence. He'd convinced Spence that you only had a few seconds to get a leech on a hook before it bit you and sucked your blood! Gary's nickname is "Rotten," and maybe you can see why. By the time Gary got through with him, Spence ranked leeches with rattlesnakes as bait.

Then one day Spence was fishing Lake Geneva, that "play" lake in Wisconsin which is hard to fish because of waterski traffic and because it's so deep and clear. Spence was in a rental boat. He noticed somebody had left some leeches in the boat, but he wasn't going to touch them.

Fishing was terrible. Finally, in desperation because fishing was so bad, Spence cautiously picked up a leech with needle-nose pliers and spent several minutes trying to get it on the hook. He no sooner put the leech down on a Lindy Rig when he caught a *nice* smallmouth. Hey, these things work! But the fish had thrown off his leech.

The next leech took longer to get on because Spence's hands were shaking. After four minutes of fighting with it, he got the hook in and put it down. His sinker touched bottom, and—*boom!*—he had another good smallmouth. Spence told me that after that fish his hands were shaking so much he spent almost 15 minutes hooking up his third leech! I'm glad Gary wasn't there to see that.

No need to worry. Bait leeches are clean and pleasant to use. For one thing, you can set the hook quicker with leeches than other baits. Once you see how well they work, you get over the initial squeamishness. When the water is cold and your hands get stiff, a writhing leech can be hard to stick with a hook. Some guys carry a little bit of fine sand so they can handle leeches better.

Leeches stick on a hook really well, so I like to use leeches when I'm trolling Lindy Rigs in weeds. Leeches are also about the easiest live bait to keep alive and in good condition. You've just got to keep them cool and supplied with fresh water every now and then.

Leeches can be effective spring, summer or fall. Leeches are not good in the extremely cold water of early spring or late fall because they "ball up" around the hook and look no more appetizing than your sinker. I'd ordinarily avoid jumbo leeches in early spring in favor of normal sized ones, but I like to have some jumbos along to experiment with. From mid-spring on through the summer and up to the cold water time of fall, jumbo leeches will usually take bigger walleyes than smaller ones.

Leeches are nice because, ordinarily, panfish don't go for them as much as they do crawlers. If they do, they don't steal your bait as often. A perch or sunfish can peck and pull on a leech without ripping it up like they will a crawler.

A leech may not look like much to you, but leeches bring in some terrific trophy walleyes every year. They're surprisingly effective on northern pike. Smallmouth *love* leeches. Largemouth like leeches, especially the biggest ones.

When you troll leeches off a live bait rig like a Lindy Rig, you can hook them in either end. The sucker end is actually the back end, but it is easier for some folks to get a hook in. The head end, the narrow end, is a little tougher, which makes it a place to put the hook in when fishing in weeds.

Leeches fished on a Lindy Rig can be hooked in either end. Most anglers hook them through the fatter, sucker, end (right). But the head end (left) is a little tougher, so hooking them there can be an advantage when fishing in weeds.

Crawlers are another bait that will turn big walleyes in spring, summer or fall, but especially in spring and summer. In the heat of summer, I'll start with crawlers more often than not.

I can sure remember doubting crawlers. They looked like a panfish bait to me. One day I was fishing crawlers strictly out of faith in Bill Binkelman; he'd said they worked, and I trusted him. I'd just turned the boat to follow a point around and my momentum was lost. My bait had time to drop down, and I got a pickup. When I landed that big walleye, one of the nicest I'd ever caught, I realized I'd been going too fast...and that Bill had been right about crawlers.

Crawlers are easy enough to keep in good condition if you take a few precautions. Keep them in bedding that is cool and moist but not soaking wet. I've already given you tips on "conditioning" crawlers (a practice started by Bill Binkelman), in the big chapter on live bait.

Crawlers naturally ride higher in the water than leeches...which is one reason they work well in summer. You can float your crawler higher by giving it a bubble of air in the mid-section with a worm blower. Insert the worm blower right behind the ring, aimed toward the tail. Otherwise, if you blow air toward the front end, you can kill the crawler. Remember, you aren't trying to pump up a beach ball! The crawler won't have any action if it is pumped up tight.

This is the right way to inflate a nightcrawler. Insert the worm blower behind the collar and aim the needle away from the head region, where the vital organs are. And remember: don't over-inflate. A little puff'l do ya!

Crawlers can be mighty frustrating to fish. If there are any bullheads, perch or sunfish around, the guy fishing a crawler is going to be pecked to death. Mid-summer walleyes have an annoying tendency to screw around with crawlers rather than taking them decisively. It can drive you crazy. But would you rather be fishing something else and getting no hits at all? Not me!

When walleyes play with crawlers instead of banging them, there are several things to try. I *don't* recommend what most people do, which is to read a paperback while the fish messes around with the crawler. Out-waiting them rarely works, and it brings everybody's fishing to a halt.

Instead, do things to make the fish hit it right the first time. Try shortening the crawler. If that doesn't work, experiment with floating jig heads (especially fluorescent jig heads) or spinners, then experiment with speed (going both faster and slower than you have been). There is usually a way you can get the fish to bang the bait. I'll also mention a way of teasing the fish into taking the bait, a little later in this chapter.

Crawlers are more effective on largemouth bass than most people realize. I remember a time when I had been fishing a certain weedline for walleyes, doing well there all summer long.

When I went back to that area in fall, suddenly my weedline was full of largemouths. Fishing at 27 feet, I took one of the best stringers of bass I'd ever seen with a Lindy Rig and a crawler. The bass had been forced out of the shallow weeds because they were then dying off. Since then, I've often seen this happen, and I've taken a lot more bass on crawlers and rigs.

Bill Binkelman was the guy who pioneered the right way of hooking a crawler—right through the "nose" of the front end. When you are moving slowly, you want the crawler to stream straight out and wriggle naturally.

Crayfish (left), waterdog (middle) and frog: all effective and overlooked live baits.

Waterdogs

Waterdogs are the immature, gilled stage of salamanders. Waterdogs have an ability to bring out aggression in large fish. You have to see this to believe it! Big bass, northerns, muskies, walleyes and even smallmouth will go after a waterdog as if it were their worst enemy. They just *destroy* them!

Now, if you're looking for *numbers* of fish, waterdogs are not the answer. A leech or some other bait is going to put far more fish in the boat, most days. Fishing waterdogs, I have had whole days without a strike, but six or eight strikes might be more normal. I fish them because those six or eight fish will almost always be trophies.

I've had the experience of fishing carefully in an area I knew had fish, catching nothing, then mopping up by going back through there with waterdogs. Spence Petros told me he once fished the dickens out of a spot without catching anything. When he switched to waterdogs he quickly took two northerns that went 18 pounds and one that went 11. I've had the same experience with other species.

It isn't always easy to find waterdogs in bait stores, let alone to find them in the right size. For smallmouth, waterdogs up to about 4 or 5 inches long. Walleyes hit best on waterdogs 4 to 6 inches long. For big northerns, waterdogs the size of young alligators are hardly too big. Get the biggest you can find.

Use big hooks. The Pike Lindy Rig, with its big hook, is about right. Or use the Big Bait Rig, which comes with a built-in stinger hook. Sometimes big fish try to crush waterdogs without actually eating them. Stinger hooks are the answer to that. You can use the standard Minnow Lindy Rig and add a stinger hook.

Frogs

Frogs are a great fall bait for walleyes or bass beating up on the frogs as they come into shallow bays to hide in the mud during the winter. I remember catching a bunch of walleyes in deep water, 35 to 70 feet, which regurgitated frogs in the livewell. Those fish had obviously been moving in to the shallows in low light times to grab frogs as they migrated.

I'll often tie up a Lindy Rig with a weedless hook, put a frog on, and anchor the boat in front of the weedline. I cast up into the weeds, then slide the frog slowly out to deeper water and down the breakoff in front of the weeds. This will produce *big* fish. I mostly am thinking about bass now, though huge walleyes will put a move on the frogs during the fall frog run.

Frogs have been hard to get recently because a disease hurt their populations. Now they're coming back. Many younger anglers who lack experience with frogs don't understand how good they can be. I don't think there is a time of year when frogs won't take bass.

Back when I was guiding, I counted on frogs as my "ace in the hole" for tough bass days. If we were trying to catch bass after a bad cold front had come through, the bass would always be tucked up way in the weeds and they'd be negative.

On days like that, I'd have a few dozen frogs in the boat. If plastic worms couldn't produce, we'd hook frogs in the lips on Lindy Rigs and drag them around on the deep edge of the weeds. It was one of those tricks that saved the day for me many times.

Crayfish

Crayfish really should be used more on Lindy Rigs than they are. They are very, very effective on smallmouth and walleyes, especially, but small crayfish are just about my favorite bait for jumbo perch.

Crayfish are a regional bait. In southern states, you'll find crayfish in every bait store. Northern anglers have been surprisingly slow to appreciate them. Most people know the soft-shelled stage (when they have just molted) is best. But regular hard-shelled crayfish catch fish, too.

Our Research Team divers have been amazed in their dives to find out how many crayfish they see. You can hardly lift a log in a lake without having crayfish scooting out, but the divers also report seeing them out in the open. They're thick as fleas in rocks. The divers also report that they see lots of evidence that fish have a special interest in crayfish.

I was reminded of the effectiveness of crayfish not long ago when fishing Lake Erie with Jim Fofrich. Using crayfish on Lindy Rigs, we had unbelievable action on smallmouth. I think our party caught 150 smallies in one day, and several times we had two or three on at once. The bass would spit up crayfish pieces as they came in.

I used to catch smallmouth in the Mississippi River when I was younger, mostly fishing them on jigs. I've also done well with crayfish on Lindy Rigs in rivers. Little soft-shelled crays are terrific for big perch. I've seen times when crayfish were better for largemouth bass or walleyes than any other bait.

Hook a crayfish through the tail for Lindy Rigging. Bring the hook up from the bottom.

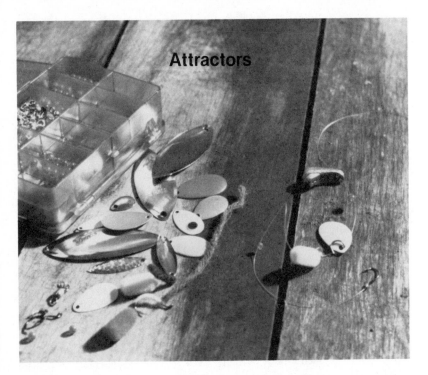

Attractors

There are various ways to add pizazz to your offering.

But let's hold up just a moment. Do you *want* to jazz up your bait? Why? If you've rigged up with the right live bait in top condition, you will rarely need to do more. In fact, messing around with your bait by gobbing scent on it, or whatever, might not be smart. The basic appeal of Lindy Rigging is that it presents *natural bait naturally*.

But many times something a little extra will produce fish. You don't need to be afraid of attractors, as long as there is a reason to use them. The two *main* times I'm likely to go to attractors are when the water is so dirty that fish might have trouble seeing my bait, or when fish are unresponsive to a "straight" presentation.

Spinners

You can add spinners for either reason. Spinners add flash, color and sound to a quieter presentation. In summer when walleyes have so much food available to them, spinners are often the only way to make them notice your bait. Spinners are effective mainly when the water is warm and you can troll faster.

What spinner color you choose depends on what you want to accomplish. Fluorescent spinner blades make a bait more conspicuous. The two most obvious choices are fluorescent chartreuse or fluorescent orange, but red, blue, purple, gold, silver, white and yellow are some colors that also work well. Silver or gold bades don't show up much at all, but their whirring can be felt by fish along their lateral line.

Spinners don't have to be huge to be effective. Little spinners the size of your smallest fingernail can spark fish interest in your bait. In really dark water, the thump and color of a bigger blade can be a big plus. You want to attract attention to your bait and help the predators find it. The darker the water, the larger and fatter your spinner blade should be.

Spinners also help lift a bait off bottom, much the way a floating rig does. This is useful when you want your bait to ride above some bottom weeds it might get lost in otherwise.

I'm selective about where I use spinners. Spinners can tangle when fished *in* weeds, but smart fishermen often use a spinner to float a bait over the tops of the weeds. For this, you would usually be casting the Lindy Rig.

I really like to use spinners when I think walleyes might be in a competitive feeding situation. Then a spinner brings out aggression in a walleye like you never thought they had!

Certain lakes, rivers or reservoirs are known to be good places to fish spinners. That has to do with how competitively the walleyes feed. It also has to do with the type of forage the fish use. A lake with a perch forage base is not as good for spinners as a lake with a smelt or ciscoe forage base.

Keep in mind that you have to move the spinner fast enough to make the blade turn. If the blade isn't turning, the spinner is a "minus" instead of a "plus." Spinners are not the ticket for slow, cautious fishing.

A final value of spinners has already been mentioned. They encourage fish to strike further forward, getting the hook right away rather than playing with the bait and finally getting it all in. Fishing with spinners, you excite aggressive strikes that let you crack back with your set right away.

I've already indicated it matters a lot which spinner you use. Changing spinners is usually troublesome, but a new style of clevis allows spinners to be changed in seconds. This clevis is used on the Little Joe Red Devil Supreme spinner.

You can add a spinner to a standard Lindy Rig by cutting off the loop knot and stringing up beads, the clevis and the spinner. Or you can simply use a spinner snell. My favorite, for most purposes, is the Little Joe Red Devil, which (like the Lindy Rig) is tied with different snells and hooks for different purposes. The Heart of Steel spinner snell is dynamite for northerns.

Some modern anglers scoff at spinners as "old fashioned" because they were so popular when our fathers were fishing, but spinners definitely deserve a place in your tackle box. In some areas, like the Missouri River reservoirs and most of Canada, spinners routinely outfish straight presentations by a big margin. I'll talk about the Missouri River fishing system in the next chapter.

Yarn

Yarn is a subtle attractor that adds a puff of bright color right ahead of your bait. It helps fish notice your bait. Some anglers (Bill Binkelman among them) believe yarn can even spark a competitive urge because it looks like your bait is running along with something attractive in its mouth. Other fish are excited by the sight of a small critter running around with a piece of candy.

Yarn is sold in many bait stores, but not all. If you find a store that caters to steelheaders, it will surely have yarn. I like the thinner yarn— the stuff about the size as the yarn women knit with—not the fat "Glow Bug" poly yarns.

Yarn can be tied to the leader ahead of the hook or even worked into the knot. Yarn rigs are great on smallmouth as well as walleyes and other fish. Yarn is easily adjusted for size. In really dirty water you can use a lot of yarn (like a piece about 2 inches long), while in clear water you can trim yarn back until it's the size of a bead.

Beads

Beads work very much like yarn. For years, some guides and expert fishermen have been slipping bright beads on the leader of their rigs. You can squeeze down the loop knot and slide most beads onto the rig that way. Beads are easier to change color with than yarn.

That spark of color at the front of the bait doesn't detract from the natural look of the bait as much as a big spinner would. Another advantage over spinners is that you can fish beads (and yarn) slowly. And you'd be amazed at how often the bead will turn on fish that ignore a straight rig.

Duane Ryks, of my Research Team, uses beads extensively in his walleye tournament fishing. He can tell stories and stories about schools of fish that ignored every bait imaginable, then turned on when a bead was added to the Lindy Rig.

Duane has several favorite colors. In dim light, he fishes pearl or fluorescent orange beads. In midday light, Duane likes blue or fluorescent red.

Most of the time, especially when fishing leeches Duane uses a single bead. But he'll go to two or even three beads when using a big bait, like a bigger minnow or a long crawler.

Scent

Scent can be an attractor. Of course, you already have the scent of the live bait. I don't as a rule believe we can improve on the scent of the natural bait. But at times, particularly in cold water, it's useful to add scent. Lindy sells flocked hooks and flocked floats that will hold that scent longer, dispersing it over a longer period of time. Most people feel it is unwise to mix scents—in other words, don't put crayfish scent on a rig with a leech on it.

You might want to use scent to hide your own odor, which you can do by smearing Chummin' Rub on your hands before you handle the bait, or just use Lindy's No Scent Soap.

Zeroing In On Schools

Fishermen working out of different sides of a boat will actually be fishing somewhat different depths of water. The rod tips might easily be 10 feet apart, which could mean that the guy on the shallow side has a sinker in 14 feet of water while the guy on the outside is fishing in 18 or 20 feet.

This varies a lot. Wide boats, long rods and steep structure exaggerate the difference in depth. If your rods are short and the structure doesn't slope quickly, inside and outside rods can be fishing just about the same depth. On top of a reef, everyone will be working the same depth.

This disparity, this *depth spread*, is usually an advantage when you are hunting for fish. Pay attention to which rod gets the fish, the inside or outside rod. That will help you pinpoint the right depth. When you know exactly where the fish are you can tighten up your spread without getting into tangles.

Fish schools don't always sit in exactly the same spot for a long time. So even when you locate a school of active fish, keep paying attention to which rods are getting the most pickups...the inside or outside rods. By watching these little details you can often follow the progress of a school as it moves up shallow to feed, then drifts back down to deeper water. You'll be able to shift your working depth accordingly.

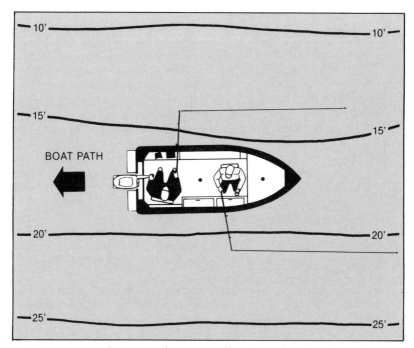

It's important to be aware that, especially along sharp-breaking structure, fishermen working out opposite sides of the boat can be fishing in very different depths. This can be a big advantage when you are looking for fish.

Feeling Bottom and Takes

I've already indicated how important it is to feel what is happening to your bait. If you pick up weeds and don't know it, you'll drag around a worthless bait. If you fail to feel a fish sucking on your crawler, you can blow the chance to catch the fish of a lifetime. Feel is *terribly* important in all live bait rigging.

To improve your feel, you can:

- get a better, more sensitive rod
- switch to Prime line,
- drop down one or two line sizes,
- drop up or down one or two sinker sizes,
- move the boat slower,
- concentrate better, or
- improve your rigging technique.

Let's look at rigging technique.

Nobody can tell exactly what's happening to a sinker if it drags steadily along bottom. Nobody. There's not that much difference in the feel of a sinker *dragging* over one surface or another.

So I pump my sinker, moving it ahead in many little regular steps. It is terribly important to do this with a regular rhythm. If you change rhythm, you lose the ability to detect tiny differences in the feel. Moving a sinker along in little steps has several advantages, but better feel is the biggest.

When I pump, I get a good feel for the sinker as I pick it up *and* as I drop it down. If the bottom is hard, like gravel, I'll feel a click as the sinker hits. If the bottom is silty, I'll feel the sinker resist me on the lift, and I'll feel it hit the spongey bottom. The rhythmic sweep of the rod also helps me feel that tiny "wrong" feeling that means a bit of weed has fouled on my sinker or hook. I can feel something wrong when there is one strand of grass on my bait. You should, too.

Don't pump too hard. The pumping affects the action of the bait. The more vigorously you pump, the more the bait surges and stops as it moves. Just as you don't want to use the same action for all jigging, you don't want to limit yourself to a single kind of pumping action when trolling a Lindy Rig. At times you will want to pump very slowly and smoothly...or not even pump at all.

I recently fished Pipestone Lake, in Ontario, with my friend, Jimmy Hayes, the manager of Pipestone Lodge. We were Lindy Rigging for smallmouth in water from 20 to 65 feet deep. That's *deep*, but we had good graphite rods and light Prime line. I bet we took 80 fish that day, with many big ones up to 4 pounds.

We could actually feel our minnows get excited when a big smallmouth came near. Jimmy and I were predicting strikes in advance just by the way our minnows were acting, by their different swimming motion. When the minnow got excited because a smallmouth was looking at it, we'd almost always get a hit right afterward. When the hit didn't come in a moment or two, we'd whip the bait up as if it wanted to escape. That would do it, every time.

That kind of feel comes only when your equipment is top quality and your concentration is total. You can't be listening to a ballgame or telling traveling salesman jokes if you're going to pick up on subtle little clues from your minnow.

Did you ever feel your line or sinker bump into the sides of a fish? If you develop your sense of feel, you will know when you're bumping fish.

The main thing to feel for, of course, is a pickup. They aren't all the same. In the last chapter, I talked about the "ka-chunk" of a fish popping the bait. That's just one type of take.

Sometimes the fish just mouth the bait and swim slowly along with the motion of the boat. You might feel a very, very slight change from a straight dead pressure (from your sinker and bait) to a slightly heavier straight dead pressure.

Other times the fish smack the bait and run with it right away. That sometimes means you have a northern. If so, you'll often feel a chomping action as the northern kills the bait. Sometimes a fish that hits and runs with the bait is a very aggressive fish that is in a big school of active fish. With those fish, you want to set quickly and get them away from the school before they ruin the school's impulse to feed.

But sometimes, contrarily enough, the fish that run are actually ultra spooky. This often happens with crawlers, and there isn't much you can do about it. Just don't assume a fish that runs with the bait is aggressive. Spooky fish sometimes act as if they were trying to get rid of the bait, moving it away. With these fish, I try to keep just barely enough tension on the line so I can keep track of the fish. Never let these fish feel you.

When To Set

How long should you wait before setting the hook after you feel a pickup?

Setting too quickly is a common beginner's mistake. The fish has grabbed the bait, but the bait isn't positioned right for the hook to do its work. Other fishermen wait so long before setting that every fish ends up being hooked down in the belly.

Your aim should be to *hook every fish, but hook them in the mouth.*

Let me expand on that. We're in an age of heavy pressure on natural resources, and walleyes are so desirable that they get more than their share of attention from anglers. These days, a lot of anglers know we have to release many fish, even nice walleyes.

Years ago a lot of anglers got into the habit of feeding line to walleyes forever, especially when fishing with crawlers. We figured that we'd always get the fish that way. Gut-hooked, maybe, but we'd get him, and we planned to keep all our fish anyway. Well, it got out of hand. There is no sense in waiting while you smoke three cigarettes and some poor cigar-sized walleye digests your bait. And those fish are mighty poor candidates to be released.

Setting the Hook

The good fishermen whose opinions I trust are setting a lot sooner than they used to, years ago. If you set and the fish isn't there, there are better answers than to wait and wait on the next pickup. Figure out some alteration of your presentation so you can get the fish to bang the bait solidly the next time. Waiting is not the cure-all for fish that don't hit well. If you wait too long, the fish will spit the bait surprisingly often.

Some pretty good fishermen don't believe in giving *any* line to the fish unless they learn it is necessary on a given day. After a pickup, these guys drop the rod tip back toward the fish as far as possible without actually releasing line. Then they set just as the boat brings the line tight on the fish. If they miss that fish, they wait a little longer on the next fish and the next one until they get it right.

The "drop back, then set" system works best when fish are really banging the bait hard. It is more suited to a longer rod, like about seven feet. Since walleyes tend to engulf leeches rather than playing with them, you can try this quick striking technique when fishing with leeches. Especially if you fish with leeches and a spinner rig (or another attractor, such as yarn or a bead), the fish usually get the whole bait on the initial pickup.

This is the set technique I use when fishing big waterdogs or oversized sucker minnows with a stinger hook. A good rig for fishing this way is Lindy's Big Bait Rig, which maybe should be called a "Big Fish Rig" since that's what it specializes in. I won't even open the bail then. In fact, I'd have the reel locked so it couldn't reverse and soften my set. On a bite with this kind of rig, when a fish hits, I just drop the rod tip back for a few moments...and then sock 'em as hard as I can. I'm counting on that stinger hook to get those fish that haven't taken the bait in all the way.

Many fishermen feed line to the fish on its initial run. They wait until the fish stops to swallow the bait and then moves off again. Then they set.

That's not a bad system either, though not all fish behave according to that script. This system works best when the fish tend to run off chomping and shaking the bait, stop, then move off steadily. What I like about this approach is that it forces you to pay attention to what the fish is doing, rather than dumping out so much line you totally lose touch with the fish.

Some people have a standard delay before setting which they then modify according to the behavior of the fish each day. They might feed line to a fish for 15 seconds or so before tightening up and setting. If they are hooking their fish too deep, they reduce the interval; if they are missing fish, they wait longer before setting.

The system just described works very well, though it is always smart to watch the line to get an idea of what the fish is up to.

Here's my system. I feed line carefully, always keeping track of how the fish is behaving. As long as the line is twitching so that it seems he's chomping the bait, I wait. When the line moves steadily, I set. The main virtue of my system is that it is strictly based on fish behavior *that day*.

I usually consider what bait I'm using when choosing how long I'll delay the set. Little minnows and leeches of any size are usually taken in by the fish all at once. Crawlers encourage fish to dink around longer. I also know that I'll have to be more patient right after a monster cold front has come through than when conditions are prime.

When you fish minnows on a Lindy Rig, you often get a complex hit. The fish will clamp down on the bait to kill it, then pauses before swallowing the minnow. But the fish hits the bait head-on. They want to kill that head. You can hook them instantly if you have your hook in the minnow's mouth *with the point exposed*. They don't chew their way up a minnow from the back, but grab the head end. So you can pop them right away.

I think a lot of guys use poor hook technique, then tell themselves they missed the fish because they set too soon. You've got to have the hook point exposed and then you have to set vigorously enough to get the hook planted.

With every system, each day on the water is a new story. You always have to start with a plan and expect to modify that plan according to what the fish do.

Straight-Line Sets

In the last chapter, I told you to avoid setting when the line is passing under the boat. I want to emphasize that point here.

You often can't help having the line passing under the boat as you fish. In wind, especially on turns, that just has to happen. But you shouldn't have the line under the boat any more than absolutely necessary.

In other words, on a long trolling run, if the line is under the boat you should change fishing position. The normal position for a right-handed backtroller has his line working off the left (port) side of the boat. But if fishing that way causes my line to go way under the boat, I'll switch and hold my rod off the starboard side. It isn't nearly as comfortable, but comfort sometimes has to come second to fishing.

Any time I get a pickup when the line is running under the boat, I know I have to work a bit before setting. You *can* whale away and try to set even though the line is in a bad position, but you'll miss the fish far more often than you'll get him. Instead, turn the boat or get up and walk until you get that line clear. Re-establish contact with the fish without tipping him off to the fact you are there. Then, if the time is right, set.

Short-Striking Fish

Sometimes fish seem to hit the back of the bait. Walleyes do this more than other fish, especially summer walleyes (when food is abundant), especially summer walleyes hitting a crawler.

Why do they do this? At times I can relate short-striking to the recent passing of a cold front. The fish are just not aggressive. If I put a tasty morsel inches from their noses, somebody in the school's going to snap his jaws. But he doesn't put himself out enough to get the whole thing.

Mike McClelland, the well-known tournament fisherman, has a theory on these "short striking" fish that makes sense. Mike claims no walleye goes to all the trouble of snapping at a bait just to bug the fishermen; they *mean to take that bait* or they wouldn't strike in the first place.

So why don't they get it solidly? You pull up your crawler, and the back half is gone.

According to Mike's theory, the fish has opened its mouth and tried to inhale the bait...but was unable to do it because the bait is attached to a tight line. The bait doesn't pop in the walleye's mouth the way the fish thought it would.

Mike's answer is to add "give" or buoyancy to the snell (leader) between the bait and the weight to make sure the fish will be successful when it tries to take in the bait. One rig Mike likes a lot is the new Lindy Floating Worm Harness. The floats in that rig keep the snell from being too tight to let a fish suck in the bait.

Mike's other rig, which is illustrated here, involves using monofilament that has intentionally been wrapped tightly around a small spool and left until it has a coiled memory. In the case of this rig, the coils in the leader act as a gentle spring, allowing the fish to take in the bait. Meanwhile, the boat is moving, taking out coils all the time. When you come tight on the leader, set the hook right away. This rig is doing very well in walleye tournaments.

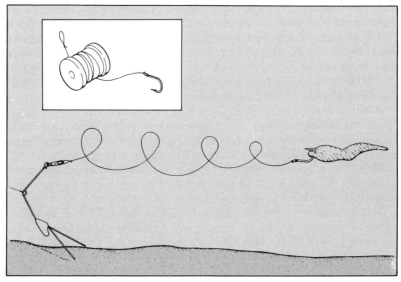

Mike McClelland of Ft. Pierre, SD, invented this neat trick of tightly spooling Lindy Rig snells. When kept for some time on a spool, the snell develops memory, which many fishermen consider "bad." But the theory behind McClelland's rig has been borne out in tournaments all over the U.S. and Canada. The coiled line acts like a shock absorber, better allowing fish to suck in a bait. The fisherman may not feel the initial hit, and doesn't drop line to the fish as in classic Lindy Rigging. When he feels anything, he assumes the fish has had the bait long enough, and sets the hook immediately. It works!

There are other ways of dealing with short strikers.

First, you can sometimes tease a fish into taking the bait, especially if you think you are dealing with playful fish that have full bellies. If the fish is going to play cat and mouse, you can too. Pull gently on the line to make the fish worry about the bait getting away. Then go slack. Then pull it playfully again. You have to go easy to avoid scaring the fish, but this trick can irritate a fish into grabbing the whole bait.

You can do something a little less drastic. When the fish hits, try keeping the line on your finger while drifting back slowly with the rod tip. You are putting just enough pressure on the bait that the fish will feel insecure about his grip. He'll often go quickly for a better grip. Then you set.

Stinger hooks are another answer. A stinger hook is just a second hook (usually a treble hook) on a short leader. The leader is attached to your rig on one end and the treble is buried near the back of the bait.

With stinger rigs you can usually set right away and get even short-strikers. The Lindy Big Bait Rig is an example of a live bait rig with a stinger.

Be careful. In some states, stinger rigs are technically illegal, though this is not the sort of violation a good warden goes around enforcing. Some fishermen believe they can add a tiny spinner to the front of the bait and call it an "artificial" bait, which is allowed to have more hooks.

Some crawler harness rigs have two sets of single hooks, with one set back about half way on the crawler. These aren't really stinger hook rigs, but you can use them the same way. Set right away. Be careful when hooking a crawler with these. A crawler in your hand is usually all bunched up and short. In the water it will relax and lengthen. If you put the second hook too far back, when the crawler stretches out it will not hang straight and look good in the water.

Another answer to short strikers is to simply shorten your crawler. Break off as much as half the crawler and see if that gives you better strikes. I shorten *plastic* crawlers by biting them off, but most guys shorten live crawlers with a knife or fingernails. Suit yourself.

Or add an attractor to the front of your bait. A spinner, bit of yarn or a floating jighead can all make your bait longer and give the fish a target that they'll hit further up.

Another thing to try, when fish aren't hitting solidly, is changing speed. Sometimes if you go slower, you get solid takes. Other days, speeding up makes the bait come by so quickly the fish bang it more firmly. In other words, going either slower or faster can make the difference.

Short strikes on crawlers or even minnows are sometimes a walleye's way of telling you that you're fishing the wrong bait. Switch to another bait to see if that's something the fish will take without dinking around with it.

Rigging On Snaggy Bottoms

Normally, Lindy sinkers are pretty snagless. But some lakes have just the size of rock that hangs up a Lindy sinker. The sinker gets wedged in between two rocks.

A guy I know heard that the DNR had shocked up a 17-pound walleye in a little lake in far northern Minnesota. He and his buddies went up there to catch that fish, though they knew the lake was snaggy. When they left several days later, they left *three gross* (that's 432) Lindy sinkers in snags in the lake. Wow! You'd think that would raise the lake level. Oh, and the walleye's still up there. It's probably a pretty nice fish by now.

It doesn't have to be that way.